KB210587

SSAT 초빈출 핵심 어휘 완결판

SSATKOREA.COM

한세희의

SSAT®

HIT VOCABULARY

한세희 (SSATKOREA 대표) 지음

For International
Private School Admissions

**MUST
HAVE**

★ ★ ★ ★ ★

미국 캐나다
명문 보딩 스쿨
합격을 위한
필수템

ERMONHOUSE

한세희의

SSAT®
HIT VOCABULARY

SSAT 초빈출 핵심 어휘 완결판

SSATKOREA.COM

한세희의

SSAT®
HIT VOCABULARY

한세희 (SSATKOREA 대표) 지음

For International
Private School Admissions

MUST
HAVE

★ ★ ★ ★ ★

미국 캐나다
명문 부딩 스쿨
합격을 위한
필수템

[
큰 꿈에 도전하는
당신의 한 걸음 한 걸음에 위안이 되었으면,
흔들리지 않는 큰 힘이 되었으면 좋겠습니다.
]

첫 SSAT 책을 낼 때부터 전설로 남을 수 있는 어휘 책 하나는 쓰고 싶다는 생각이 있었습니다. 그러다 어느 날 문득 깨달은 것이 있습니다. 끊임없는 변화의 소용돌이 속에서도 중심으로 남는 것들은 그때나 지금이나 항상 그 자리를 지킨다는 것이지요. 그 덕에 시류에 휘둘리지 않는 기본이자, 핵심을 걸러낼 수 있는 안목이 생겼다고나 할까요?

제가 이 책으로 공부하실 여러분께 드리고 싶은 말씀은 세 가지입니다.

첫째, 단어는 매우 강력한 무기입니다. 이제 한 해 한 해 지날 때마다 뼈저리게 느끼실 겁니다. 어휘력이 당신에게 얼마나 큰 힘이 될 수 있는지를 말이지요. 어차피 인생에서 한 번은 제대로 정리해 둬야 하는 어휘. 이제 강한 무기 하나 손에 넣을 때가 되었지요?

둘째, 외우고 잊어버리는 것은 당연한 이치이니 그것으로 괴로워 마십시오. 단, 이것만 기억해 주세요. 운동으로 근육을 단련 시키면 더 큰 힘을 낼 수 있는 것처럼, 여러분의 단어 근육도 훈련을 시키면 시킬수록 더 빨리 외우고, 더 오래 기억하게 만들 수 있습니다. 외우면 외울수록, 더 빨리 더 잘 외우게 됩니다.

셋째, 조급해 하지 말고, 실패했다는 생각이 들 때는 그냥 그 자리에서 다시 일어나서 나아가면 됩니다. 단어는 시간차를 두고 여섯 번 정도 보고, 쓰고, 또 봐야 자기 것이 된다고 합니다. 한 번 외웠는데 생각이 안 난다고 괴로워하지 말고, 그 시간에 한 번만 더 보세요. 불안함은 해야 할 일을 하고 있지 않기 때문에 생기는 것

입니다. SSAT 때문에 너무 걱정되어서 잠도 안 온다고요? 그럼 그냥 책을 펴서 열 개만 외워보세요. 집중해서 하는 그 시간에는 걱정도 불안함도 사라집니다. 그렇게 연습의 횟수가 늘어나면 자신감까지 생겨나게 되죠. 그렇게 불안함을 줄이고 자신감을 키워 나가는 것이죠.

이 책에는 현존하는 SSAT의 가장 중요한 어휘들만을 담았다고 자부합니다. 요리로 치면 아주 싱싱하고 좋은 재료들을 잘 선별해 가져다 놓은 것이죠. 그리고 그 하나하나의 단어에 맞추어 어떤 부분을 꼭 알아야 하는지 포인트를 짚어주는 강의도 따로 준비했습니다. 즉, 맛있는 요리를 위한 조리법도 영상으로 준비해 놓았다는 뜻입니다. 또한 단어를 외울 때는 문제로 나오는 포인트를 연결시킬 줄 알아야 실제 점수 상승으로 연결된다는 점도 잊지 마세요. 마지막으로 재료도 좋고, 요리 비법을 알았다 해도 실제 요리 연습 없이는 좋은 요리를 만들기 어렵겠죠? 단어가 어느 정도 쌓이면 실전 문제 풀이 연습은 선택이 아니라 필수입니다.

이 책으로 공부하고 나면, SSAT가 더 이상 두렵지 않을 것이라고 믿습니다. 그리고 이 작은 책 한 권으로 당신의 인생이 완전히 달라질 수 있기를, 상상도 못했던 좋은 기회를 잡아 더 큰 꿈을 이룰 수 있기를 기대합니다. 큰 꿈에 도전하는 당신의 한 걸음 한 걸음에 위안이 되었으면, 흔들리지 않는 큰 힘이 되었으면 좋겠습니다.

책이 나오기까지 격려와 응원을 아낌없이 보내주신 사랑하는 가족들과 친구들, 함께 일하는 기쁨을 알게 해준 나의 동료들, 좋은 인연으로 힘이 되어주신 헤르몬 하우스 여러분들, 그리고 특별히 오랜 시간 애써 주신 이연수 디자이너님께 감사의 말씀을 전합니다.

하나님께 이 모든 영광과 감사를 돌립니다.

한 세 희 드림

저에게 Hit Vocab은
보물상자 같더라고요.

안녕하세요 후배님들! 저는 이번에 필립스 엑시터 아카데미에 합격한 이예원 입니다. 저는 일반 중학교에서 미국 보딩 스쿨로 간 경우라 도움이 되실 만한 약간의 팁을 이야기해 볼게요.

제 SSAT 첫 주는 말 그대로 혼돈의 카오스였어요. 어느 정도 예상은 했었지만 한세희 선생님의 수업은 그야말로 상상을 초월했어요. 선생님이 던지시는 질문에 아이들 사이에서는 거침없이 답변들이 튀어나오고, Reading을 풀 때는 시, 소설, 연설문, 논설문 등 다양한 스타일의 낯선 지문들이 나와 이해가 잘되지 않았어요. 그러나 뭐니 뭐니 해도 제일 힘들었던 것은 단어였어요. 충격적인 첫 점수를 받고 포기하고 싶었지만 그때마다 선생님과 선배들이 끝까지 버티라고 응원해 준 기억이 떠올라 그렇게 버티며 공부했어요. 두 달 정도 지나니 어느 순간부터 술술 보이기 시작하더라고요. 그래도 여름에 좀 게을리해서인지 첫 시험 점수는 마음에 들지 않았어요. 또 제 주변 친구들 대다수가 외국인 학교나 주니어 보딩 출신으로 첫 시험 한 번에 97~99% 퍼센트 성적을 내는 걸 보고, 일반 중학교에 재학 중이었던 저는 더 주눅이 들었어요. 어느 순간 제가 꿈꿔왔던 탑 보딩들이 너무나도 멀게만 느껴지고, 제가 한 군데라도 붙을 수는 있을까 걱정이 될 정도였어요. 그래도 중간 중간 한세희 선생님께서 할 수 있다고, 내년에 하겠다는 생각은 하지도 말고 끝까지 밀어보라고 해주신 말들이 큰 동기 부여와 힘이 되었어요.

제가 제대로 공부를 시작한 건 학교 인터뷰 후였어요. 인터뷰 투어가 끝날 때쯤

제가 지원했던 너무 좋은 학교들을 보고, 여름에 더 열심히 공부할걸 하고 후회했어요. 그리고 인터뷰 투어의 마지막 날, 제 드림 스쿨인 엑시터에서 온 이메일을 보고 SSAT 2월 성적도 받는다는 것을 알게 되었어요. 인터뷰를 직접 가보니 조금이라도 더 높은 학교에 가고 싶다는 야망과 욕심이 생겼어요. 그래서 저는 다시 2월 시험을 준비하게 됐어요. 이번에는 제발 꼭 한세희 선생님의 Hit Vocab을 제패하자는 마인드로 임했어요. 그렇게 Hit Vocab을 모두 외웠어요. 또 수학에서 약간 점수가 깎인 것이 아까워서 [한세희의 SSAT] 책에 있는 수학 용어도 다시 한번 모조리 외웠어요. 마지막 며칠 동안 한세희 선생님의 모의고사 책을 2-3개씩 풀었어요. 그렇게 해서 본 시험으로 드디어!! 엑시터에 지원할수 있었고, 합격할 수 있었답니다!

저에게 Hit Vocab은 보물 상자 같더라고요. 그것만 외워도 시험에 엄청 많이 나오니까 제발 외워주세요! Hit Vocab을 외우는 것이 Verbal 뿐 아니라, Reading 점수, 나아가 Total 점수까지 올리는 가장 빠른 길이라는 것을 잊지 마세요.

공부를 시작하시는 후배들에게 가장 해주고 싶은 조언은 첫째, Hit Vocab은 기본이니 반드시 꼭 외우기! 둘째, 한세희쌤의 수업 열심히 듣기(실제 시험에서는 수업시간에 한세희 선생님께서 알려 주셨던 세세한 꿀팁들이 완전 도움이 됐어요.)! 그리고 마지막으로 멘탈 관리에요! '포기하고, 내년에 할까? 내가 에시터를 갈 수는 있을까?'라는 생각은 버리시고, 버티고 버티며 Hit Vocab부터 제패하자는 마인드로 공부하세요! 후배님들 모두 파이팅!

[
한세희 선생님의 SSAT 수업과 끝없는 격려 덕분에
포기하지 않고 노력할 수 있었고,
결국 첫 실제 시험에서 만점을 받을 수 있었습니다.
]

　우리 가족은 7학년인 나를 기숙학교에 보낼 생각을 한 번도 해본 적이 없었습니다. 그러나 지난 여름, 아버지가 여러 사람들에게서 보딩스쿨 출신들의 성공담과 추천을 들으신 후, 처음으로 이 길을 고민하게 되었습니다. Junior TOEFL, 지원 에세이, 인터뷰까지 모든 과정이 순식간에 지나갔고, 저는 여러 주니어 보딩스쿨에서 합격 통지를 받았습니다. 하지만 정작 저는 이 길이 저에게 맞는지 확신이 서지 않았습니다.

　그런 저를 부모님은 스스로도 걱정되고 불안했을 텐데도 무던히 응원해 주셨고, 새로운 도전을 해보라며 격려해 주셨습니다. 결국 부모님의 지지 덕분에, 저는 미국 최고의 주니어 보딩스쿨 중 하나로 손꼽히는 페센든(Fessenden)에 7학년으로 입학할 것을 결정했습니다.

　첫날 캠퍼스에 도착한 순간, 저는 페센든에 오기로 한 결정이 제 인생에서 가장 잘한 선택 중 하나라는 것을 깨달았습니다. 뛰어난 학업 환경은 저를 더욱 성숙한 학생으로 성장시켜 주었고, 스포츠팀 활동을 통해 새로운 종목을 경험하며 팀워크와 도전 정신을 배울 수 있었습니다. 기숙사 생활을 하면서 독립심을 기르고, 친구들과 함께 잊을 수 없는 추억을 만들었습니다. 하지만 또 한 번 새로운 도전이 다가왔습니다. 바로 고등학교 입학이었습니다.

　여름방학 동안 저는 다양한 학교를 조사하며 입학 과정을 알아보았습니다. 전반적인 절차는 주니어 보딩스쿨 지원 과정과 비슷했지만, 한 가지 커다란 장애물이 있었습니다. SSAT.

주변의 추천을 받아 한세희 선생님의 수업을 듣기 시작했습니다. 미국에서 공부한 경험이 있었기에 SSAT가 크게 어렵지 않을 것이라고 생각했지만, 첫 시험 결과는 제 예상을 완전히 빗나갔습니다. 전체 점수 30%. 예상 밖의 낮은 점수에 충격을 받았고, SSAT 공부에 대한 의욕도 점점 떨어졌습니다. 매일 수업이 끝난 후 성적을 확인할 때마다 실망감이 커졌고, 포기하고 싶다는 생각도 들었습니다.

그러나 한세희 선생님과 선배들의 꾸준한 격려 덕분에 저는 포기하지 않고 계속 노력할 수 있었습니다. 함께 공부하는 친구들도 서로를 응원하며 끝까지 도전할 수 있도록 힘이 되어 주었습니다. 그리고 몇 주간의 꾸준한 노력 끝에, 제 점수는 서서히 오르기 시작했고, 결국 첫 실제 시험에서 만점을 받는 성과를 거두었습니다.

SSAT 공부는 단순히 시험 점수만을 위한 것이 아니었습니다. 여름이 끝나고 새 학기가 시작되자, SSAT를 통해 익힌 고급 어휘와 독해 능력 덕분에 학교 영어 수업에서 글을 더 쉽게 이해할 수 있었고, 글쓰기 실력 또한 크게 향상되었습니다. 특히, 고등학교 지원 에세이를 작성할 때 SSAT에서 배운 표현들이 큰 도움이 되었습니다. 그리고 마침내 저는 엑시터(Exeter)와 앤도버(Andover)를 포함한 여러 명문 보딩스쿨에서 합격 통지를 받았습니다.

저는 결국 엑시터로 다음 스텝을 결정했습니다. 엑시터는 학업적으로 매우 도전적인 환경을 제공할 것으로 생각합니다. 그렇지만 페센든에서 배운 독립심과 우정, 그리고 한세희 선생님과 함께했던 값진 성장의 시간들이 고등학교에서도 큰 힘이 되어 줄 것이라 믿기에, 저는 새로운 여정을 향해 한 걸음 더 나아갈 준비가 되었습니다.

> 한세희 선생님의 SSAT 수업을 듣게 되면서
> 제 태도와 공부 방식이 완전히 바뀌었습니다.

　올가을, 저는 꿈에 그리던 Choate Rosemary Hall에 10학년으로 입학합니다. 지난 4년 동안 Rumsey Hall에서 생활하며 많은 것을 배웠지만, 제 학업과 입시 과정에서 결정적인 전환점을 만든 것은 한세희 선생님의 SSAT 수업이었습니다.

　처음 SSAT를 시작했을 때, 제 점수는 28%에 불과했습니다. 미국에서 공부한 경험이 있었기에 SSAT가 크게 어렵지 않을 것이라 생각했지만, 첫 시험 결과는 제 예상을 완전히 빗나갔습니다. 낮은 점수는 저를 실망하게 했고, 공부에 대한 의욕도 점점 떨어졌습니다.

　하지만, 그때 한세희 선생님의 SSAT 수업을 듣게 되면서 제 태도와 공부 방식이 완전히 바뀌었습니다.

　한세희 선생님의 수업은 단순한 문제 풀이가 아니라, 논리적인 사고력과 전략적인 접근법을 가르치는 과정이었습니다. 특히, 선생님은 단어 암기가 지겨울 때마다 SSAT를 위한 공부가 아니라, 영어 실력을 키운다는 마음가짐으로 접근하라고 강조하셨습니다. 덕분에 단순 암기식 학습이 아니라, 장기적으로 도움이 되는 학습법을 익히게 되었습니다. 이러한 변화 덕분에 제 점수는 점진적으로 상승하기 시작했고, 결국 두 번째 시험에서는 목표 점수를 기록하며 보다 편안한 마음으로 입시를 준비할 수 있었습니다.

　만약 한세희 선생님의 SSAT 수업이 없었다면, 저는 이 과정을 끝까지 해낼 수 없었을지도 모릅니다. 선생님의 체계적인 지도와 끊임없는 격려 덕분에 저는 포기하지 않고 끝까지 노력할 수 있었습니다.

Choate Rosemary Hall
이원석

주니어 보딩스쿨이나 국제학교는 단순한 학업 공간이 아니라, 즐거운 순간과 도전, 그리고 때로는 스트레스를 함께 겪으며 성장하는 작은 사회입니다. 저는 이 공동체에서 스스로 주인의식을 가지고, 작은 것부터 실천하는 태도가 얼마나 중요한지 배웠습니다.

이러한 경험은 결국 제 자신에게 도움이 되어, 커뮤니티에 대한 책임감을 갖고 헌신하는 태도로 전교 회장과 같은 리더십 포지션으로 이어졌고, 친구들과 선생님들에게서 신뢰와 존경을 얻을 수 있었습니다. 그리고 이러한 과정들은 입시에서도 강력한 강점이 되었습니다.

입시는 단순히 성적과 시험 점수로만 평가되지 않습니다. 탑 보딩스쿨이 원하는 학생은 얼마나 인간적이며, 학교 공동체에 긍정적인 영향을 줄 수 있는 사람인지를 중요하게 평가합니다. 다시 말해, 학교 안에서 어떤 가치를 창출했는지가 입시의 중요한 요소가 된다는 것입니다.

이런 이유로 저는 외부 활동 없이, 모든 EC(Extracurricular) 활동을 학교 안에서 집중적으로 수행했습니다. 제가 속한 공동체에서 의미 있는 기여를 하는 것이야말로, 입시에서도 가장 큰 경쟁력이 될 것이라 믿었기 때문입니다.

Rumsey Hall에서의 4년, 그리고 SSAT 공부 과정에서 저는 한 가지 확실한 교훈을 얻었습니다. 모든 행동은 마음가짐에서 시작된다는 것입니다.

SSAT 공부 역시 마찬가지입니다. 겸손하고, 긍정적인 태도를 유지하면서 성실하게 노력한다면, 반드시 원하는 결과를 얻을 수 있습니다. 단순히 점수를 올리는 것이 목표가 아니라, 자신을 성장시키는 과정으로 받아들인다면, 결과는 자연스럽게 따라오게 됩니다.

여러분, 끝까지 화이팅!!

[SSAT 99%라는 점수는 나와는
다른 세상 이야기라고만 생각했어요.]

안녕하세요! 저는 미국 주니어 보딩에서 Brooks로 진학하게 된 한정원입니다. 처음 한세희 선생님 반에서 SSAT를 시작했을 때는, SSAT 99%라는 점수는 나와는 다른 세상 이야기라고만 생각했어요. 충격적인 첫 모의고사 점수를 보고 정말 앞으로 열심히 해야겠다고 다짐했어요. SSAT와 어드미션 에세이를 같이 준비하다 보니 힘들었지만 한세희 선생님과 꾸준히 상담하며 포기하지 않고 열심히 계속하다 보니 SSAT 99%라는 좋은 결과가 나왔어요.

저는 SSAT를 시작하면서부터 Reading을 집중적으로 했어요. 주니어 보딩에 다니느라 방학이 끝나고 미국에 돌아가면 Reading 문제들을 풀 시간도 없을 것 같고 학교를 다니면서 공부하기가 쉽지 않을 것 같아서요. 선생님 말씀대로 저는 일단 Math를 99%에 맞춰 놓고 Reading을 올리는 데 신경을 썼습니다. 또 Verbal은 상대적으로 Reading 보다 올리기가 쉽기 때문에 선생님이 주시는 Hit Vocab과 [한세희의 SSAT]책에 있는 Analogies 유형들도 잘 정리하면 잘 볼 수 있어요. 선생님과 한 달 정도 공부했을 때 모의고사 점수가 90% 초반이 나와서 힘든 순간도 있었지만 할 수 있다는 선생님의 격려와 선배들의 응원에 포기하지 않고 열심히 했습니다. 미국에 돌아가서는 한세희 선생님께서 만들어 주신 자료들을 복습하고, 오답 노트를 만들어 매일 조금씩 공부하였어요. 단어장을 만들어 학교에서 돌아다니면서 외우고, 시간이 날 때마다 문제들을 풀었어요.

시험 전에는 자주 나오는 시들과 시에 자주 쓰이는 단어들을 외웠어요. 한세희 선생님께서 따로 시에 자주 사용되는 어휘 리스트도 주셔서 그것을 외웠는 데 도움이 많이 되었어요. 선생님께서 종종 말씀해 주셨던 한 가지 팁을 드리자면 SSAT는 Omit을 어떻게 하느냐가 굉장히 중요해요. 저도 처음 시험 볼 때는 Omit을 하나도 하지 않아서 점수가 예상 보다 낮게 나왔었어요. 그 뒤로는 Omit하는 방법을 비롯해 문제풀이 전략을 연습해 좋은 결과를 얻었습니다.

SSAT, GPA, Interview 모두 너무 중요하지만, 제가 하나 더 드리고 싶은 팁은 학교에서 Leadership Position과 Extracurricular 활동에 적극적으로 참여 하라는 것입니다. 저는 다른 부분들은 다 괜찮았는데 학교 활동에서 조금 조용하고 소극적이었던 것이 아쉬웠어요. 또한 Recommendation도 중요하기 때문에 학교에서 친구들, 선생님들과 잘 지내야 하고 수업도 열심히 들어야 해요.

저는 Brooks에 가기로 했습니다. 제가 Brooks 고른 이유는 인터뷰 때문이에요. 인터뷰 때 선생님과 정말 재미있는 시간을 보냈고, 그 이후에도 계속 연락을 주고받았어요. 지원했던 모든 학교 중에서 Brooks 인터뷰할 때 제일 편했고 가장 저 다웠던 것 같아요.

이 글이 SSAT를 시작하는 많은 후배님들에게 도움이 됐으면 좋겠고, 제가 잘 진학 할 수 있도록 도와주신 모든 분들께 감사드립니다. 아무리 힘들어도 포기하지 마시고 열심히 하셔서 좋은 결과를 보시길 바래요! 후배님들 파이팅!

이 책의 구성

Check Point 1
레슨 번호를 확인하세요. 동영상 강의를 들으실 때는 이것으로 순서를 찾으시면 편리합니다.

MIDDLE LEVEL **Lesson 1-1**

abolish
[uh-**bol**-ish

v. to put
institutio

(법률, 제도

*The Su
to abo*

1 abandon		6 accelerate	
abash		7 accompany	

Check Point 2
이번 수업에서 배울 열 개의 단어입니다.
시작하기 전 빠르게 한번 훑어 보세요.

1 abandon		6 accelerate
2 abash		7 accompany
3 abolish		8 accomplished

Check Point 3
각 단어는 [단어/발음기호/영어 뜻/한글 뜻/예문/동의어] 순으로 구성되어 있습니다.
공부할 때는 동의어를 같이 외우며 SSAT 점수를 빠르게 올릴 수 있어요. 모두 외우고 나서는 예문을 꼭 읽어 어떤 식으로 활용되었는지 확인하세요. 동영상 강의를 보면서 단어를 어떻게 외울지, 어떻게 시험에 출제되는지 확인하면 훨씬 더 효과적입니다.

abandon
[uh-**ban**-duhn]

v. to give up completely
(사람, 물건, 장소, 지위 등을) 버리다, 버리고 떠나다

*The criminal **abandoned** the old car in the empty parking lot.*

ab
[uh-

adj
풍부

S
th

Check Point 4
배운 단어를 즉시 활용하여 ISEE Sentence Completion 연습도 할 수 있습니다. 또한, SSAT와 ISEE에서 반복적으로 등장하는 필수 어휘를 한 번에 익히고 실전에 적용할 수 있어, 두 시험을 동시에 대비하는 데 최적화된 학습 효과를 제공합니다.

ISEE Sentence Completion 1-2

MIDDLE

1
2

Directions : Fill in the blanks to complete the sentences.

Check Point 5
정답은 해당 페이지 하단에서 확인하실 수 있습니다.

1. admirable	
2. adequate	5. affirm
3. affront	6. adjoin
4. adorn	7. acute

🖐 Answers

Analogy 1. Person

Analogy에는 사람 관련 문제가 전체의 10%정도 출제됩니다. 여기서는 가장 중요한 위
실제 출제되는 문제 유형은 [A is to B]의 형태이지만 여기서는 편의상 [A : B]로 표기

A는 B하는 사람

A는 B하는 사람	
entor : advise	nomad : w
: 조언하다	유목민 : 방랑하
aggart : boast	arbiter : se

POP QUIZ

1. Abolitionist is to bondage as
(A) iconoclast is to convention
(B) weaver is to weep
(C) superintendent is to manage
(D) glutton is to food
(E) miser is to money

age
(C) caretaker is to solicitous
(D) toady is to unassuming
(E) coward is to gallant

Answer 1.A 2.C

Check-up 1-1

Directions   Each of the following questions consists of one
You are to select the one word or phrase whose

1. ABANDON

(C) demand
(D) endow
(E) obtain

Answer 1.C 2.E 3.B 4.D 5.A 6.D 7.B 8.B 9.C 10.E

29

MIDDLE LEVEL SSAT VOCABULARY

UPPER LEVEL SSAT VOCABULARY

MIDDLE

한세희의 SSAT HIT VOCABULARY

LEVEL

1 abandon   6 accelerate

2 abash   7 accompany

3 abolish   8 accomplished

4 abridge   9 acknowledge

5 abundant   10 acquire

Carpe diem.
(Seize the day.)
오늘을 즐겨라.

SSATKOREA.com

abolish
[uh-**bol**-ish]

v. to put an end to (a system, practice, or institution)

(법률, 제도, 관습 등을) 폐지하다, 없애다

*The Supreme Court believed it was time to **abolish** the outdated law.*

syn. eliminate, demolish, destroy

abridge
[uh-**brij**]

v. to shorten by omissions while retainig the basic contents

줄이다, 축약하다

*The editor wanted to **abridge** his epic 1000-page history to a 10-page summary instead.*

syn. shorten, abbreviate, curtail

abandon
[uh-**ban**-duhn]

v. to give up completely

(사람, 물건, 장소, 지위 등을) 버리다

*The criminal **abandoned** the old car in the empty parking lot.*

syn. desert, forsake, relinquish

abundant
[uh-**buhn**-duhnt]

adj. existing or available in large quantities

풍부한, 많은

*Since the apple crops were **abundant** this year, apple prices are affordable.*

syn. plentiful, copious, ample

abash
[uh-**bash**]

v. to cause another person to feel awkward, embarrassed, or ashamed

(다른 사람을) 당황시키다, 부끄럽게 만들다

*The villain vowed to **abash** his opponent in any way possible.*

syn. embarrass, disconcert, confuse

accelerate
[ak-**sel**-uh-reyt]

v. to increase in speed

가속하다, 속도를 높이다

*Many accidents happen when drivers **accelerate** on sharp curves.*

syn. speed up, quicken, expedite

accompany
[uh-**kuhm**-puh-nee]

v. to go along or in company with

(사람과) 같이 가다, 동행하다

*I'd like you to **accompany** me.*

syn. escort, attend, partner

accomplished
[uh-**kom**-plisht]

adj. skilled in activity

숙달된, 노련한, 학식이 깊은

*Johann Sebastian Bach had three children who all became highly **accomplished** musicians.*

syn. skilled, adept, proficient

acknowledge
[ak-**nol**-ij]

v. to admit to be real or true, to show or express appreciation for

(사실로) 인정하다

*The boys **acknowledged** that they had accidentally broken the window.*

syn. accept, admit, concede

acquire
[uh-**kwahyuhr**]

v. to obtain or receive

(노력으로) 습득하다, 얻다

*Through experience, she **acquired** a sense of calm in a crisis.*

syn. obtain, gain, attain

Directions : Fill in the blanks to complete the sentences.

1. After years of dedication and hard work, she became an _____ writer, respected by her peers.

   (A) accomplished   (B) abundant
   (C) abashed   (D) abridge

2. The movement was instrumental in the effort to _____ slavery.

   (A) abolish   (B) abridge
   (C) accompany   (D) acknowledge

3. Critics argued that the new policy might _____ the rights of marginalized groups.

   (A) accomplish   (B) accelerate
   (C) abridge   (D) abandon

4. We were told to _____ ship during the emergency.

   (A) abolish   (B) accompany
   (C) abandon   (D) acknowledge

5. The company implemented new strategies to _____ its growth in the global market.

   (A) accelerate   (B) acquire
   (C) abridge   (D) abash

1. (A)   2. (A)   3. (C)   4. (C)   5. (A)

 Answers

11 acute	16 admirable
12 adaptable	17 adorn
13 adept	18 affable
14 adequate	19 affront
15 adjoin	20 aggravate

Alea iacta est.
(The die is cast.)
주사위는 던져졌다.

SSATKOREA.com

acute
[uh-**kyoot**]

adj. deeply perceptive or very clever
(매우) 예리한

*She has an **acute** understanding of algebra, so she always gets 100% on tests.*

syn. sharp, keen, clever

adaptable
[uh-**dap**-tuh-b*uh*l]

adj. able and usually willing to change
(새로운 환경에) 적응할 수 있는

*Successful people are highly **adaptable** to changes.*

syn. flexible, versatile, malleable

adept
[uh-**dept**]

adj. very skilled
능숙한, 솜씨 좋은

*Carry is an **adept** speaker; he never loses a debate.*

syn. skilled, proficient, expert

adequate
[**ad**-i-kwit]

adj. fully sufficient or suitable
(특정한 필요에) 충분한, 적절한

*Ten dollars is **adequate** to buy lunch.*

syn. sufficient, enough, acceptable

adjoin
[uh-**join**]

v. to be next to
인접하다, 붙어 있다

*Reading rooms **adjoin** the assembly room.*

syn. abut, border, attach

admirable
[**ad**-mer-uh-b*uh*l]

adj. deserving respect or approval
감탄스러운, 존경스러운

*She is an **admirable** teacher, with great power of lucid exposition.*

syn. praiseworthy, commendable, laudable

adorn
[uh-**dawrn**]

v. to decorate or add beauty to

꾸미다, 장식하다

*Children **adorn** their Christmas trees with tinsel and lights.*

syn. decorate, beautify, embellish

affable
[**af**-*uh*-b*uh*l]

adj. friendly, easy to talk to, and pleasant in manner

상냥한, 붙임성 있는, 친근한

*Her **affable** smile made everyone feel welcome at the party.*

syn. friendly, approachable, pleasant

affront
[uh-**fruhnt**]

n. an insult

모욕, (마음의) 상처

*Revenge for an **affront** massacred all the men capable of bearing arms in the city.*

syn. insult, indignity, provocation

aggravate
[ag-**ruh**-veyt]

v. to cause to become worse

악화시키다, 더 나쁘게 만들다

*Military intervention **aggravate** regional tensions.*

syn. worsen, exacerbate, intensify

ISEE Sentence Completion 1-2

Directions : Fill in the blanks to complete the sentences.

1. Adding unnecessary details will only _____ the problem and delay the solution.

   (A) affront   (B) adjoin
   (C) aggravate   (D) adorn

2. The patient complained of _____ pain after the surgery.

   (A) adequate   (B) acute
   (C) affable   (D) affront

3. The decorations were carefully chosen to _____ the hall with festive charm.

   (A) affront   (B) adorn
   (C) adjoin   (D) aggravate

4. Her response was seen as a _____ to the committee, causing a heated debate.

   (A) affront   (B) adorn
   (C) affable   (D) aggravate

5. His kind and _____ personality made him popular among his peers.

   (A) affable   (B) acute
   (C) admirable   (D) adaptable

1. (C)   2. (B)   3. (B)   4. (A)   5. (A)

  Answers

21	agile	26	alias
22	agitate	27	alliance
23	agony	28	allude
24	agreeable	29	alter
25	airborne	30	amass

Memento mori.
(Remember that you will die.)
죽음을 기억하라.

SSATKOREA.com

agile
[**aj**-*uh*l]

adj. quick and well-coordinated in movement

날렵한, 민첩한

*On water skis, she was **agile** and made sharp turns.*

syn. nimble, quick, dexterous

agitate
[**aj**-i-teyt]

v. to move or force into violent, irregular action

(마음을) 뒤흔들다, 불안하게 만들다

*When he watched a horror movie at bedtime, he was too **agitated** to sleep.*

syn. provoke, disturb, trouble

agony
[**ag**-uh-nee]

n. extreme and generally prolonged pain

극도의 고통, 괴로움

*That level of **agony** was something he never wanted to go through again.*

syn. anguish, suffering, torture

agreeable
[uh-gree-*uh*-b*uh*l]

adj. enjoyable or pleasing

기분 좋은, 받아들일 만한

*The weather was so **agreeable** that we decided to have a picnic.*

syn. pleasant, friendly, enjoyable

airborne
[**air**-bawrn]

adj. carried by the air

공기 중에 떠 있는, 비행 중인

*The **airborne** virus infected all of the people on the cruise.*

syn. flying, aloft, soaring

alias
[**ey**-lee-*uh*s]

n. an assumed name

가명, 별명

*He travelled under an **alias**: Luke Skywalker.*

syn. pseudonym, moniker, nickname

alliance

[uh-**lahy**-*uh*ns]

n. the act of allying or state of being allied

동맹, 연합

*By the tension between the two, their **alliance** was brittle at best.*

syn. association, union, partnership

allude

[uh-**lood**]

v. to make an allusion

암시하다, 시사하다, 넌지시 말하다

*He **alluded** to his rival's past failure.*

syn. imply, refer, suggest

alter

[**awl**-ter]

v. to cause to change

바꾸다, 고치다

*He pronounced the words that would forever **alter** his life.*

syn. change, adjust, modify

amass

[uh-**mas**]

v. to collect as one's own

모으다, 축적하다

*His family has **amassed** great wealth from their investments in real estate.*

syn. accumulate, gather, collect

ISEE Sentence Completion 1-3

Directions : Fill in the blanks to complete the sentences.

1. We need to _____ the plan to account for the unexpected weather conditions.

   (A) allude   (B) alter
   (C) amass   (D) alliance

2. The spy operated under an _____ to protect their identity.

   (A) airborne   (B) alias
   (C) alliance   (D) amass

3. The two companies decided to form an _____ to expand their market reach.

   (A) agony   (B) alias
   (C) alliance   (D) alter

4. She has an _____ mind that allows her to solve puzzles faster than anyone else.

   (A) amass   (B) alter
   (C) agile   (D) agree

5. Over the years, she managed to _____ significant wealth through her investments.

   (A) amass   (B) alliance
   (C) alter   (D) agreeable

31	ambiguous	36	antagonistic
32	amiable	37	anticipate
33	amorphous	38	apex
34	ample	39	apologetic
35	annex	40	appease

Vice versa
(With the order reversed)
반대로, 역으로.

SSATKOREA.com

amorphous
[*uh*-**mawr**-f*uh*s]

adj. without a clear shape or form
형태가 없는, 무정형의

*The clouds in the sky were **amorphous**, constantly changing their shapes.*

syn. shapeless, formless, vague

ample
[**am**-p*uh*l]

adj. plentiful and enough
충분한, 풍부한

*His parents have left **ample** stores of food and water for him.*

syn. bountiful, plentiful, abundant

ambiguous
[am-big-**yoo**-*uh*s]

adj. open to or having several possible meanings
모호한, 애매한, 불확실한

*His answers are intentionally **ambiguous**.*

syn. unclear, equivocal, obscure

annex
[uh-**neks**]

v. to attach, append, or add
합병하다, 합치다, 더하다

*The first ten amendments were **annexed** to the Constitution.*

syn. add, attach, incorporate

amiable
[**ey**-mee-uh-b*uh*l]

adj. having pleasant, good-natured personal qualities
친절한, 쾌활한, 친근한

*Her teacher had an **amiable** personality, always ready with a kind word and a smile.*

syn. kind, friendly, agreeable

antagonistic
[an-tag-uh-**nis**-tik]

adj. opposing, especially mutually
적대적인, 반감을 가진

*The moral in this story appears to be **antagonistic** to ideas of monarchy.*

syn. hostile, opposing, combative

anticipate

[an-**tis**-uh-peyt]

v. to foretaste or foresee

예상하다, 예측하다

*There was every reason to **anticipate** the success.*

syn. foresee, expect, predict

apex

[**ey**-peks]

n. the highest point or peak of something

정점, 꼭대기, 절정

*The climbers were excited when they finally reached the **apex** of the mountain after hours of hiking.*

syn. peak, summit, culmination

apologetic

[*uh*-pol-uh-**jet**-ik]

adj. showing regret or remorse for having done something wrong or for causing offense

사과하는, 미안해하는

*He gave her an **apologetic** smile after accidentally stepping on her foot.*

syn. regretful, sorry, remorseful

appease

[uh-**peez**]

v. to bring to a state of peace

달래다, 고통을 줄여주다

*"Look, you did all you could do," I said trying to **appease** her.*

syn. soothe, pacify, assuage

ISEE Sentence Completion 1-4

Directions : Fill in the blanks to complete the sentences.

1. She worked tirelessly for years to _____ of her career and become a respected leader.

   (A) annex   (B) appease
   (C) apex   (D) annex

2. Her _____ personality made her well-liked by everyone in the community.

   (A) antagonistic   (B) amorphous
   (C) amiable   (D) ample

3. His _____ statement left everyone confused about his true intentions.

   (A) ambiguous   (B) amiable
   (C) ample   (D) apologetic

4. This new policy provides _____ opportunities for growth in the industry.

   (A) amorphous   (B) apologetic
   (C) ample   (D) ambiguous

5. The speaker tried to _____ the crowd by addressing their concerns immediately.

   (A) anticipate   (B) appease
   (C) annex   (D) ambiguous

Answers
1. (C) 2. (C) 3. (A) 4. (C) 5. (B)

41 appliance   46 arid

42 approve   47 arouse

43 apt   48 ashamed

44 arable   49 aspire

45 arduous   50 assert

Per aspera ad astra.
(Through hardships to the stars.)
역경을 넘어 별들에게로.

──────── SSATKOREA.com

appliance
[uh-**plahy**-*uh*ns]

n. a device or machine often used in the home
기기, 가전제품

*All household **appliances**, such as a stove, fan, or refrigerator, are now on sale.*

syn.   device, gadget, gear

approve
[uh-**proov**]

v. to consent or agree to
찬성하다, 승인하다, 인정하다

*The committee **approved** the proposed budget.*

syn.   accept, ratify, approve

apt
[apt]

adj. quick to learn
~을 잘하는, 적성이 있는

*He was **apt** at dancing.*

syn.   capable, skilled, talented

arable
[**ar**-uh-b*uh*l]

adj. suitable for farming
농사지을 수 있는, 경작 가능한

*In Great Britain, 15% of all **arable** land is unproductive.*

syn.   farmable, cultivable, tillable

arduous
[**ahr**-joo-*uh*s]

adj. difficult, needing a lot of effort and energy
몹시 힘든, 고된

*It was a long and **arduous** trip.*

syn.   difficult, challenging, strenuous

arid
[**ar**-id]

adj. extremely dry
매우 건조한

*An **arid** stony plateau lacks water.*

syn.   dry, dehydrated, parched

arouse

[uh-**rouz**]

v. to stir to action or strong response

(느낌이나 태도를) 불러일으키다

*A warm touch began to **arouse** him.*

syn.   stimulate, excite, awaken

ashamed

[uh-**sheymd**]

adj. feeling shame

부끄러운, 수치스러운

*He was **ashamed** that he'd made so little effort.*

syn.   embarrassed, abashed, humiliated

aspire

[uh-**spahy***uhr*]

v. to be eagerly desirous

바라다, 열망하다

*As an actor, he **aspired** to work on Broadway.*

syn.   strive, aim, yearn

assert

[uh-**surt**]

v. to state strongly or positively

주장하다, 확고히 말하다

*The defense attorney **asserted** that he believed strongly in his client's innocence.*

syn.   declare, insist, maintain

ISEE Sentence Completion 1-5

Directions : Fill in the blanks to complete the sentences.

1. From a young age, he was encouraged to _____ to greatness by setting ambitious goals.

   (A) arouse   (B) aspire
   (C) approve   (D) assert

2. The desert is known for its _____ climate, with very little rainfall throughout the year.

   (A) arduous   (B) aspire
   (C) arable   (D) arid

3. Hiking through the dense jungle was an _____ journey that tested their endurance.

   (A) arid   (B) arduous
   (C) assert   (D) apt

4. The farmers relied on the _____ land to grow their crops successfully.

   (A) arable   (B) appliance
   (C) arduous   (D) ashamed

5. The blender is a commonly used _____ in most modern kitchens.

   (A) appliance   (B) aspire
   (C) arable   (D) arduous

Answers
1. (B) 2. (D) 3. (B) 4. (A) 5. (A)

Analogy 1. Person

Analogy에는 사람 관련 문제가 전체의 10%정도 출제됩니다. 여기서는 가장 중요한 몇가지 유형과 자주 출제되는 단어를 살펴 보도록 합시다.
실제 출제되는 문제 유형은 [A is to B]의 형태이지만 여기서는 편의상 [A : B]로 표기 합니다.

A는 B하는 사람

mentor : advise
멘토 : 조언하다

nomad : wander
유목민 : 방랑하다

braggart : boast
자랑꾼 : 자랑하다

arbiter : settle
중재자 : 해결하다

A의 특징이 B

acrobat : agile
곡예사 : 민첩한

philanthropist : benevolent
박애주의자 : 인정 많은

boor : vulgar
무례한 사람 : 상스러운

sage : wise
현명한 사람 : 현명한

B는 A가 좋아하거나 추구하는 것

glutton : food
대식가 : 음식

miser : money
구두쇠 : 돈

bibliophile : book
애서가 : 책

hedonist : pleasure
쾌락주의자 : 쾌락

B는 A가 싫어하거나 피하려는 것

vegetarian : meat
채식주의자 : 고기

pacifist : violence
평화주의자 : 폭력

iconoclast : convention
인습 타파주의자 : 관습

anarchist : government
무정부주의자 : 정부

POP QUIZ

1. Anarchist is to government as
- (A) iconoclast is to convention
- (B) weaver is to weep
- (C) superintendent is to manage
- (D) glutton is to food
- (E) miser is to money

2. Sage is to wise as
- (A) opponent is to annihilated
- (B) liar is to candid
- (C) boor is to vulgar
- (D) toady is to unassuming
- (E) coward is to gallant

Check-up 1-1

Directions   Each of the following questions consists of one word followed by five words or phrases. You are to select the one word or phrase whose meaning is closest to the word in capital letters.

1. ABANDON
(A) impact
(B) convene
(C) desert
(D) revitalize
(E) veil

2. ABASH
(A) donate
(B) handle
(C) reflect
(D) resolve
(E) embarrass

3. ABOLISH
(A) generate
(B) eliminate
(C) stare
(D) doze
(E) liberate

4. ABRIDGE
(A) protest
(B) locate
(C) quote
(D) shorten
(E) annoy

5. ABUNDANT
(A) plentiful
(B) artistic
(C) noble
(D) fatal
(E) hasty

6. ACCELERATE
(A) take over
(B) hand in
(C) count on
(D) speed up
(E) let up

7. ACCOMPANY
(A) detect
(B) escort
(C) determine
(D) produce
(E) discourage

8. ACCOMPLISHED
(A) athletic
(B) skilled
(C) clumsy
(D) structural
(E) obsolete

9. ACKNOWLEDGE
(A) achieve
(B) protest
(C) accept
(D) demand
(E) steal

10. ACQUIRE
(A) falter
(B) ask
(C) demand
(D) endow
(E) obtain

33

Check-up 1-2

1. ACUTE
(A) lively
(B) empty
(C) sharp
(D) inborn
(E) dull

2. ADAPTABLE
(A) flexible
(B) generous
(C) merciful
(D) messy
(E) unkempt

3. ADEPT
(A) inept
(B) skilled
(C) tamed
(D) insane
(E) magnanimous

4. ADEQUATE
(A) excellent
(B) sufficient
(C) redundant
(D) distinct
(E) obese

5. ADJOIN
(A) abut
(B) detach
(C) lessen
(D) ponder
(E) agree

6. ADMIRABLE
(A) sacred
(B) proud
(C) miserable
(D) inclement
(E) praiseworthy

7. ADORN
(A) decorate
(B) disband
(C) change
(D) worsen
(E) create

8. AFFABLE
(A) standoffish
(B) distant
(C) repulsive
(D) despicable
(E) friendly

9. AFFRONT
(A) nobility
(B) strength
(C) depth
(D) pleasure
(E) insult

10. AGGRAVATE
(A) retract
(B) worsen
(C) bellow
(D) ameliorate
(E) compensate

Check-up 1-3

Directions   Each of the following questions consists of one word followed by five words or phrases.
You are to select the one word or phrase whose meaning is closest to the word in capital letters.

1. AGILE
(A) fierce
(B) soiled
(C) breathless
(D) nimble
(E) spiritual

2. AGITATE
(A) humiliate
(B) provoke
(C) disagree
(D) endure
(E) furnish

3. AGONY
(A) anguish
(B) truce
(C) approval
(D) initiate
(E) expound

4. AGREEABLE
(A) epic
(B) sickly
(C) pleasant
(D) abashed
(E) unanimous

5. AIRBORNE
(A) articulate
(B) genteel
(C) contagious
(D) flying
(E) cluttered

6. ALIAS
(A) stranger
(B) accomplice
(C) pseudonym
(D) backer
(E) patron

7. ALLIANCE
(A) avalanche
(B) association
(C) blizzard
(D) rebellion
(E) worker

8. ALLUDE
(A) vend
(B) conflict
(C) inspire
(D) imply
(E) save

9. ALTER
(A) invest
(B) change
(C) peddle
(D) investigate
(E) insinuate

10. AMASS
(A) accumulate
(B) conspire
(C) aggress
(D) refer
(E) attack

35

Check-up 1-4

Directions   Each of the following questions consists of one word followed by five words or phrases.
You are to select the one word or phrase whose meaning is closest to the word in capital letters.

1. AMBIGUOUS
(A) contented
(B) unclear
(C) conflicting
(D) obvious
(E) evident

2. AMIABLE
(A) happy
(B) kind
(C) dim
(D) clever
(E) satisfied

3. AMORPHOUS
(A) ingenious
(B) sincere
(C) comical
(D) shapeless
(E) frivolous

4. AMPLE
(A) grave
(B) scalding
(C) ascending
(D) bountiful
(E) wanting

5. ANNEX
(A) add
(B) appease
(C) soothe
(D) reveal
(E) call

6. ANTAGONISTIC
(A) welcoming
(B) hospitable
(C) balmy
(D) dominant
(E) hostile

7. ANTICIPATE
(A) foresee
(B) ascend
(C) publish
(D) communicate
(E) release

8. APEX
(A) virtue
(B) abyss
(C) homage
(D) peak
(E) quintessence

9. APOLOGETIC
(A) erratic
(B) pompous
(C) superior
(D) unassuming
(E) regretful

10. APPEASE
(A) impair
(B) ameliorate
(C) deceive
(D) mar
(E) soothe

Check-up 1-5

Directions   Each of the following questions consists of one word followed by five words or phrases.
You are to select the one word or phrase whose meaning is closest to the word in capital letters.

1. APPLIANCE
(A) device
(B) plot
(C) tier
(D) bottleneck
(E) complaint

2. APPROVE
(A) dishearten
(B) accept
(C) determine
(D) produce
(E) detect

3. APT
(A) fainthearted
(B) inept
(C) mousy
(D) capable
(E) various

4. ARABLE
(A) farmable
(B) soggy
(C) ache
(D) parched
(E) mountainous

5. ARDUOUS
(A) replaced
(B) smug
(C) difficult
(D) uncovered
(E) distinguished

6. ARID
(A) dry
(B) soaked
(C) financial
(D) drowned
(E) pecuniary

7. AROUSE
(A) whisper
(B) stare
(C) glare
(D) fret
(E) stimulate

8. ASHAMED
(A) incognito
(B) lackluster
(C) peevish
(D) embarrassed
(E) pout

9. ASPIRE
(A) address
(B) strive
(C) accost
(D) aggress
(E) perspire

10. ASSERT
(A) emancipate
(B) inspire
(C) improvise
(D) declare
(E) insert

Answer 1.A 2.B 3.D 4.A 5.C 6.A 7.E 8.D 9.B 10.D

51 assist	56 authentic
52 associate	57 authority
53 assure	58 avid
54 astounding	59 baffle
55 astute	60 banish

Fortuna audaces iuvat.
(Fortune favors the bold.)
운명은 용감한 자를 돕는다.

SSATKOREA.com

assist
[uh-**sist**]

v. to give support or aid to
도와주다, 돕다

*She had the sudden urge to **assist** her friend.*

syn.   aid, help, support

associate
[uh-**soh**-shee-eyt]

v. to connect in the mind
연관을 짓다, 연상하다

*Even a prisoner was unwilling to **associate** with him.*

syn.   connect, correlate, combine

assure
[*uh*-**shoor**]

v. to make certain
보증하다, 장담하다, 단언하다

*'It'll be all right,' Meg **assured** her sister.*

syn.   convince, ensure, persuade

astounding
[uh-**stoun**-ding]

adj. causing surprise and wonder
크게 놀라게 하는, 놀라운

*She made an **astounding** success.*

syn.   astonishing, amazing, incredible

astute
[uh-**stoot**]

adj. showing an ability to accurately assess situations or people
통찰력 있는, 기민한, 날카로운

*He is an **astute** businessman who is skillful at using his knowledge to his own advantage.*

syn.   shrewd, sharp, acute

authentic
[aw-**then**-tik]

adj. not false or copied
진짜의, 진품의

*The expert doesn't know if the painting is **authentic**.*

syn.   genuine, real, reliable

authority
[uh-**thawr**-i-tee]

n. the power or right to give orders, make decisions, and enforce obedience

권위, 권력, 권한, 직권

*Only the principal has the **authority** to sign this document.*

syn. power, authorization, control

avid
[**av**-id]

adj. showing a great interest in or desire for something

몹시 탐내는, 열심인, 열광적인

*He is an **avid** reader.*

syn. eager, enthusiastic, ardent

baffle
[**baf**-*uhl*]

v. to confuse, frustrate, or perplex

당황하게 하다, 꺾어버리다, 좌절시키다

*A boy's awkward behavior **baffles** his mom.*

syn. perplex, puzzle, bewilder

banish
[**ban**-ish]

v. to force to leave

추방하다, 유배를 보내다

*Roger Williams was **banished** from Massachusetts Bay Colony.*

syn. exile, expel, deport

ISEE Sentence Completion 2-1

Directions : Fill in the blanks to complete the sentences.

1. The king decided to _____ the traitor from the kingdom to ensure peace.

   (A) baffle   (B) assure
   (C) assist   (D) banish

2. Her _____ observation during the meeting helped resolve a complicated issue.

   (A) authentic   (B) astute
   (C) astounding   (D) baffle

3. The scientist's discovery produced _____ results that shocked the world.

   (A) authentic   (B) astute
   (C) astounding   (D) avid

4. The tour provided an _____ experience of the local culture.

   (A) astounding   (B) authentic
   (C) avid   (D) baffle

5. She's an _____ reader, devouring several books each month.

   (A) avid   (B) assist
   (C) authentic   (D) associate

Answers

1. (D)   2. (B)   3. (C)   4. (B)   5. (A)

61 barrier	66 bestow
62 barter	57 bland
63 bellow	68 blatant
64 beneficial	69 bleak
65 benign	70 bliss

Dum spiro, spero.
(While I breathe, I hope.)
숨 쉬는 한, 희망이 있다.

SSATKOREA.com

barrier
[**bar**-ee-er]

n. anything that restrains or obstructs progress or access

장애물, 장벽

The police put a barrier across the road to stop the traffic.

syn. obstacle, obstruction, barricade

barter
[**bahr**-ter]

v. to trade by exchange of commodities

물물교환하다, 물건을 교환하다

The Native Americans bartered not only with natural resources, but also with handcrafted goods.

syn. trade, exchange, haggle

bellow
[**bel**-oh]

v. to emit a hollow, loud, animal cry **as a** bull or cow

(우렁찬 소리로) 고함치다, 소리 지르다

The boss was bellowing into the phone, giving orders to his employees.

syn. roar, holler, yell

beneficial
[ben-uh-**fish**-uhl]

adj. advantageous or helpful

도움이 되는, 이익이 되는

Ladybugs are beneficial insects, eating the pesky aphids.

syn. helpful, advantageous, profitable

benign
[bih-**nahyn**]

adj. having a kindly disposition

상냥한, 유순한, 양성의

The gracious king was benign and generous.

syn. kind, harmless, mild

bestow
[bih-**stoh**]

v. to present as a gift

수여하다, 부여하다

The trophy was bestowed upon the winner.

syn. endow, give, allot

bland
[bland]

adj. pleasantly gentle or agreeable

부드러운, 단조로운, 재미없는

Avocado's bland taste and creamy texture make it easy to add to almost any salad.

syn. mild, temperate, dull

blatant
[bleyt-nt]

adj. brazenly obvious

명백하고 뻔뻔한

The math prodigy made a blatant error in simple addition.

syn. flagrant, obvious, conspicuous

bleak
[bleek]

adj. bare and desolate

차가운, 쓸쓸한

In the winter the landscape is bleak and the house is drafty.

syn. desolate, dreary, barren

bliss
[blis]

n. supreme happiness

행복, 환희

Before learning about climate change, I was carefree—perhaps ignorance is bliss.

syn. happiness, euphoria, ecstasy

ISEE Sentence Completion 2-2

Directions : Fill in the blanks to complete the sentences.

1. After the wildfire, the once-lush forest was left _____, with nothing but charred trees and ash.

   (A) bleak   (B) barrier
   (C) benign   (D) bliss

2. Eating fresh fruits and vegetables is _____ to your overall health.

   (A) bizarre   (B) benign
   (C) beneficial   (D) bliss

3. The soup lacked spices and had a very _____ flavor, disappointing the diners.

   (A) bland   (B) bleak
   (C) bellow   (D) barter

4. Spending a weekend at the beach, away from all worries, felt like pure _____.

   (A) bliss   (B) benign
   (C) bleak   (D) blatant

5. His statement was a _____ lie, and everyone in the room knew it instantly.

   (A) bizarre   (B) blatant
   (C) blissful   (D) benign

1. (A) 2. (C) 3. (A) 4. (A) 5. (B)
Answers

71 blunder   76 brash

72 bolster   77 brawl

73 boon   78 brazen

74 boundary   79 breach

75 bounteous   80 brittle

Temet nosce.
(Know yourself.)
너 자신을 알라.

SSATKOREA.com

blunder
[**bluhn**-der]

n. a huge, stupid or careless mistake
큰 실수, 실책

*Blessed are the forgetful, for they get the better even of their **blunders**.*

syn.   mistake, error, blooper

bolster
[**bohl**-ster]

v. to support with or as with a pillow or cushion
북돋다, 개선하다, 강화하다

*Mom's hug **bolstered** the kid's confidence.*

syn.   support, reinforce, strengthen

boon
[boon]

n. something to be thankful for
유용한 것, 요긴한 것, 도움이 되는 깃

*This mobile battery is a **boon** for cellphone users.*

syn.   advantage, godsend, blessing

boundary
[**boun**-duh-ree]

n. something that indicates bounds or limits
경계, 한계, 제한점

*The two neighbors had a violent dispute on the **boundary**.*

syn.   border, limit, edge

bounteous
[**boun**-tee-*uhs*]

adj. generous and abundant
너그러운, 풍부한

*The king gave **bounteous** gifts to the poor.*

syn.   abundant, generous, liberal

brash
[brash]

adj. impulsive and brazen
성급한, 자신만만한, 경솔한

*The **brash** young man was too confident and aggressive.*

syn.   bold, hasty, rash, impetuous

brawl

[brawl]

n. a noisy fight

싸움, 소동

Josh had been in a drunken street brawl.

syn. fight, scuffle, clash

brazen

[brey-*zuh*n]

adj. bold and without shame

철면피의, 뻔뻔스런

The crime was so brazen and daring.

syn. unashamed, shameless, unabashed

breach

[breech]

v. to break or act contrary to a law

(법을) 위반하다, (약속을) 저버리다

The company unilaterally breached a contract.

syn. violate, infringe, break

brittle

[brit-l]

adj. fragile and breakable

약한, 깨지기 쉬운, 불안정한

As a man ages, his bones grow more brittle.

syn. fragile, frail, feeble

ISEE Sentence Completion 2-3

Directions : Fill in the blanks to complete the sentences.

1. The client is suing the company for a serious _____ of contract regarding the delayed delivery.

   (A) boon   (B) blunder
   (C) brawl   (D) breach

2. The politician's slip of the tongue was seen as a major _____ during the debate.

   (A) blunder   (B) breach
   (C) brawl   (D) boon

3. His _____ decision to invest all his savings in a risky venture worried his family.

   (A) brash   (B) boon
   (C) blunder   (D) brittle

4. The police were quick to intervene in the chaotic _____ that broke out downtown.

   (A) breach   (B) blunder
   (C) brawl   (D) boundary

5. The company was accused of making a _____ lie to cover up its financial losses.

   (A) brazen   (B) brittle
   (C) bounteous   (D) boon

Answers

1. (D) 2. (A) 3. (A) 4. (C) 5. (A)

81 camouflage   86 clumsy

82 candor   87 coarse

83 capitulate   88 colossal

84 chaotic   89 combative

85 clarify   90 combine

Omnia vincit amor.
(Love conquers all.)
사랑은 모든 것을 이긴다.

SSATKOREA.com

camouflage
[**kam**-uh-flahzh]

v. to disguise by means of camouflage
위장하다, 변장하다

*They **camouflaged** ships by painting them gray.*

syn. disguise, cover, conceal

candor
[**kan**-der]

n. the quality of being frank, open, and sincere
솔직함, 신실함

*He spoke with **candor** about his past life.*

syn. honesty, straightforwardness, frankness

capitulate
[kuh-**pich**-uh-leyt]

v. to surrender unconditionally or on stipulated terms
항복하다, 복종하다, 굴복하다

*The city **capitulated** after a three-month siege.*

syn. surrender, concede, defeat

chaotic
[key-**ot**-ik]

adj. utterly confused
대혼란의, 무법의

***Chaotic** conditions followed the war.*

syn. disorderly, unorganized, tumultuous

clarify
[**klar**-uh-fahy]

v. to make clear and intelligible
명확하게 하다, 분명히 말하다

*She was unable to **clarify** her situation.*

syn. explain, expound, elucidate

clumsy
[**kluhm**-zee]

adj. awkward in movement or action
솜씨없는, 손재주가 없는, 어색한

*His accent was pretty good, but his speech pattern was really **clumsy**.*

syn. awkward, uncoordinated, ungainly

coarse

[kohrs]

adj. not fine or rude

거친, 상스러운, 굵은

*She prefers **coarse** grind to fine grind coffee.*

syn.   crude, vulgar, rough

colossal

[kuh-**los**-*uhl*]

adj. extraordinarily great in size, extent, or degree

거대한, 광대한, 대량의

*It was a **colossal** bronze image of Athena, which was visible far out at sea.*

syn.   gigantic, huge, enormous

combative

[k*uh*m-**bat**-iv]

adj. ready or inclined to fight

호전적인, 싸우기 좋아하는

*His **combative** disposition led him to numerous difficulties.*

syn.   aggressive, hostile, belligerent

combine

[kuhm-**bahyn**]

v. to bring into or join in a close union or whole

결합하다, 조합하다

*The choreography **combines** artistry and athletics.*

syn.   merge, unite, blend

ISEE Sentence Completion 2-4

Directions : Fill in the blanks to complete the sentences.

1. The teacher asked the students to _____ their ideas to ensure everyone understood the main point of the project.

   (A) combine   (B) clarify
   (C) camouflage   (D) capitulate

2. The new student felt _____ during her first day at school, accidentally knocking over books and tripping in the hallway.

   (A) clumsy   (B) chaotic
   (C) coarse   (D) colossal

3. The ancient statue was so _____ in size that it towered over all the visitors at the museum.

   (A) clumsy   (B) colossal
   (C) combative   (D) chaotic

4. His tone was so _____ when he spoke to his teammates that they were offended and refused to cooperate.

   (A) coarse   (B) chaotic
   (C) colossal   (D) candor

5. The two clubs decided to _____ their efforts to organize a larger, more successful school event.

   (A) capitulate   (B) clarify
   (C) camouflage   (D) combine

Answers

1. (B) 2. (A) 3. (B) 4. (A) 5. (D)

91 comfort		96 conceal	
92 commotion		97 concede	
93 compassionate		98 conceit	
94 complimentary		99 condemn	
95 composed		100 confide	

Status quo
(The current state)
현재 상태

SSATKOREA.com

comfort
[**kuhm**-fert]

v. to soothe, console, or reassure
위로하다, 애도하다

There was no use to try to comfort her.

syn. console, reassure, soothe

commotion
[kuh-**moh**-shuhn]

n. a violent or tumultuous motion
난동, 소란

What's all the commotion in the study hall?

syn. tumult, furor, uproar

compassionate
[k*u*hm-**pash**-*uh*-nit]

adj. demonstrating empathy and care
농정심 있는, 자비로운

A compassionate person always finds ways to help those in need.

syn. humane, caring, kind

complimentary
[kom-pluh-**men**-tuh-ree]

adj. given free as a gift or courtesy
무료의, 서비스의

The hotel provided complimentary breakfast for all guests.

syn. free, gratis, on the house

composed
[kuhm-**pohzd**]

adj. having one's feelings and expression under control
침착한, 조용한, 차분한

The captain's composed face reassured the nervous passengers.

syn. collected, calm, serene

conceal
[kuhn-**seel**]

v. to hide, to keep secret
감추다, 비밀로 하다

He was always trying to conceal that passion.

syn. hide, cover, disguise

concede
[kuhn-**seed**]

v. to acknowledge as true, just, or proper

(마지못해) 인정하다, 수긍하다

*Dad finally **conceded** that mom was right.*

syn. admit, accept, acknowledge

conceit
[konsi-t]

n. excessive pride in oneself

자만심, 자부심

*He is full of **conceit**, always boasting about his achievements.*

syn. arrogance, vanity, egotism

condemn
[k*uh*n-**dem**]

v. to express strong disapproval of something

비난하다, 규탄하다

*The teacher **condemned** cheating during exams, saying it was unfair to others.*

syn. criticize, blame, denounce

confide
[kuhn-**fahyd**]

v. to tell confidentially

비밀을 털어놓다

*Lucy dared not **confide** the secret to her family.*

syn. entrust, disclose, reveal

ISEE Sentence Completion 2-5

Directions : Fill in the blanks to complete the sentences.

1. Emma sought to _____ her nervous friend before the big audition by reminding her how well she had prepared.

   (A) conceal   (B) complimentary
   (C) comfort   (D) concede

2. The sudden _____ in the cafeteria caused the teachers to rush in and restore order.

   (A) composed   (B) commotion
   (C) comfort   (D) condemn

3. Even though Lily was excellent at math, her _____ made it hard for others to enjoy her company.

   (A) comfort   (B) confide
   (C) concede   (D) conceit

4. The hotel offers _____ breakfast to all guests staying in deluxe rooms.

   (A) concede   (B) conceal
   (C) complimentary (D) conceit

5. Despite the stressful situation, Sarah remained _____ and calmly handled the emergency.

   (A) commotion   (B) comfort
   (C) confide   (D) composed

Analogy 2. Tools & Function

Tools & Function은 도구와 그 기능을 연결짓는 관계입니다.

A는 B하기 위한 것	
loom : weave 베틀 : 천을 짜다	**locomotive : travel** 증기 기관차 : 이동하다
magnifying glass : enlarge 돋보기 : 확대하다	**lamp : illuminate** 램프 : 밝히다
tripod : support 삼각대 : 지지하다	**buffer : polish** 버퍼 : 광내다
colander : drain 체 : 물기를 빼다	**drill : bore** 드릴 : 구멍을 뚫다
mortar : grind 절구 : 갈다	**awl : pierce** 송곳 : 구멍을 뚫다
cleaver : cut 큰 식칼 : 자르다	**jack : raise** 잭(자동차 타이어를 갈 때처럼 무거운 것을 들어 올릴 때 쓰는 기구) : 들어올리다
chisel : carve (조각용) 끌 : 조각하다	**shovel : dig** 삽 : 파다
stove : cook 스토브 : 요리하다	**blade : cut** 칼날 : 자르다
vessel : contain 용기, 그릇 : 담다, 포함하다	**hammer : pound** 망치 : 두드리다

1. Tripod is to support as

    (A) razor is to fix
    (B) blade is to cut
    (C) shears is to cull
    (D) tongs is to tweezers
    (E) podium is to speech

2. Magnifying glass is to enlarge as

    (A) telescope is to prolong
    (B) stethoscope is to physician
    (C) ladder is to rung
    (D) vessel is to contain
    (E) crater is to apple

Check-up 2-1

Directions   Each of the following questions consists of one word followed by five words or phrases.
You are to select the one word or phrase whose meaning is closest to the word in capital letters.

1. ASSIST
(A) aid
(B) preserve
(C) add
(D) odd
(E) annex

2. ASSOCIATE
(A) appease
(B) connect
(C) smuggle
(D) falsify
(E) muffle

3. ASSURE
(A) hoard
(B) sanction
(C) validate
(D) disapprove
(E) convince

4. ASTOUNDING
(A) grimy
(B) soiled
(C) sooty
(D) astonishing
(E) sullen

5. ASTUTE
(A) stout
(B) meandering
(C) shrewd
(D) dull
(E) blunt

6. AUTHENTIC
(A) intrepid
(B) deafening
(C) bogus
(D) practical
(E) genuine

7. AUTHORITY
(A) elite
(B) power
(C) complexion
(D) knack
(E) reaper

8. AVID
(A) tepid
(B) eager
(C) opinionated
(D) flexible
(E) supple

9. BAFFLE
(A) perplex
(B) crumble
(C) banish
(D) fabricate
(E) collapse

10. BANISH
(A) concede
(B) accelerate
(C) exile
(D) invert
(E) descend

49

Check-up 2-2

1. BARRIER
- (A) timber
- (B) obstacle
- (C) risk
- (D) pastime
- (E) nectar

2. BARTER
- (A) donate
- (B) negotiate
- (C) tear
- (D) rip
- (E) trade

3. BELLOW
- (A) frown
- (B) compose
- (C) roar
- (D) dent
- (E) clash

4. BENEFICIAL
- (A) extinct
- (B) sparse
- (C) sluggish
- (D) hostile
- (E) helpful

5. BENIGN
- (A) illustrate
- (B) forecast
- (C) kind
- (D) anticipate
- (E) compete

6. BESTOW
- (A) cultivate
- (B) distract
- (C) reap
- (D) comply
- (E) endow

7. BLAND
- (A) essential
- (B) constructive
- (C) available
- (D) mild
- (E) destructive

8. BLATANT
- (A) flagrant
- (B) cordial
- (C) belligerent
- (D) illicit
- (E) surreptitious

9. BLEAK
- (A) torrid
- (B) contiguous
- (C) desolate
- (D) candid
- (E) mammoth

10. BLISS
- (A) folly
- (B) artisan
- (C) happiness
- (D) apprentice
- (E) ignorance

Check-up 2-3

Directions   Each of the following questions consists of one word followed by five words or phrases.
You are to select the one word or phrase whose meaning is closest to the word in capital letters.

1. BLUNDER
(A) mischief
(B) mission
(C) mishap
(D) mislead
(E) mistake

2. BOLSTER
(A) support
(B) slide
(C) credit
(D) debate
(E) submit

3. BOON
(A) nest
(B) stroke
(C) label
(D) discipline
(E) advantage

4. BOUNDARY
(A) harness
(B) border
(C) disgust
(D) scheme
(E) result

5. BOUNTEOUS
(A) opaque
(B) sleeve
(C) lucid
(D) abundant
(E) wanting

6. BRASH
(A) bold
(B) sheepish
(C) embarrassed
(D) omnipotent
(E) lithe

7. BRAWL
(A) zest
(B) fight
(C) fiction
(D) spearhead
(E) indicator

8. BRAZEN
(A) pungent
(B) incendiary
(C) toothsome
(D) pliable
(E) unashamed

9. BREACH
(A) derive
(B) violate
(C) render
(D) institute
(E) romain

10. BRITTLE
(A) callous
(B) evanescent
(C) congenial
(D) fragile
(E) vicarious

51

Check-up 2-4

Each of the following questions consists of one word followed by five words or phrases. You are to select the one word or phrase whose meaning is closest to the word in capital letters.

1. CAMOUFLAGE
(A) illustrate
(B) forecast
(C) scrub
(D) disguise
(E) compete

2. CANDOR
(A) honesty
(B) fidelity
(C) faithfulness
(D) sympathy
(E) detachment

3. CAPITULATE
(A) anticipate
(B) surrender
(C) entitle
(D) recede
(E) infer

4. CHAOTIC
(A) gruesome
(B) ungainly
(C) tattered
(D) discursive
(E) disorderly

5. CLARIFY
(A) cower
(B) decorate
(C) explain
(D) intimidate
(E) pollute

6. CLUMSY
(A) awkward
(B) belligerent
(C) hilarious
(D) unlawful
(E) stealthy

7. COARSE
(A) crude
(B) deft
(C) fanciful
(D) beneficial
(E) massive

8. COLOSSAL
(A) tiny
(B) conflicting
(C) gigantic
(D) impetuous
(E) colloquial

9. COMBATIVE
(A) torrid
(B) aggressive
(C) peripheral
(D) candid
(E) mammoth

10. COMBINE
(A) merge
(B) muffle
(C) compensate
(D) acquit
(E) commence

Check-up 2-5

Directions   Each of the following questions consists of one word followed by five words or phrases.
              You are to select the one word or phrase whose meaning is closest to the word in capital letters.

1. COMFORT

(A) dwindle
(B) soar
(C) wither
(D) console
(E) translate

2. COMMOTION

(A) emphasis
(B) tumult
(C) option
(D) game
(E) distinction

3. COMPASSIONATE

(A) relevant
(B) intriguing
(C) humane
(D) concerned
(E) successive

4. COMPLIMENTARY

(A) private
(B) expensive
(C) optional
(D) required
(E) free

5. COMPOSED

(A) ardent
(B) consecutive
(C) dense
(D) collected
(E) edible

6. CONCEAL

(A) employ
(B) hide
(C) envelop
(D) locate
(E) ebb

7. CONCEDE

(A) refuse
(B) admit
(C) leak
(D) stir
(E) pardon

8. CONCEIT

(A) hilarity
(B) philanthropy
(C) arrogance
(D) fury
(E) humility

9. CONDEMN

(A) gratify
(B) flee
(C) criticize
(D) oppose
(E) how

10. CONFIDE

(A) usurp
(B) bellow
(C) retract
(D) taper
(E) entrust

Answer 1.D 2.B 3.C 4.E 5.D 6.B 7.B 8.C 9.C 10.E

101 confound	106 conspicuous
102 confront	107 conspire
103 congenial	108 constant
104 conjecture	109 constraint
105 conquest	110 contemporary

Per se
(By itself)
그 자체로

SSATKOREA.com

congenial
[kuhn-**jeen**-yuhl]

adj. agreeable, suitable, or pleasing in nature or character

마음이 잘 맞는, 친절한, 기분 좋은

*She wants to be back in the more **congenial** company.*

syn. friendly, pleasant, agreeable

conjecture
[kuhn-**jek**-cher]

n. inference formed without proof or sufficient evidence

추측, 짐작

*He tried to make a **conjecture** on her intentions.*

syn. guess, surmise, supposition

confound
[kon-**found**]

v. to cause confusion or surprise

당황하게 하다

*The sudden rise of the Arctic temperature has **confounded** many meteorologists.*

syn. confuse, baffle, puzzle

conquest
[**kon**-kwest]

n. the act of invading, taking over, and ruling another area or group

정복, 극복

*He continued to expand his kingdom by **conquest**.*

syn. defeat, takeover, seizure

confront
[kuhn-**fruhnt**]

v. to oppose directly and openly

직면하다, 대면하다, 대결하다

*The girl had to **confront** her fears.*

syn. face, challenge, oppose

conspicuous
[kuhn-**spik**-yoo-uhs]

adj. very noticeable

눈에 잘 띄는, 남의 눈을 끄는

*Her red hair made her **conspicuous** in her class.*

syn. remarkable, noticeable, discernible

conspire

[kuhn-**spahy**_uhr_]

v. to make secret plans with others to do something that is illegal or harmful

음모를 꾸미다, 공모하다

*They **conspired** to rebel.*

syn.   plot, scheme, unite

constant

[**kon**-st_uh_nt]

adj. not changing or varying, continuing without pause

불변의, 변함없는, 계속되는

*Toddlers need **constant** attention.*

syn.   steady, regular, unceasing

constraint

[k_uh_n-**streynt**]

n. a limit or restriction on actions or ideas

제한점, 한계

*The project team has suffered from **constraints** of time and money.*

syn.   restriction, limitation, inhibition

contemporary

[k_uh_n-**tem**-puh-rer-ee]

adj. of or relating to present and recent time

동시대의, 현세의

*He was **contemporary** with the Alexander the Great.*

syn.   modern, present-day, current

ISEE Sentence Completion 3-1

Directions : Fill in the blanks to complete the sentences.

1. Without sufficient data, it's difficult to do more than _____ about the possible outcome.

   (A) constant   (B) conjecture
   (C) confront   (D) conspire

2. The manager encouraged the team to _____ the issue directly rather than avoiding it.

   (A) congenial   (B) confront
   (C) conspire   (D) conjecture

3. Her innovation in design led to a _____ success, gaining widespread attention.

   (A) constant   (B) congenial
   (C) conspicuous   (D) contemporary

4. The gallery's latest exhibit features pieces of _____ art by renowned modern artists.

   (A) contemporary   (B) conspicuous
   (C) congenial   (D) constant

5. The retreat offered a _____ environment, making it ideal for relaxation and creativity.

   (A) conspicuous   (B) congenial
   (C) constant   (D) contemporary

111 contend	116 convenient
112 content	117 conventional
113 contentious	118 converse
114 contract	119 cooperate
115 contrive	120 coordinate

Veni, vidi, vici.
(I came, I saw, I conquered.)
왔노라, 보았노라, 이겼노라.

SSATKOREA.com

contentious
[**kuhn**-ten-shus]

adj. likely to cause disagreement or argument
논쟁을 좋아하는, 논쟁이 많이 벌어지는

*She has a **contentious** nature, always looking for a debate.*

syn. argumentative, controversial, disputable

contract
[kon-trakt]

n. a formal or legal, written agreement between two or more people
계약

*The **contract** gives a female executive maternity leave rights.*

syn. agreement, pact, deal

contend
[k*uh*n-**tend**]

v. to strive in rivalry
겨루다, 다투다, 주장하다

*The governor **contends** with great difficulties.*

syn. compete, fight, argue

contrive
[k*uh*n-**trahyv**]

v. to plan with ingenuity
고안하다, 설계하다

*The rebel **contrived** a plot to seize power.*

syn. invent, devise, plan

content
[**kuhn**-tent]

adj. satisfied and at peace with what one has or a situation
(현재 상황에) 만족하는

*She is **content** with her job for now.*

syn. happy, contented, satisfied

convenient
[kuhn-**veen**-y*uh*nt]

adj. well suited to a person's needs, plans, or comfort
편리한, 알맞은, 사용하기 쉬운

*Put things where they will be most **convenient** for you.*

syn. handy, appropriate, suited

conventional
[k*uh*n-**ven**-shuh-nl]

adj. common, traditional, or accepted by most people

습관적인, 관습에 따른

Conventional symbols are universally used.

syn. traditional, customary, accustomed

converse
[k*uh*n-**vurs**]

v. to carry on a conversation

대화하다

*She speaks several languages fluently, so people want to meet and **converse** with her.*

syn. talk, chat, communicate

cooperate
[koh-**op**-uh-reyt]

v. to work or act together for a common purpose or benefit

협력하다

*The two companies agreed to **cooperate** with each other.*

syn. work together, collaborate, team up

coordinate
[koh-**awr**-dn-it]

v. to bring order and organization to

조정하다, 조화를 이루게 하다

*When you dance, try to **coordinate** your steps*

syn. organize, arrange, align

ISEE Sentence Completion 3-2

Directions : Fill in the blanks to complete the sentences.

1. _____ wisdom often provides general advice, but it may not suit every situation.

   (A) contentious   (B) convenient
   (C) conventional   (D) coordinate

2. The event organizers worked together to _____ activities across different venues.

   (A) contend   (B) coordinate
   (C) contrive   (D) content

3. After achieving her goals, she couldn't help but feel _____ with her accomplishments.

   (A) content   (B) contentious
   (C) contrive   (D) coordinate

4. The discussion quickly turned into a _____ debate with both sides strongly disagreeing.

   (A) contract   (B) conventional
   (C) convenient   (D) contentious

5. They managed to _____ a solution to the problem despite limited resources.

   (A) contrive   (B) cooperate
   (C) converse   (D) contend

121 correspondence 126 craven

122 corroborate 127 creed

123 counteract 128 crucial

124 courtesy 129 cultured

125 cower 130 cunning

Mens sana in corpore sano.
(A healthy mind in a healthy body.)
건강한 몸에 건강한 정신.

SSATKOREA.com

correspondence
[kawr-*uh*-**spon**-d*uh*ns]

n. an exchange of written communication, such as letters or emails

(편지나 이메일 같은) 서면 의사소통의 교환

*The historian studied the **correspondence** between the two diplomats to understand their negotiation tactics.*

syn. communication, connection, consistency

corroborate
[kuh-**rob**-uh-reyt]

v. to make more certain

확인하다, 확증하다

*The story was **corroborated** by evidence.*

syn. validate, verify, confirm

counteract
[koun-ter-**akt**]

v. to reduce the effect by doing something that produces an opposite effect

(나쁜 영향에) 대응하다, 반작용하다

*Volunteering is a good way to **counteract** loneliness.*

syn. neutralize, offset, counterbalance

courtesy
[**kur**-tuh-see]

n. showing politeness in how one behaves with others

예의, 공손함

*You could at least have had the **courtesy** to let me know.*

syn. politeness, manners, etiquette

cower
[**kou**-er]

v. to crouch, as in fear or shame

움츠리다, 위축하다

*A shot went off, and people **cowered** under tables.*

syn. cringe, shrink, crouch

craven
[**krey**-vuhn]

adj. extremely cowardly or lacking in courage

비겁한, 겁쟁이의

*The soldier's refusal to help his team in danger was seen as a **craven** act.*

syn. cowardly, timid, spineless

creed
[kri:d]

n. beliefs or principles that guide someone's actions, often related to religion or philosophy

신념, 믿음, 신조

*His **creed** is to always treat others with kindness and respect.*

syn. belief, doctrine, philosophy

crucial
[**kroo**-sh*uh*l]

adj. very important or significant

결정적인, 매우 중요한

*The meetings are **crucial** for the success of the plan.*

syn. essential, vital, decisive

cultured
[**k*uh*l**-cherd]

adj. enlightened or refined

교양 있는, 세련된, 고상한

*You all seem so elegant and **cultured**, and you've even written books.*

syn. educated, refined, sophisticated

cunning
[**k*uh*n**-ing]

n. the quality of being skillful at achieving goals through cleverness

교활함, 간사함

*The fox used its **cunning** to trick the hunter and escape from the trap.*

syn. guile, craftiness, cleverness

ISEE Sentence Completion 3-3

Directions : Fill in the blanks to complete the sentences.

1. His _____ plan to outsmart the competition involved careful calculation and strategy.

   (A) cunning   (B) crestfallen
   (C) courteous   (D) cryptic

2. The animal began to _____ in fear when it heard the loud thunder.

   (A) cower   (B) counteract
   (C) corroborate   (D) cunning

3. The board's _____ decision could determine the future of the entire company.

   (A) cunning   (B) cryptic
   (C) crucial   (D) crestfallen

4. The note contained a _____ message that left everyone puzzled about its meaning.

   (A) cryptic   (B) courteous
   (C) cunning   (D) craven

5. The lawyer presented written _____ as proof of the agreement between the two parties.

   (A) courtesy
   (B) correspondence
   (C) crestfallen
   (D) cryptic

Answers

1. (A)   2. (A)   3. (C)   4. (A)   5. (B)

131	damp	136	deceive
132	daring	137	deceptive
133	dawdle	138	deferential
134	dearth	139	defiance
135	debacle	140	dejected

Fide et fortitudine.
(By faith and fortitude)
믿음과 용기로

SSATKOREA.com

damp
[damp]

adj. slightly wet

축축한, 젖은

*The rain had made the floors **damp**.*

syn. moist, humid, clammy

daring
[**dair**-ing]

adj. disposed to venture or take risks

담대한, 용감한, 겁 없는

*The **daring** artist is willing to do which might shock or anger other people.*

syn. audacious, venturesome, bold

dawdle
[dawd-l]

v. to waste time

시간을 낭비하다, 빈둥빈둥 지내다

*He knew that he might not live for another six months, so there was no time to **dawdle**.*

syn. linger, loiter, procrastinate

dearth
[durth]

n. an inadequate supply

부족, 결핍

*There was a **dearth** of reliable information on the issue.*

syn. shortage, paucity, insufficiency

debacle
[dey-**bah**-k*uhl*]

n. a general breakup or dispersion

파괴, 붕괴, 재해

*His first performance was a **debacle**.*

syn. disaster, ruin, fiasco

deceive
[dih-**seev**]

v. to mislead by a false appearance or statement

기만하다, 사기 치다

*We easily **deceive** ourselves.*

syn. mislead, swindle, defraud

deceptive
[dih-**sep**-tiv]

adj. apt or tending to deceive

남을 속이는, 믿을 수 없는, 현혹하는

*Appearances can be **deceptive**.*

syn. delusive, fallacious, specious

deferential
[def-*uh*-**ren**-sh*uh*l]

adj. showing respect or submission to someone

경의를 표하는, 공손한

*He was always **deferential** toward his grandparents.*

syn. respectful, humble, submissive

defiance
[dih-**fahy**-*uh*ns]

adj. daring or bold resistance to authority or to any opposing force

과감한 저항, 대담한 반항

*He held up a clenched fist in **defiance**.*

syn. resistance, opposition, noncompliance

dejected
[dih-**jek**-tid]

adj. depressed in spirits

기가 죽은, 풀 죽은, 의기소침한

*He was thoroughly **dejected** and miserable.*

syn. discouraged, despondent, dispirited

ISEE Sentence Completion 3-4

Directions : Fill in the blanks to complete the sentences.

1. The organization faced a _____ of resources, making it difficult to continue its operations.

   (A) debacle   (B) dearth
   (C) defiance   (D) deceptive

2. The company's _____ in handling its investments led to a significant financial loss.

   (A) dearth   (B) damp
   (C) debacle   (D) daring

3. The product had a _____ appearance that made it look more valuable than it actually was.

   (A) daring   (B) deceptive
   (C) dejected   (D) defiant

4. His bold act of _____ against the unjust rule earned him admiration from his peers.

   (A) defiance   (B) dearth
   (C) debacle   (D) daring

5. After hearing the bad news, she was in a _____ mood for the rest of the day.

   (A) dejected   (B) damp
   (C) daring   (D) deceptive

Answers
1. (B)   2. (C)   3. (B)   4. (A)   5. (A)

141 delegate   146 denounce

142 deliberate   147 deplete

143 delicacy   148 detached

144 deluge   149 deteriorate

145 demure   150 deviate

Scientia potentia est.
(Knowledge is power.)
지식은 힘이다.

SSATKOREA.com

delicacy
[del-i-*kuh*-see]

n. a rare or luxurious food that is considered highly desirable and special

진미, 별미

*Caviar is considered a **delicacy** in many countries.*

syn.   treat, specialty, luxury

deluge
[**del**-yooj]

n. the rising of a body of water and its overflowing onto normally dry land

홍수, 범람

*The **deluge** was caused by a huge amount of rainfall in a day.*

syn.   flood, inundation, overwhelm

delegate
[**del**-i-git]

n. a person appointed or elected to represent others

대표자

*The **delegates** voted to support the resolution.*

syn.   representative, deputy, envoy

demure
[dih-**myoor**]

adj. modest and reserved
얌전한, 점잖은

*The dress was elegant and **demure**, perfect for the formal event.*

syn.   modest, shy, reserved

deliberate
[dih-**lib**-er-it]

adj. carefully thought out in advance
신중한, 찬찬한

*It was a calculated and **deliberate** move.*

syn.   intentional, measured, calculated

denounce
[dih-**nouns**]

v. to condemn or censure openly or publicly

비난하다, 고발하다

*The governor publicly **denounced** the president's handling of the crisis.*

syn.   condemn, criticize, censure

deplete
[dih-**pleet**]

v. to decrease seriously or exhaust the abundance or supply of

고갈시키다, 다 써버리다

*Water pollution **depletes** the world of natural resources.*

syn. exhaust, use up, reduce

detached
[dih-**tacht**]

adj. emotionally uninvolved

무심한, 거리감 있는

*He stayed **detached** during the argument, refusing to take sides.*

syn. distant, uninvolved, aloof

deteriorate
[dih-**teer**-ee-*uh*-reyt]

v. To become worse or decline in quality, condition, or value over time

악화되다, 나빠지다

*If we don't take care of the environment, it will **deteriorate** quickly.*

syn. decline, worsen, degenerate

deviate
[**dee**-vee-eyt]

v. to move away from an established path, plan, or norm

벗어나다, 빗나가다, 일탈하다

*The driver had to **deviate** from the usual route because of road construction.*

syn. stray, depart, diverge

ISEE Sentence Completion 3-5

Directions : Fill in the blanks to complete the sentences.

1. The group leader decided to _____ tasks to each team member to ensure the project was completed on time.

   (A) demolish   (B) detach
   (C) denounce   (D) delegate

2. If we continue to use resources at this rate, we will _____ the supply and leave nothing for future generations.

   (A) delegate   (B) deplete
   (C) demolish   (D) detach

3. After several days of heavy rain, the dam overflowed, causing a _____ that flooded the entire valley.

   (A) demolish   (B) delegate
   (C) deluge   (D) device

4. Unlike her outgoing friends, Sarah preferred to stay quiet and _____ at social gatherings.

   (A) demure   (B) delegate
   (C) deteriorate   (D) deviate

5. The committee took a _____ approach to choosing the winner, carefully evaluating every candidate's application.

   (A) device   (B) delicate
   (C) demolish   (D) deliberate

Analogy 3. Degree

Degree는 강도의 차이를 구별하는 관계를 말합니다. 크게 그 품사에 따라 Noun/ Adjective / Verb 의 세 기지 유형으로 구분됩니다. 매우 자주 출제되는 유형이므로 단어를 외울때 이 Degree 유형에 자주 출제되는 것인 경우에는 뜻과 함께 강도의 여부도 함께 기억해야 합니다.

Adjective 〈 Adjective 형용사 degree

happy < ecstatic
행복한 < 황홀한

sad < inconsolable
슬픈 < 너무 슬픈

singed < charred
그을린, 살짝 태운 < 새까맣게 탄, 숯이 된

shocked < traumatic
충격받은 < 정신적으로 큰 외상을 입은

Verb 〈 Verb 동사 degree

nudge < shove
가볍게 찌르다 < 거칠게 밀치다

glance < stare
흘끗 보다 < 응시하다

request < command
요청하다 < 명령하다

embarrass < humiliate
당황하게 하다 < 수치스럽게 하다

Noun 〈 Noun 명사 degree

daydream < hallucination
공상 < 환각

sleep < coma
잠 < 혼수상태

tweezers < tongs
족집게 < 집게

gully < canyon
도랑 < 협곡

POP QUIZ

1. Singed is to charred as
(A) happy is to jubilant
(B) warm is to mild
(C) frigid is to algid
(D) shocked is to traumatic
(E) sad is to inconsolable

2. Request is to command as
(A) berate is to admonish
(B) demonstrate is to abash
(C) idolize is to worship
(D) nudge is to shove
(E) suggest is to influence

3. Ripple is to wave as
(A) coma is to sleep
(B) canyon is to gully
(C) breeze is to squall
(D) cello is to viola
(E) tongs is to tweezers

4. Sleepy is to comatose as
(A) detestable is to abominable
(B) hideous is to dreary
(C) embarrassed is to humiliated
(D) inflated is to deflated
(E) abridged is to abbreviated

Check-up 3-1

Each of the following questions consists of one word followed by five words or phrases.
You are to select the one word or phrase whose meaning is closest to the word in capital letters.

1. CONFOUND
(A) tickle
(B) confuse
(C) illustrate
(D) snip
(E) accost

2. CONFRONT
(A) chatter
(B) trip
(C) rage
(D) fling
(E) face

3. CONGENIAL
(A) feasible
(B) boring
(C) fair
(D) friendly
(E) prevented

4. CONJECTURE
(A) guess
(B) overlook
(C) recall
(D) absorb
(E) swipe

5. CONQUEST
(A) display
(B) spite
(C) bump
(D) delegate
(E) defeat

6. CONSPICUOUS
(A) jocular
(B) remarkable
(C) cogent
(D) empirical
(E) inherent

7. CONSPIRE
(A) plot
(B) frown
(C) spit
(D) complain
(E) grant

8. CONSTANT
(A) hilarious
(B) solitary
(C) steady
(D) feisty
(E) loathsome

9. CONSTRAINT
(A) aim
(B) restriction
(C) object
(D) stream
(E) pace

10. CONTEMPORARY
(A) dangerous
(B) filthy
(C) modern
(D) conspicuous
(E) manifold

65

Check-up 3-2

1. CONTEND
- (A) strengthen
- (B) cultivate
- (C) replace
- (D) consume
- (E) compete

2. CONTENT
- (A) shapeless
- (B) happy
- (C) gloomy
- (D) finicky
- (E) amorphous

3. CONTENTIOUS
- (A) decrepit
- (B) sparse
- (C) aforementioned
- (D) argumentative
- (E) noxious

4. CONTRACT
- (A) agreement
- (B) comment
- (C) subject
- (D) input
- (E) strap

5. CONTRIVE
- (A) instruct
- (B) address
- (C) invent
- (D) equip
- (E) devote

6. CONVENIENT
- (A) tepid
- (B) superfluous
- (C) discordant
- (D) fallacious
- (E) handy

7. CONVENTIONAL
- (A) fallow
- (B) traditional
- (C) sanguine
- (D) comatose
- (E) seminal

8. CONVERSE
- (A) talk
- (B) subtract
- (C) rouse
- (D) enlarge
- (E) fasten

9. COOPERATE
- (A) make out
- (B) pull over
- (C) work together
- (D) put off
- (E) watch out

10. COORDINATE
- (A) stimulate
- (B) organize
- (C) imply
- (D) allow
- (E) acknowledge

Check-up 3-3

Directions — Each of the following questions consists of one word followed by five words or phrases. You are to select the one word or phrase whose meaning is closest to the word in capital letters.

1. CORRESPONDENCE
(A) communication
(B) interpretation
(C) migration
(D) treason
(E) exclusion

2. CORROBORATE
(A) imitate
(B) validate
(C) solve
(D) describe
(E) split

3. COUNTERACT
(A) civilize
(B) neutralize
(C) establish
(D) punch
(E) industrialize

4. COURTESY
(A) lid
(B) mess
(C) curve
(D) dyo
(E) politeness

5. COWER
(A) approve
(B) accomplish
(C) hesitate
(D) cringe
(E) heal

6. CRAVEN
(A) peeved
(B) cowardly
(C) agreeable
(D) provoking
(E) disrespectful

7. CREED
(A) clergy
(B) shelter
(C) belief
(D) significance
(E) hospitality

8. CRUCIAL
(A) essential
(B) urbane
(C) parochial
(D) fulsome
(E) profuse

9. CULTURED
(A) educated
(B) clandestine
(C) impious
(D) freaky
(E) seemly

10. CUNNING
(A) pride
(B) guile
(C) shame
(D) eminence
(E) assumption

67

Check-up 3-4

Each of the following questions consists of one word followed by five words or phrases. You are to select the one word or phrase whose meaning is closest to the word in capital letters.

1. DAMP
(A) tortuous
(B) conscious
(C) exemplary
(D) omnivorous
(E) moist

2. DARING
(A) audacious
(B) humid
(C) narrow-minded
(D) versatile
(E) prosperous

3. DAWDLE
(A) bounce
(B) reinforce
(C) damn
(D) prohibit
(E) linger

4. DEARTH
(A) status
(B) statute
(C) shortage
(D) surplus
(E) excess

5. DEBACLE
(A) disaster
(B) survey
(C) landscape
(D) curse
(E) favor

6. DECEIVE
(A) cope
(B) mislead
(C) deal
(D) flee
(E) sympathize

7. DECEPTIVE
(A) delusive
(B) felicitous
(C) canine
(D) arrogant
(E) pretentious

8. DEFERENTIAL
(A) different
(B) assertive
(C) bashful
(D) discourteous
(E) respectful

9. DEFIANCE
(A) resistance
(B) malfunction
(C) delegate
(D) comparison
(E) commencement

10. DEJECTED
(A) akin
(B) bovine
(C) constructive
(D) discouraged
(E) complicit

Check-up 3-5

Directions   Each of the following questions consists of one word followed by five words or phrases.
You are to select the one word or phrase whose meaning is closest to the word in capital letters.

1. DELEGATE
- (A) stature
- (B) rim
- (C) orbit
- (D) contrast
- (E) representative

2. DELIBERATE
- (A) winsome
- (B) covetous
- (C) dismal
- (D) pompous
- (E) intentional

3. DELICACY
- (A) prestige
- (B) treat
- (C) hazard
- (D) stature
- (E) audacity

4. DELUGE
- (A) conduct
- (B) ambition
- (C) flood
- (D) border
- (E) cable

5. DEMURE
- (A) modest
- (B) curious
- (C) outgoing
- (D) combative
- (E) awesome

6. DENOUNCE
- (A) accompany
- (B) define
- (C) enable
- (D) condemn
- (E) deposit

7. DEPLETE
- (A) digest
- (B) examine
- (C) regret
- (D) mystify
- (E) exhaust

8. DETACHED
- (A) awaken
- (B) approximate
- (C) distant
- (D) humane
- (E) baffled

9. DETERIORATE
- (A) splice
- (B) diffuse
- (C) encourage
- (D) revamp
- (E) decline

10. DEVIATE
- (A) depict
- (B) signify
- (C) outcome
- (D) understudy
- (E) stray

Answer 1.E 2.E 3.B 4.C 5.A 6.D 7.E 8.C 9.E 10.E

151	devious	156	disclose
152	dexterous	157	disgrace
153	dignified	158	disguise
154	dilemma	159	dishearten
155	dim	160	dismay

Pro bono
(For the public good)
공익을 위하여.

SSATKOREA.com

devious
[**dee**-vee-*uhs*]

adj. departing from the most direct way
정직하지 못한, 속이는

*She has **devious** ways of making money.*

syn.　dishonest, sneaky, deceitful

dexterous
[**dek**-str*uhs*]

adj. attracting notice or attention, worthy of notice
손재주가 매우 좋은, 솜씨 좋은

*Power users are **dexterous** at using new gadgets.*

syn.　agile, nimble, adroit

dignified
[**dig**-nuh-fahyd]

adj. characterized or marked by dignity of aspect or manner
위엄 있는, 품위 있는

*She maintained a **dignified** silence as a queen.*

syn.　glorified, stately, majestic

dilemma
[dih-**lem**-uh]

n. a situation requiring a choice between equally undesirable alternatives
딜레마, 곤경, 궁지

*The ranchers often face the **dilemma** of feeding themselves or their cattle.*

syn.　quandary, predicament, plight

dim
[dim]

adj. not bright or having low light
흐릿한, 어둑한

*The room was **dim**, lit only by a small candle.*

syn.　dark, dull, faint

disclose
[dih-**sklohz**]

v. to make known
밝히다, 폭로하다

*She **disclosed** her rival's gossips to the press.*

syn.　reveal, debunk, unveil

disgrace
[dis-**greys**]

n. the loss of respect, honor, or esteem

불명예, 망신, 수치

*He's a **disgrace** to his family.*

syn. ignominy, dishonor, shame

disguise
[dis-**gahyz**]

v. to hide an opinion, a feeling, etc.

변장하다, 가장하다

*He tried to **disguise** his voice with holding a handkerchief to the mouthpiece.*

syn. camouflage, conceal, hide

dishearten
[dis-**hahr**-tn]

v. to make a person lose confidence, hope, and energy

낙심시키다, 실망시키다

*He was very **disheartened** by the results of the test.*

syn. discourage, dispirit, demoralize

dismay
[dis-**mey**]

v. to break down the courage of completely, as by sudden danger or trouble

실망하게 하다, 경악하게 만들다

*They were **dismayed** by the condition of the hotel.*

syn. appall, horrify, shock

ISEE Sentence Completion 4-1

***Directions* :** Fill in the blanks to complete the sentences.

1. Many voters felt _____ after realizing the promises made during the campaign were empty.

   (A) disgrace   (B) dignified
   (C) dexterous   (D) disillusioned

2. The politician was accused of using _____ tactics to gain an unfair advantage in the election.

   (A) devious   (B) dexterous
   (C) dignified   (D) disillusioned

3. After completing their mission, the team decided to _____ and go their separate ways.

   (A) disguise   (B) disclose
   (C) disband   (D) dismay

4. His actions were so dishonorable that they brought _____ upon his entire family.

   (A) disgrace   (B) disband
   (C) dilemma   (D) dexterous

5. The committee faced an ethical _____ when deciding between two equally compelling options.

   (A) dismay   (B) dilemma
   (C) disgrace   (D) disguise

Answers
1. (D) 2. (A) 3. (C) 4. (A) 5. (B)

---

161 disrupt	166 distraction
162 dissuade	167 distress
163 distasteful	168 divisive
164 distend	169 docile
165 distort	170 dominant

Pacta sunt servanda.
(Agreements must be kept.)
계약은 지켜져야 한다.

——————— SSATKOREA.com

disrupt
[dis-**ruhpt**]

v. to break apart or disturb the normal flow of something

붕괴시키다, 중단시키다

*The storm **disrupted** traffic flow.*

syn. interrupt, disturb, interfere with

dissuade
[dih-**sweyd**]

v. to deter by advice or persuasion

(~을 하지 않도록) ~를 설득하다

*Her family tried to **dissuade** him from studying abroad.*

syn. discourage, foil, frustrate

distasteful
[dis-**teyst**-*fuhl*]

adj. unpleasant, offensive, or causing dislike

불쾌한, 혐오스러운

*People complained about the **distasteful** odor.*

syn. unpleasant, disagreeable, obnoxious

distend
[dih-**stend**]

v. to expand by stretching, as something hollow or elastic

팽창시키다, 부풀리다

*Air is introduced into the stomach to **distend** it.*

syn. swell, dilate, bulge

distort
[dih-**stawrt**]

v. to twist awry or out of shape, to give a false, perverted, or disproportionate meaning to

비틀다, 왜곡시키다

*The pipe will **distort** as you bend it.*

syn. twist, garble, falsify

distraction
[dih-**strak**-sh*uh*n]

n. the act of distracting

집중을 방해하는 것

*Her kids drive her to **distraction** at times.*

syn. diversion, interruption, disturbance

distress

[dih-**stres**]

n. great pain, anxiety, or sorrow

고통, 괴로움

*Ted was obviously in **distress** after the bankruptcy.*

syn. trouble, suffering, affliction

divisive

[dih-**vahy**-siv]

adj. forming or expressing division or distribution

분열을 초래하는

*The highly **divisive** issues cause disagreement or hostility between people.*

syn. dissenting, alienating, discordant

docile

[**dos**-*uhl*]

adj. easily managed or handled

고분고분한, 유순한

*The **docile** workers were ready to accept control or instruction.*

syn. compliant, obedient, pliant

dominant

[**dom**-uh-n*uh*nt]

adj. occupying or being in a commanding or elevated position

우세한, 지배적인

*The company is in the most **dominant** position in the market.*

syn. prevailing, leading, primary

ISEE Sentence Completion 4-2

Directions : Fill in the blanks to complete the sentences.

1. The policy became a _____ issue, splitting public opinion into opposing sides.

   (A) divisive   (B) docile
   (C) dominant   (D) distasteful

2. The puppy's _____ nature made it easy to train and a joy to have at home.

   (A) distress   (B) divisive
   (C) dominant   (D) docile

3. The police were called to _____ the crowd after the protest became unruly.

   (A) disperse   (B) distort
   (C) divisive   (D) distress

4. Overeating can cause the stomach to _____, leading to discomfort and pain.

   (A) disperse   (B) distend
   (C) distort   (D) docile

5. The company emerged as a _____ force in the industry, setting trends and leading innovation.

   (A) distress   (B) docile
   (C) divisive   (D) dominant

Answers

1. (A)   2. (D)   3. (A)   4. (B)   5. (D)

171 domineering   176 dynamic

172 drought   177 eager

173 drowsy   178 economical

174 durable   179 edible

175 dwindle   180 efficient

Si vis pacem, fac bellum.
(If you want peace, make war.)
평화를 원하거든 전쟁을 준비하라.

SSATKOREA.com

domineering
[dom-uh-**neer**-ing]

adj. inclined to rule arbitrarily or despotically
거만한, 지배하려 드는, 폭군적인

*She found him arrogant and **domineering**.*

syn. overbearing, authoritarian, imperious

drought
[drout]

n. a period of dry weather, especially a long one that is injurious to crops
가뭄

*The rain ended a six-month **drought**.*

syn. scarcity, deficiency, aridity

drowsy
[**drou**-zee]

adj. half-asleep
졸리는, 나른하게 만드는

*A glass of wine can make her **drowsy**.*

syn. sleepy, lethargic, soporific

durable
[**door**-uh-b*uhl*]

adj. able to resist, wear, decay, etc.
내구성이 있는, 오래가는

*Gold is strong and **durable**.*

syn. lasting, resistant, imperishable

dwindle
[**dwin**-dl]

v. to become smaller and smaller
줄어들다, 작아지다

*Traffic **dwindled** when the construction was over.*

syn. diminish, decrease, reduce

dynamic
[dahy-**nam**-ik]

adj. pertaining to or characterized by energy or effective action
정력적인, 활발한

*His performance is **dynamic** and passionate in every move.*

syn. active, energetic, vigorous

eager

[ee-ger]

adj. keen or ardent in desire or feeling

열렬한, 간절히 바라는

The young boys are eager for new knowledge.

syn. enthusiastic, avid, fervent

economical

[ek-uh-nom-i-kuhl]

adj. avoiding waste or extravagance

경제적인, 절약하는

This pipe is economical in metal and therefore light in weight.

syn. frugal, prudent, careful

edible

[ed-uh-buhl]

adj. fit to be eaten as food

먹을 수 있는, 식용의

They tried to find edible mushrooms.

syn. consumable, digestible, palatable

efficient

[ih-fish-uhnt]

adj. performing or functioning in the best possible manner with the least waste of time and effort

능률적인, 효율적인

LED lamps are efficient at converting electricity into light.

syn. effective, adept, able

ISEE Sentence Completion 4-3

Directions : Fill in the blanks to complete the sentences.

1. The family decided to take an _____ approach to their vacation, choosing affordable destinations and saving on expenses.

   (A) domineering (B) economical
   (C) efficient   (D) dynamic

2. The company focused on creating products that were _____ enough to last for years without breaking.

   (A) durable   (B) dynamic
   (C) domineering (D) efficient

3. The chef assured everyone that the decorative flowers on the plate were completely _____ and safe to eat.

   (A) dynamic   (B) durable
   (C) edible   (D) efficient

4. The students were _____ to participate in the science fair, excited to showcase their creative experiments.

   (A) durable   (B) eager
   (C) domineering (D) edible

5. The leader's _____ attitude made it difficult for others to share their opinions during group discussions.

   (A) domineering (B) dynamic
   (C) eager   (D) efficient

181	egress	186	enact
182	elaborate	187	enclose
183	emerging	188	encounter
184	empower	189	endurance
185	emulate	190	enhance

Justitia omnibus.
(Justice for all.)
모두를 위한 정의.

SSATKOREA.com

egress
[ee-gres]

n. the act or an instance of going, especially from an enclosed place

출구, 떠남, 나감

The passengers go through a narrow egress.

syn. exit, out

elaborate
[ih-lab-er-it]

adj. worked out with great care and nicety of detail

정교한, 정성들인

It requires more elaborate procedures than those just described.

syn. complicated, complex, intricate

emerging
[ih-mur-jing]

adj. coming into existence or rising in importance

떠오르는, 신흥의, 부상하는

She is an emerging artist in the music industry.

syn. developing, rising, appearing

empower
[em-pou-er]

v. to give power or authority to

권한을 주다

Nobody was empowered to sign checks on the boss's behalf.

syn. authorize, entitle, permit

emulate
[em-yuh-leyt]

v. to try to equal or excel

모방하다, 따라가다

Only a few people tried to emulate his greatness.

syn. imitate, copy, mirror

enact
[en-akt]

v. to make into an act or statue

제정하다, 법으로 만들다

This new legislation was enacted in 2012 to attract foreign investments.

syn. legislate, approve, perform

enclose
[en-**klohz**]

v. to shut or hem in

두르다, 에워싸다

Pure darkness enclosed space.

syn. surround, hem, encompass

encounter
[en-**koun**-ter]

v. to come upon or meet with, especially unexpectedly

우연히 만나다, 맞닥뜨리다

You will encounter numerous problems.

syn. meet, come across, run into

endurance
[en-**door**-uhns]

n. the ability or strength to continue or last

인내, 참을성

Sean showed great endurance in the face of pain.

syn. persistence, tenacity, perseverance

enhance
[en-**hans**]

v. to raise to a higher degree

높이다, 향상시키다

He refused to do more things to enhance his reputation.

syn. improve, reinforce, intensify

ISEE Sentence Completion 4-4

Directions : Fill in the blanks to complete the sentences.

1. The new lighting system was installed to _____ the stadium's visibility during evening games.

   (A) endurance   (B) empower
   (C) enhance   (D) emulate

2. The city council voted to _____ a law requiring all public buildings to have wheelchair access.

   (A) enhance   (B) encounter
   (C) enclose   (D) enact

3. The artist's design was so _____ that it took months to complete, with every detail carefully crafted.

   (A) elaborate   (B) emerging
   (C) empower   (D) encounter

4. During their hike, the group had an unexpected _____ with a bear, which they handled calmly.

   (A) enact   (B) encounter
   (C) endurance   (D) enhance

5. The new policy aimed to _____ students by giving them a stronger voice in school decisions.

   (A) empower   (B) emulate
   (C) enhance   (D) endure

Answers
1. (C)   2. (D)   3. (A)   4. (B)   5. (A)

191 enlarge	196 eradicate
192 enormous	197 erratic
193 entice	198 etiquette
194 entreat	199 evade
195 epoch	200 evident

Veritas vos liberabit.
(The truth will set you free.)
진리가 너를 자유롭게 하리라.

SSATKOREA.com

enlarge
[en-**lahrj**]

v. to make larger
확장하다, 확대하다

*We **enlarged** our swimming pool.*

syn. magnify, expand, extend

enormous
[ih-**nawr**-m*uh*s]

adj. greatly exceeding the common size, extent, etc.
거대한, 매우 큰

*Your possibilities are **enormous**.*

syn. colossal, mammoth, gigantic

entice
[en-**tahys**]

v. to lead on by exciting hope or desire
유도하다, 유인하다

*The performance group needs to **entice** a new audience into the theater.*

syn. tempt, lure, allure

entreat
[en-**treet**]

v. to ask (a person) earnestly
간청하다, 애원하다

*Her husband **entreated** her not to leave.*

syn. implore, beg, plead

epoch
[ep-*uh*k]

n. a particular period of time marked by distinctive features, events, etc.
시대, 기간

*The art style is very common in the Victorian **epoch**.*

syn. era, age, period

eradicate
[ih-**rad**-i-keyt]

v. to remove or destroy utterly
제거하다, 뿌리뽑다

*This disease has been **eradicated** from the world.*

syn. eliminate, remove, obliterate

erratic
[ih-**rat**-ik]

adj. deviating from the usual or proper course in conduct or opinion

불규칙한, 일정치 않은

*The old man's breath was **erratic**.*

syn. unpredictable, inconsistent, idiosyncratic

etiquette
[et-i-kit]

n. rules of conduct or acceptable behavior in specific situations

예의, 에티켓

*It is important to maintain **etiquette** in public places.*

syn. manners, politeness. courtesy

evade
[ih-**veyd**]

v. to escape from by trickery or cleverness

피하다, 모면하다

*He tried to kiss her, but she **evaded** him.*

syn. avoid, elude, shun

evident
[ev-i-duhnt]

adj. plain or clear to the sight

명백한, 분명한

*Queen's frown made it **evident** to all that she was displeased.*

syn. apparent, clear, obvious

ISEE Sentence Completion 4-5

Directions : Fill in the blanks to complete the sentences.

1. During the test, the student tried to _____ answering the question by pretending to reread the instructions.

   (A) entice   (B) evade
   (C) eradicate   (D) evident

2. The young child tried to _____ her parents to let her stay up late by promising to clean her room the next day.

   (A) eradicate   (B) enlarge
   (C) evade   (D) entreat

3. The company decided to _____ its headquarters to accommodate the growing number of employees.

   (A) entice   (B) enlarge
   (C) eradicate   (D) evade

4. The teacher had to address the student's _____ behavior, which made it hard for the class to stay focused.

   (A) erratic   (B) entice
   (C) evident   (D) enormous

5. It is important to follow proper _____ when attending formal events to show respect for the host.

   (A) enormous   (B) evident
   (C) etiquette   (D) entice

Answers

1. (B) 2. (D) 3. (B) 4. (A) 5. (C)

Analogy 4. Study

학문과 연구대상 또는 학자와 연구 대상을 연결짓는 관계입니다.

학문 : 연구대상

botany : plant
식물학 : 식물

zoology : animal
동물학 : 동물

aesthetics : beauty
미학 : 아름다움

petrology : rock
암석학 : 암석

phonetics : sound
음성학 : (언어의) 소리

semantics : meaning
의미론 : (언어의) 의미

학자 : 연구대상

archeologist : artifact
고고학자 : 유물

ornithologist : bird
조류학자 : 새, 조류

meteorologist : weather
기상학자 : 날씨

physicist : physics
물리학자 : 물리학

astronomer : space
천문학자 : 우주

spelunker : cave
동굴 탐험가 : 동굴

POP QUIZ

1. Phonetics is to sound as
(A) semantics is to meaning
(B) aesthetic is to sedatives
(C) petrology is to oil
(D) phonetics is to telephone
(E) abacus is to computer

2. Archeologist is to artifact as
(A) astronomer is to sun
(B) physician is to physics
(C) meteorologist is to space
(D) analyst is to finance
(E) spelunker is to cave

Check-up 4-1

Directions   Each of the following questions consists of one word followed by five words or phrases. You are to select the one word or phrase whose meaning is closest to the word in capital letters.

1. DEVIOUS
(A) apparent
(B) dishonest
(C) fatal
(D) obvious
(E) irresistible

2. DEXTEROUS
(A) vacant
(B) intelligent
(C) agile
(D) suitable
(E) primary

3. DIGNIFIED
(A) opposite
(B) current
(C) jagged
(D) finicky
(E) glorified

4. DILEMMA
(A) definition
(B) quandary
(C) curiosity
(D) objective
(E) cycle

5. DIM
(A) dark
(B) weighty
(C) sound
(D) radiant
(E) solid

6. DISCLOSE
(A) govern
(B) promote
(C) grasp
(D) reveal
(E) doze

7. DISGRACE
(A) conference
(B) ignominy
(C) survey
(D) attitude
(E) nursery

8. DISGUISE
(A) camouflage
(B) confess
(C) tackle
(D) drift
(E) credit

9. DISHEARTEN
(A) launch
(B) arrange
(C) steer
(D) crumple
(E) discourage

10. DISMAY
(A) scatter
(B) appall
(C) injure
(D) vanish
(E) frustrate

Check-up 4-2

Each of the following questions consists of one word followed by five words or phrases. You are to select the one word or phrase whose meaning is closest to the word in capital letters.

1. DISRUPT
(A) stress
(B) urge
(C) interrupt
(D) volunteer
(E) starve

2. DISSUADE
(A) defend
(B) flutter
(C) tan
(D) influence
(E) discourage

3. DISTASTEFUL
(A) mental
(B) unpleasant
(C) vigorous
(D) positive
(E) gradual

4. DISTEND
(A) contain
(B) rely
(C) elect
(D) swell
(E) thrive

5. DISTORT
(A) amaze
(B) twist
(C) arouse
(D) memorize
(E) reverse

6. DISTRACTION
(A) cocoon
(B) diversion
(C) prank
(D) tentacle
(E) talent

7. DISTRESS
(A) dangle
(B) smuggle
(C) trouble
(D) forsake
(E) humiliate

8. DIVISIVE
(A) dissenting
(B) novel
(C) average
(D) marine
(E) individual

9. DOCILE
(A) transparent
(B) frail
(C) compliant
(D) sufficient
(E) mature

10. DOMINANT
(A) exceptional
(B) recessive
(C) obstinate
(D) prevailing
(E) eager

Check-up 4-3

MIDDLE 1 2 3 4 5 6 7 8 9 10

Directions   Each of the following questions consists of one word followed by five words or phrases. You are to select the one word or phrase whose meaning is closest to the word in capital letters.

1. DOMINEERING
(A) deliberate
(B) overbearing
(C) amiable
(D) artificial
(E) parallel

2. DROUGHT
(A) feature
(B) spine
(C) scarcity
(D) court
(E) cylinder

3. DROWSY
(A) spacious
(B) eventual
(C) vast
(D) ancient
(E) sleepy

4. DURABLE
(A) scarce
(B) lasting
(C) flexible
(D) annual
(E) abreast

5. DWINDLE
(A) behold
(B) diminish
(C) deprive
(D) detest
(E) pierce

6. DYNAMIC
(A) energetic
(B) stout
(C) vain
(D) active
(E) crude

7. EAGER
(A) humble
(B) petty
(C) enthusiastic
(D) familiar
(E) temporary

8. ECONOMICAL
(A) frugal
(B) precious
(C) entire
(D) threadbare
(E) famished

9. EDIBLE
(A) instant
(B) prompt
(C) shallow
(D) consumable
(F) frequent

10. EFFICIENT
(A) utter
(B) foremost
(C) apt
(D) considerable
(E) effective

UPPER 1 2 3 4 5 6 7 8 9 10

83

Check-up 4-4

Directions Each of the following questions consists of one word followed by five words or phrases. You are to select the one word or phrase whose meaning is closest to the word in capital letters.

1. EGRESS
(A) fanatic
(B) exit
(C) lack
(D) entrance
(E) entry

2. ELABORATE
(A) mammoth
(B) content
(C) severe
(D) complicated
(E) fortunate

3. EMERGING
(A) furious
(B) capital
(C) developing
(D) stingy
(E) external

4. EMPOWER
(A) authorize
(B) despise
(C) increase
(D) attend
(E) observe

5. EMULATE
(A) wander
(B) imitate
(C) chord
(D) consider
(E) applaud

6. ENACT
(A) ail
(B) cherish
(C) legislate
(D) coax
(E) develop

7. ENCLOSE
(A) implore
(B) approach
(C) refine
(D) surround
(E) astonish

8. ENCOUNTER
(A) intend
(B) permit
(C) revise
(D) astound
(E) meet

9. ENDURANCE
(A) forlorn
(B) keen
(C) widespread
(D) persistence
(E) distant

10. ENHANCE
(A) utilize
(B) recognize
(C) improve
(D) arrest
(E) seize

Check-up 4-5

Each of the following questions consists of one word followed by five words or phrases.
You are to select the one word or phrase whose meaning is closest to the word in capital letters.

1. ENLARGE
(A) achieve
(B) magnify
(C) separate
(D) approve
(E) obtain

2. ENORMOUS
(A) melancholy
(B) destructive
(C) exquisite
(D) sensitive
(E) colossal

3. ENTICE
(A) attract
(B) slay
(C) plead
(D) distribute
(E) ensure

4. ENTREAT
(A) represent
(B) implore
(C) confirm
(D) shun
(E) forbid

5. EPOCH
(A) tour
(B) hamlet
(C) era
(D) fare
(E) trio

6. ERADICATE
(A) eliminate
(B) eject
(C) boast
(D) summon
(E) create

7. ERRATIC
(A) unpredictable
(B) tragic
(C) hearty
(D) crafty
(E) apparent

8. ETIQUETTE
(A) visage
(B) panorama
(C) facades
(D) manners
(E) appliances

9. EVADE
(A) inhale
(B) exclaim
(C) alter
(D) occupy
(F) avoid

10. EVIDENT
(A) charming
(B) disillusioned
(C) muddled
(D) staunch
(E) apparent

85

201 excessive	206 expand
202 exclude	207 expert
203 exemplary	208 explicit
204 exhaust	209 expound
205 exhort	210 exquisite

Amor fati.
(Love of fate)
운명을 사랑하라.

SSATKOREA.com

excessive
[ik-**ses**-iv]

adj. going beyond the usual, necessary, or proper limit or degree
지나친, 과도한

She was drinking **excessive** amounts of wine.

syn. immoderate, intemperate, imprudent

exclude
[ik-**sklood**]

v. to keep from being a part of something
제외하다, 빼다

Women had been **excluded** from many scientific societies.

syn. expel, forbid, ban, boycott

exemplary
[ig-**zem**-pluh-ree]

adj. worthy of imitation
모범적인

Her works are **exemplary** of certain feminist arguments.

syn. outstanding, model, ideal

exhaust
[ig-**zawst**]

v. to drain of strength or energy
(에너지나 기력을) 다 써버리다

This long journey had **exhausted** her.

syn. reduce, deplete, consume

exhort
[ig-**zawrt**]

v. to urge, advise, or caution earnestly
열심히 권하다, 촉구하다

The social media has been **exhorting** people to turn out for the showing.

syn. urge, encourage, enjoin

expand
[ik-**spand**]

v. to make larger in size, amount, volume, or scope
넓히다, 확장하다

Baby birds cannot **expand** and contract their lungs.

syn. increase, enlarge, magnify

expert
[ek-spurt]

n. a person who has a lot of knowledge about a subject

전문가

*They are accredited as **experts** in legal and financial advice.*

syn. veteran, master, specialist, authority

explicit
[ik-**splis**-it]

adj. clear, direct, and specific as to leave no doubt about the meaning

명백한, 확실한

*The writer's intentions were not made **explicit**.*

syn. obvious, apparent, clear

expound
[ik-**spound**]

v. to set forth or state in detail

자세히 설명하다

*She declined to **expound** on her decision.*

syn. explain, elaborate, clarify

exquisite
[ik-**skwiz**-it]

adj. of special beauty or charm, or rare and appealing excellence

매우 아름다운, 정교한

*They were surprised with her **exquisite** taste in painting.*

syn. beautiful, elegant, delicate

ISEE Sentence Completion 5-1

***Directions* :** Fill in the blanks to complete the sentences.

1. Her _____ behavior during the crisis earned her admiration from colleagues.

   (A) excessive   (B) exquisite
   (C) explicit   (D) exemplary

2. If we continue to use natural resources at this rate, we will _____ them before long.

   (A) exhaust   (B) expound
   (C) exclude   (D) expand

3. Traveling abroad is a great way to _____ your horizons and experience new cultures.

   (A) expand   (B) exhaust
   (C) expound   (D) exclude

4. The guide provided _____ instructions to ensure everyone understood the safety rules.

   (A) exquisite   (B) explicit
   (C) expert   (D) excessive

5. The professor began to _____ on his ideas, explaining them in greater depth.

   (A) exclude   (B) expand
   (C) expound   (D) exhort

Answers
1. (D)   2. (A)   3. (A)   4. (B)   5. (C)

211	extend	216	famine
212	exuberant	217	fathom
213	facade	218	faux
214	fallacy	219	fecund
215	falsify	220	fervent

Ignorantia est beatitudo.

(Ignorance is bliss)

모르는 것이 약이다.

SSATKOREA.com

extend
[ik-**stend**]

v. to stretch out

늘이다, 더 길게 만들다

*Middle schools may consider **extending** the class day from five to seven periods.*

syn. lengthen, expand, magnify

exuberant
[ig-**zoo**-ber-*uh*nt]

adj. effusively and almost uninhibitedly enthusiastic

활기 넘치는

*This type of arch is a flamboyant and **exuberant** architectural invention.*

syn. ebullient, buoyant, cheerful

facade
[f*uh*-**sahd**]

n. a superficial or deceptive outward appearance that hides the true nature of something

(진실을 감추기 위한) 겉모습, 허울

*Behind her cheerful **facade**, she was feeling very nervous.*

syn. pretense, front, exterior

fallacy
[**fal**-uh-see]

n. a deceptive, misleading, or false notion or belief

오류, 틀린 생각

*The most common **fallacy** is to suppose that wealth brings happiness.*

syn. misconception, false belief, error

falsify
[**fawl**-suh-fahy]

v. to make false or incorrect,

속이다, 위조하다

*The hypothesis is **falsified** by the evidence.*

syn. misrepresent, fake, counterfeit

famine
[**fam**-in]

n. extreme and general scarcity of food purpose, intent, etc.

기근, 기아

*Widespread **famine** had triggered this violent protest.*

syn. starvation, hunger, drought

fathom
[**fath**-*uh*m]

v. to understand or comprehend something deeply

헤아리다, 이해하다

*She couldn't **fathom** why her best friend suddenly stopped talking to her.*

syn. understand, comprehend, grasp

faux
[foh]

adj. artificial or fake

가짜의, 모조의

***Faux** fur is used in place of real fur for items like stuffed animals, fashion accessories, and throws.*

syn. fake, ersatz, artificial

fecund
[**fee**-kuhnd]

adj. capable of producing abundant offspring or vegetation

다산의, 비옥한

The farmer was happy to see that his fields were fecund and full of healthy crops.

syn. fertile, prolific, productive

fervent
[**fur** *vuhnt*]

adj. having or showing great warmth or intensity of spirit, feeling, enthusiasm, etc.

열렬한, 강렬한

*The government confronted a **fervent** opposite of tax reform.*

syn. zealous, passionate, intense

ISEE Sentence Completion 5-2

Directions : Fill in the blanks to complete the sentences.

1. The argument was dismissed because it was based on a logical _____.

   (A) fallacy   (B) famine
   (C) facade   (D) faux

2. The city held an _____ celebration after the team won the championship.

   (A) facade   (B) fecund
   (C) faux   (D) exuberant

3. It was difficult to _____ the meaning of his cryptic message.

   (A) fathom   (B) falsify
   (C) fervent   (D) fecund

4. The jacket was made of _____ leather but looked just like the real thing.

   (A) fallacy   (B) facade
   (C) faux   (D) fervent

5. Behind her cheerful smile was a false _____ that masked her true feelings.

   (A) fecund   (B) fallacy
   (C) facade   (D) famine

Answers

1. (A)   2. (D)   3. (A)   4. (C)   5. (C)

221	fierce	226	fledgling
222	fiery	227	flippant
223	flamboyant	228	flounder
224	flatter	229	flutter
225	flawless	230	foible

Ceteris paribus.
(All other things being equal.)
다른 조건이 같다면.

SSATKOREA.com

fierce
[feers]

adj. very violent or powerful
사나운, 험악한

*A tiger is a **fierce** predator.*
syn.   ferocious, aggressive, intense

fiery
[**fahy***uhr*-ee]

adj. burning brightly and strongly
불타는 듯한, 불의

*The crowd was agitated by the **fiery** speech.*
syn.   passionate, blazing, flaming

flamboyant
[flam-**boi**-*uh*nt]

adj. strikingly bold or brilliant
화려한, 현란한

*Her **flamboyant** fashion styles are brightly colored, oddly patterned, or unusual.*
syn.   showy, extravagant, ostentatious

flatter
[**flat**-er]

v. to give a compliment, especially for the purpose of gaining something
아첨하다, 알랑거리다

*She was **flattering** him to avoid doing what he wanted.*
syn.   compliment, adulate, fawn

flawless
[**flaw**-lis]

adj. having no defects or faults, especially none that diminish the value of something
흠 하나 없는, 나무랄 데 없는

*She greeted him in almost **flawless** English.*
syn.   perfect, impeccable, unblemished

fledgling
[**flej**-ling]

n. a young bird that has grown feathers and is learning to fly or a beginner
(막 날기 시작한) 어린 새, 신출내기, 초보자

*The **fledgling** has just developed wings not enough for flight.*
syn.   beginner, novice, rookie

flippant

[**flip**-*uh*nt]

adj. frivolously disrespectful, shallow, or lacking in seriousness

경솔한, 건방진

*He frowned as he heard the boy's **flippant** remark.*

syn. frivolous, facetious, disrespectful

flounder

[**floun**-der]

v. to struggle with stumbling, or plunging movements

몸부림치다, 허우적거리다, 허둥대다

*The little boy was **floundering** at the edge of the shallow brook.*

syn. struggle, stumble, wallow

flutter

[**fluht**-er]

v. to wave, flap, or toss about

파닥거리다, 펄럭이다

*The butterfly's wings began to **flutter** as it landed on the flower.*

syn. flap, tremble, quiver

foible

[**foi**-b*uh*l]

n. a minor weakness or failing of character

약점

*Family members have to tolerate each other's little **foibles**.*

syn. flaw, defect, weakness

Directions : Fill in the blanks to complete the sentences.

1. There was a _____ of hope that the trapped miners would be rescued in time.

   (A) flounder   (B) flutter
   (C) fierce   (D) flamboyant

2. The swimmer began to _____ in the water, struggling to stay afloat.

   (A) flounder   (B) flatter
   (C) foible   (D) flutter

3. The two companies engaged in _____ competition to secure the lucrative contract.

   (A) fierce   (B) fiery
   (C) flippant   (D) flutter

4. The performer wore a _____ costume filled with bright colors and sparkling sequins that captured everyone's attention.

   (A) fiery   (B) flawless
   (C) flippant   (D) flamboyant

5. The performer wore a _____ costume filled with bright colors and sparkling sequins that captured everyone's attention.

   (A) fiery   (B) flawless
   (C) flippant   (D) flamboyant

1. (B) 2. (A) 3. (A) 4. (D) 5. (D)

Answers

231	force	236	fragment
232	forthright	237	frenzied
233	fortify	238	fretful
234	foundation	239	frugal
235	fragile	240	fruitful

De facto.
(In fact)
사실상의

SSATKOREA.com

force
[fawrs, fohrs]

v. to compel or oblige to do something
강요하다, 억지로 하게 하다

*The police officer **forced** a suspect to confess.*

syn.   coerce, impel, compel

forthright
[**fawrth**-rahyt]

adj. going straight to the point
솔직 담백한

*His **forthright** manner can be mistaken for rudeness.*

syn.   straightforward, honest, frank

fortify
[**fawr**-tuh-fahy]

v. to protect or strengthen against attack
강화하다, 요새처럼 만들다

*The bright intellect was **fortified** by the profound knowledge.*

syn.   strengthen, reinforce, toughen

foundation
[foun-**dey**-shuhn]

n. the beginning point and support from which something develops
기초, 기반, (건물의) 토대

*No good building exists without a good **foundation**.*

syn.   basis, base, groundwork, infrastructure

fragile
[**fraj**-uhll]

adj. easily broken, shattered, or damaged
부서지기 쉬운, 손상되기 쉬운

*Be careful not to drop it; it's very **fragile**.*

syn.   brittle, frail, feeble

fragment
[**frag**-muhnt]

n. a part broken off or detached
조각, 파편

*I heard only a **fragment** of their conversation.*

syn.   piece, bit, particle

frenzied

[**fren**-zeed]

adj. wildly excited or enthusiastic

광분한, 매우 화난, 미친듯한

There was no getting away from his frenzied assault.

syn. frantic, wild, frenetic

fretful

[**fret**-*fuhl*]

adj. irritable or peevish

안달하는, 초조해하는, 짜증 잘내는

Babies soon become fretful when they are tired or hungry.

syn. irritable, fidgeting, distressed

frugal

[**froo**-*guhl*]

adj. economical in use or expenditure

절약하는, 검소한

She lived a very frugal life, avoiding all luxuries.

syn. thrifty, economical, careful

fruitful

[**froot**-*fuhl*]

adj. producing good results

생산적인, 유익한

He lived a fruitful life as a man can only die once.

syn. productive, prolific, fertile

ISEE Sentence Completion 5-4

Directions : Fill in the blanks to complete the sentences.

1. The student was very _____ about her opinion and did not hesitate to express her thoughts clearly.

   (A) force
   (B) fragile
   (C) frenzied
   (D) forthright

2. The small child handled the antique vase carefully because it was very _____.

   (A) forthright
   (B) fragile
   (C) frugal
   (D) fruitful

3. The general decided to _____ the city's walls to protect it from enemy attacks.

   (A) foundation
   (B) fragment
   (C) fortify
   (D) frenzied

4. After weeks of studying, Emily's hard work proved to be _____ when she got a perfect score on her test.

   (A) fruitful
   (B) fretful
   (C) force
   (D) frugal

5. The toddler became _____ when he didn't get the toy he wanted.

   (A) forthright
   (B) fretful
   (C) frenzied
   (D) fruitful

241	frustrate	246	futile
242	fulfill	247	gallant
243	fumble	248	genesis
244	furnish	249	genre
245	furtive	250	genuine

Ad majorem Dei gloriam.
(For the greater glory of God.)
하느님의 더 큰 영광을 위하여.

SSATKOREA.com

frustrate
[**fruhs**-treyt]

v. to disappoint or thwart
좌절감을 주다, 불만스럽게 만들다

*The failure didn't **frustrate** him.*

syn. thwart, foil, dissuade

fulfill
[fool-**fil**]

v. to carry out, or bring to realization,
as a prophecy or promise
(의무나 약속을) 다하다, 이루다

*I have a promise to **fulfill** as well.*

syn. achieve, attain, realize, satisfy

fumble
[**fuhm**-b*uhl*]

v. to feel or grope about clumsily
(찾느라고 손으로) 더듬거리다

*He bit his lip and began to **fumble**
with his tie.*

syn. grope for, mishandle, bumble

furnish
[**fur**-nish]

v. to put furniture and other needed
items in a building
(가구를) 비치하다

*I'll **furnish** my own place according
to my own taste.*

syn. equip, supply, provide

furtive
[**fur**-tiv]

adj. done in a quiet and secretive way
은밀한, 엉큼한

*He cast a **furtive** glance at her.*

syn. secretive, surreptitious, clandestine

futile
[**fyoot**-l]

adj. incapable of producing any result
헛된, 소용없는

*The teacher described these activities
as **futile**.*

syn. useless, vain, fruitless

gallant

[gal-*uh*nt]

adj. brave, spirited, noble-minded, or chivalrous

용감한, 용맹한

*The general is famous for his **gallant** and successful defense in the war.*

syn. brave, valiant, valorous

genesis

[jen-uh-sis]

n. an origin, creation, or beginning

시작, 창조, 기원

*It was the **genesis** of the Great Empire.*

syn. origin, source, formation

genre

[zhahn-ruh]

n. a class or category of artistic endeavor having a particular form

장르, 분야, 카테고리

*What **genre** does the movie fall into - fantasy or action?*

syn. category, class, sort

genuine

[jen-yoo-in]

adj. possessing the claimed or attributed character, quality, or origin

진짜의, 진품의

*Is it **genuine** or fake?*

syn. authentic, real, actual, sincere

ISEE Sentence Completion 5-5

Directions : Fill in the blanks to complete the sentences.

1. They decided to _____ the room with modern furniture and bright decor.

   (A) frustrate (B) furnish
   (C) fulfill (D) fumble

2. He cast a _____ glance at the envelope, not wanting anyone to notice his interest.

   (A) furtive (B) futile
   (C) gallant (D) genre

3. The explorers made a _____ attempt to cross the harsh desert, but it ended in failure.

   (A) genesis (B) gallant
   (C) futile (D) furnish

4. The soldier's _____ gesture of risking his life to save a comrade earned him a medal.

   (A) gallant (B) furtive
   (C) genuine (D) futile

5. She worked tirelessly to _____ her lifelong dream of becoming a doctor.

   (A) furtive (B) frustrate
   (C) fumble (D) fulfill

Answers

1. (B) 2. (A) 3. (C) 4. (A) 5. (D)

Analogy 5. Doctors

의학을 다루는 여러 의사와 그들이 연구하거나 치료하는 대상을 연결짓는 관계입니다.

cardiologist : heart
심장 전문의 : 심장

psychiatrist : mind
정신과 전문의 : 정신, 심리

dermatologist : skin
피부과 의사 : 피부

ophthalmologist : eyes
안과의사 : 눈

geriatrician : elderly
노인병 의사 : 노인들

pediatrician : children
소아과 의사 : 아이들

anatomist : dissection
해부학자 : 해부

chiropractor : spine
척추 지압사 : 척추

orthodontist : teeth
치과 교정 의사 : 치아

orthopedist : skeleton
정형외과 의사 : 뼈대, 골격

physician : medical practice
내과의사 : 의료

surgeon : surgery
외과의사 : 수술

veterinarian : animals
수의사 : 동물

radiologist : X-ray
방사선 전문의 : X-ray

pathologist : disease
병리학자 : 질병

neurologist : nervous system
신경과 전문의 : 신경계

1. Psychiatrist is to mind as
- (A) husbandry is to farmer
- (B) surgeon is to rehabilitation
- (C) dermatologist is to skin
- (D) pollster is to garment
- (E) physiatrist is to operation

2. Geriatrician is to elderly as
- (A) neurologist is to liver
- (B) toxicologist : blood
- (C) coroner is to specimen
- (D) podiatrist is to brain
- (E) pediatrician is to children

Check-up 5-1

Directions   Each of the following questions consists of one word followed by five words or phrases.
You are to select the one word or phrase whose meaning is closest to the word in capital letters.

1. EXCESSIVE
(A) abrupt
(B) quaint
(C) immoderate
(D) modest
(E) typical

2. EXCLUDE
(A) expel
(B) elevate
(C) decay
(D) intrude
(E) cease

3. EXEMPLARY
(A) dreary
(B) sullen
(C) outstanding
(D) fragile
(E) dejected

4. EXHAUST
(A) ease
(B) conclude
(C) blend
(D) reduce
(E) recommend

5. EXHORT
(A) relent
(B) dispute
(C) urge
(D) console
(E) encircle

6. EXPAND
(A) cower
(B) parch
(C) banish
(D) locate
(E) increase

7. EXPERT
(A) elder
(B) veteran
(C) benefit
(D) terror
(E) torment

8. EXPLICIT
(A) obvious
(B) valiant
(C) provocative
(D) approximate
(E) evident

9. EXPOUND
(A) explain
(B) communicate
(C) persuade
(D) afford
(E) recite

10. EXQUISITE
(A) capable
(B) complete
(C) essential
(D) recent
(E) beautiful

Answer 1.C 2.A 3.C 4.D 5.C 6.E 7.B 8.A 9.A 10.E

Check-up 5-2

1. EXTEND
- (A) paralyze
- (B) prune
- (C) descend
- (D) lengthen
- (E) somber

2. EXUBERANT
- (A) ebullient
- (B) drab
- (C) overdue
- (D) dormant
- (E) animated

3. FACADE
- (A) chamber
- (B) passage
- (C) pretense
- (D) feud
- (E) venture

4. FALLACY
- (A) treachery
- (B) profundity
- (C) misconception
- (D) trickery
- (E) perfidy

5. FALSIFY
- (A) evaporate
- (B) reject
- (C) reveal
- (D) misrepresent
- (E) vary

6. FAMINE
- (A) bent
- (B) starvation
- (C) provision
- (D) incumbency
- (E) stipulation

7. FATHOM
- (A) replace
- (B) suspect
- (C) migrate
- (D) understand
- (E) dismay

8. FAUX
- (A) fake
- (B) dormant
- (C) obscure
- (D) bland
- (E) major

9. FECUND
- (A) primitive
- (B) rigorous
- (C) fertile
- (D) intense
- (E) fruitless

10. FERVENT
- (A) alert
- (B) zealous
- (C) substantial
- (D) overdue
- (E) feeble

Check-up 5-3

Directions   Each of the following questions consists of one word followed by five words or phrases. You are to select the one word or phrase whose meaning is closest to the word in capital letters.

1. FIERCE
(A) formal
(B) methodical
(C) somber
(D) ferocious
(E) tropical

2. FIERY
(A) tempestuous
(B) absurd
(C) puny
(D) ample
(E) passionate

3. FLAMBOYANT
(A) bland
(B) puny
(C) compatible
(D) tropical
(E) showy

4. FLATTER
(A) ban
(B) compliment
(C) scurry
(D) invade
(E) forego

5. FLAWLESS
(A) perfect
(B) meager
(C) painstaking
(D) bracing
(E) carnivorous

6. FLEDGLING
(A) crew
(B) milestone
(C) beginner
(D) landmark
(E) chasm

7. FLIPPANT
(A) obsolete
(B) frivolous
(C) previous
(D) equivalent
(E) edible

8. FLOUNDER
(A) mope
(B) struggle
(C) release
(D) insert
(E) depend

9. FLUTTER
(A) flinch
(B) smite
(C) cower
(D) bore
(E) flap

10. FOIBLE
(A) shaft
(B) rod
(C) gust
(D) flaw
(E) gulf

Check-up 5-4

Each of the following questions consists of one word followed by five words or phrases. You are to select the one word or phrase whose meaning is closest to the word in capital letters.

1. FORCE
(A) coerce
(B) falsify
(C) implicate
(D) burnish
(E) verify

2. FORTHRIGHT
(A) akin
(B) related
(C) straightforward
(D) optional
(E) aforementioned

3. FORTIFY
(A) nourish
(B) reinforce
(C) hibernate
(D) engage
(E) affect

4. FOUNDATION
(A) basis
(B) tournament
(C) cable
(D) nation
(E) process

5. FRAGILE
(A) compassionate
(B) brittle
(C) notable
(D) rebellious
(E) monstrous

6. FRAGMENT
(A) piece
(B) habit
(C) moisture
(D) recreation
(E) pattern

7. FRENZIED
(A) optimistic
(B) solitary
(C) frantic
(D) meddlesome
(E) harsh

8. FRETFUL
(A) nostalgic
(B) compatible
(C) significant
(D) irritable
(E) superior

9. FRUGAL
(A) thrifty
(B) burly
(C) ridiculous
(D) stupendous
(E) foolhardy

10. FRUITFUL
(A) nonchalant
(B) productive
(C) brilliant
(D) jubilant
(E) visible

Check-up 5-5

Directions   Each of the following questions consists of one word followed by five words or phrases.
You are to select the one word or phrase whose meaning is closest to the word in capital letters.

1. FRUSTRATE
(A) exceed
(B) trudge
(C) persist
(D) extinguish
(E) thwart

2. FULFILL
(A) plunge
(B) yield
(C) achieve
(D) mock
(E) confuse

3. FUMBLE
(A) lean on
(B) give in
(C) grope for
(D) call up
(E) take over

4. FURNISH
(A) concern
(B) equip
(C) repent
(D) prepare
(E) recall

5. FURTIVE
(A) premature
(B) steadfast
(C) secretive
(D) minor
(E) desperate

6. FUTILE
(A) patient
(B) scalding
(C) vertical
(D) useless
(E) obscure

7. GALLANT
(A) evasive
(B) flimsy
(C) hilarious
(D) numerous
(E) brave

8. GENESIS
(A) malice
(B) interval
(C) span
(D) origin
(E) resident

9. GENRE
(A) deed
(B) cathedral
(C) myriad
(D) category
(E) carnival

10. GENUINE
(A) cumbersome
(B) boisterous
(C) authentic
(D) moral
(E) subsequent

101

261 gimmick

256 gracious

252 glare

257 greedy

253 gloomy

258 grotesque

254 gossip

259 guarded

255 graceful

260 guile

Post hoc, ergo propter hoc.
(After this, therefore because of this).
이후에 일어났으므로, 그 때문에 일어났다.

SSATKOREA.com

gimmick
[**gim**-ik]

n. an ingenious or novel device or scheme

속임수 장치, 책략

Some food companies give small gifts with children's meals as a sales gimmick.

syn. finesse, scheme, trick

glare
[glair]

v. to stare with a fiercely or angrily piercing look

노려보다, 쏘아보다

He glared at his opponent with an angry face.

syn. stare, frown, gape

gloomy
[glu-mi]

adj. dark, dim, or lacking light

(어눕고 우울한) 어두운, 침울한

The weather was gloomy, with dark clouds covering the sky.

syn. dim, dark, depressing

gossip
[**gos**-*uh*p]

n. idle talk or rumor, especially about the personal or private affairs of others

소문

The magazine was full of gossip about celebrities.

syn. rumor, scandal, news

graceful
[greys-*fuh*l]

adj. characterized by elegance or beauty of form, manner, movement, or speech

우아한, 매우 솜씨 좋은

Her movements were graceful and elegant.

syn. skilled, agile, charming

gracious
[grey-sh*uh*s]

adj. pleasantly kind, benevolent, and courteous

친절한, 품위 있는

The gracious lady was very well-mannered and kind.

syn. courteous, polite, elegant, civil

greedy
[**gree**-dee]

adj. excessively or inordinately desirous of wealth, profit, etc.

욕심 많은, 탐욕스러운

The greedy merchant wants to have more money than is fair.

syn. gluttonous, ravenous, voracious

grotesque
[groh-**tesk**]

adj. odd or unnatural in shape, appearance, or character

모습이 이상하고 무서운, 기괴한

The grotesque statue was so unnatural and unpleasant.

syn. malformed, deformed, misshapen

guarded
[**gahr**-did]

adj. cautious and careful

조심스러운, 신중한

The guarded inspector was so careful not to show his feelings.

syn. cautious, careful, circumspect

guile
[gahyl]

n. insidious cunning in attaining a goal

속임수

I love children's innocence and lack of guile.

syn. cunning, craftiness, craft, artfulness

ISEE Sentence Completion 6-1

Directions : Fill in the blanks to complete the sentences.

1. The sky was covered with thick, dark clouds, creating a _____ atmosphere before the storm arrived.

   (A) graceful   B) guarded
   (C) gloomy   (D) grotesque

2. The flashy advertisement relied on a clever _____ to attract attention, but the product itself wasn't very impressive.

   (A) gimmick   (B) gossip
   (C) guile   (D) glare

3. His _____ desire for wealth made him overlook the needs of others, causing him to lose friends over time.

   (A) grotesque   (B) guarded
   (C) gracious   (D) greedy

4. After being hurt in the past, Emily was more _____ when sharing personal information with new friends.

   (A) gracious   (B) guarded
   (C) gimmick   (D) grotesque

5. Emma carried herself in a _____ manner, impressing everyone with her poise and elegance.

   (A) greedy   (B) guarded
   (C) graceful   (D) grotesque

Answers
1. (C)   2. (A)   3. (D)   4. (B)   5. (C)

261	harass	266	heed
262	harbor	267	Herculean
263	hazard	268	heritage
264	heave	269	hierarchy
265	hectic	270	hindrance

Sine qua non.
(Without which not)
없으면 안 되는 필수 요소.

SSATKOREA.com

harass
[huh-**ras**]

v. to disturb persistently
괴롭히다, 못살게 굴다

*They **harassed** him by attacking him repeatedly.*

syn. badger, vex, irritate

harbor
[**hahr**-ber]

v. to shelter, protect, or give refuge
숨겨 주다, 보호하다

*The village **harbored** refugees during the war.*

syn. shelter, protect, refuge

hazard
[**haz**-erd]

n. an unavoidable danger or risk, even though often foreseeable
위험

*His casual remark was a real **hazard** to his reputation.*

syn. danger, risk, peril

heave
[heev]

v. to raise or lift with effort or force
들어올리다

*They push, pull and **heave** the luggage.*

syn. raise, lift, hoist

hectic
[**hek**-tik]

adj. very busy, full of activity, or chaotic
매우 바쁜, 정신없이 분주한

*I had a **hectic** schedule for the last two weeks.*

syn. frantic, crazy, frenzied

heed
[heed]

v. to give careful attention to
(남의 충고에) 주의를 기울이다

*It is important to **heed** the lessons of failure.*

syn. care, listen, observe

Herculean
[hur-kyuh-lee-uhn]

adj. very difficult to accomplish

엄청난 힘이 필요한, 매우 힘든

Completing the project required a Herculean effort.

syn. arduous, monumental, strenuous

heritage
[**her**-i-tij]

n. property, traditions, or values passed down from previous generations

유산, 전통

He inherited a beautiful estate as part of his family's heritage.

syn. legacy, inheritance, tradition

hierarchy
[**hahy**-uh-rahr-kee]

n. An organization of people or things arranged in order of rank, power, or status

위계질서, 서열

The company's hierarchy places the CEO at the top.

syn. ranking, order, structure

hindrance
[**hin** druhns]

n. an impeding, stopping, preventing, or the like

방해, 장애

To be honest, he was more of a hindrance than a help.

syn. obstruction, deterrent, impediment

ISEE Sentence Completion 6-2

Directions : Fill in the blanks to complete the sentences.

1. The journalist continued to _____ the politician with difficult questions during the interview.

   (A) hazard   (B) harbor
   (C) harass   (D) heed

2. The family decided to _____ the stray dog, providing it with food and a safe place to stay.

   (A) harass   (B) harbor
   (C) hazard   (D) heed

3. The storm posed a serious _____ to the residents, forcing them to evacuate the area immediately.

   (A) harass   (B) heave
   (C) heed   (D) hazard

4. It's important to _____ the warnings on the package to avoid any potential harm.

   (A) harass   (B) heed
   (C) hazard   (D) hectic

5. The athlete's accomplishment was seen as a _____ effort, requiring immense strength and perseverance.

   (A) Herculean   (B) heritage
   (C) hectic   (D) hazard

Answers
1. (C) 2. (B) 3. (D) 4. (B) 5. (A)

271	hollow	276	hue
272	honorable	277	humility
273	horde	278	hurl
274	hospitable	279	hypnotic
275	hostile	280	hypocritical

Sic transit gloria mundi.
(Thus passes the glory of the world.)
세상의 영광은 이렇게 지나간다.

SSATKOREA.com

hollow
[**hol**-oh]

adj. having a space or cavity inside
빈, 속이 움푹 꺼진

*Most bones are **hollow** to provide the light and strong body.*

syn. empty, void, unfilled

honorable
[**on**-er-uh-b*uh*l]

adj. in accordance with or characterized by principles of honor
명예로운, 고상한

*We will end this war with an **honorable** peace.*

syn. reputable, principled, virtuous

horde
[hawrd]

n. a large group, multitude, number
무리, 떼

*A **horde** of children ran over the office building.*

syn. mob, crowd, throng

hospitable
[**hos**-pi-tuh-b*uh*l]

adj. receiving or treating guests or strangers warmly and generously
친절한, 환대하는

*The **hospitable** host is friendly, generous, and welcoming to guests.*

syn. cordial, congenial, friendly

hostile
[**hos**-tl]

adj. of, relating to, or characteristic of an enemy
적대적인, 강력히 반대하는

*Their **hostile** looks showed that he was unwelcome.*

syn. antagonistic, adverse, belligerent

hue
[hyoo]

n. a gradation or variety of a color
색채, 색

*Black will take no other **hue**.*

syn. color, shade, tone

humility

[hyoo-**mil**-i-teeor]

n. a modest view of one's importance

겸손, 겸허

*She showed **humility** by sharing credit for the group's success.*

syn. modesty, meekness, humbleness

hurl

[hurl]

v. to throw forcefully

던지다

*The mob **hurled** a brick violently and with a love of force.*

syn. fling, throw, lob

hypnotic

[hip-**not**-ik]

adj. inducing sleep or hypnosis

최면의, 최면을 거는

*He has been hypnotized deeply, so he was in a total **hypnotic** state.*

syn. spellbinding, sleep-inducing

hypocritical

[hip-uh-**krit**-i-k*uh*l]

adj. of the nature of hypocrisy, or pretense of having virtues, beliefs, principles, etc.

위선적인, 가식적인

*She accused the statesman of being **hypocritical**.*

syn. insincere, deceitful, pretending

ISEE Sentence Completion 6-3

Directions : Fill in the blanks to complete the sentences.

1. His decision to donate his prize money to charity was seen as an _____ gesture.

   (A) hypocritical   (B) honorable
   (C) hospitable   (D) hypnotic

2. A _____ of people gathered at the concert, making it difficult to move through the crowd.

   (A) humility   (B) hollow
   (C) hue   (D) horde

3. His _____ attitude made it difficult for others to work with him on the project.

   (A) hostile   (B) honorable
   (C) hollow   (D) hospitable

4. The painting had a beautiful _____ of blue that gave it a serene quality.

   (A) hue   (B) hue
   (C) humility   (D) hypnotic

5. His claims about fairness were criticized as _____ behavior because his actions said otherwise.

   (A) hypocritical   (B) hollow
   (C) hostile   (D) hypnotic

1. (B) 2. (D) 3. (A) 4. (B) 5. (A)

Answers

281	illuminate	286	Implement
282	illustrious	287	improvise
283	impassive	288	impulse
284	impeccable	289	inadequate
285	impetuous	290	inadvertent

Fiat lux.
(Let there be light.)
빛이 있으라.

SSATKOREA.com

illuminate
[ih-**loo**-muh-neyt]

v. to supply or brighten with light
비추다, 밝히다

The red glow of the sunset illuminated the sky.

syn. brighten, light up, clarify

illustrious
[ih-**luhs**-tree-*uhs*]

adj. highly distinguished
유명한, 저명한

The composer was one of many illustrious visitors to the town.

syn. renowned, eminent, acclaimed

impassive
[im-**pas**-iv]

adj. without emotion, apathetic
무표성한, 아무런 감정이 없는

His impassive face is not showing any emotion.

syn. unemotional, expressionless, apathetic

impeccable
[im-**pek**-uh-b*uh*l]

adj. without fault or error
흠 잡을 데 없는, 완벽한

Her appearance was impeccable, showing perfect taste.

syn. flawless, faultless, unblemished

impetuous
[im-**pech**-oo-*uhs*]

adj. likely to do something suddenly, without considering the results of the actions
성급한, 충동적인

It would be foolish and impetuous to resign over such a small matter.

syn. impulsive, rash, hasty

implement
[**im**-pl*uh*-m*uh*nt]

v. to put into action or use
실행하다, 시행하다

The school decided to implement a new rule about using phones.

syn. execute, enforce, carry out

improvise
[**im**-pruh-vahyz]

v. to compose and perform or deliver without previous preparation

(연주나 연설 등을) 즉흥적으로 하다

*The jazz pianist **improvised** on the melody without having planned it in advance.*

syn. extemporize, contrive, devise

impulse
[**im**-puhls]

n. the influence of a particular feeling, mental state, etc.

(갑작스러운) 충동

*She is likely to decide on **impulse** without being careful.*

syn. impetus, stimulus, throb

inadequate
[in-**ad**-i-kwit]

adj. not adequate or sufficient

불충분한, 부적당한

*Undernutrition is a condition of malnutrition caused by **inadequate** food supply.*

syn. insufficient, deficient, incompetent

inadvertent
[in-uhd-**vur**-tnt]

adj. unintentional

고의가 아닌, 우연의, 의도하지 않은

Most mistakes are 'inadvertent' and 'unintentional.'

syn. unwitting, accidental, unintentional

ISEE Sentence Completion 6-4

Directions : Fill in the blanks to complete the sentences.

1. The manager decided to _____ the plan immediately to address the issue.

   (A) illuminate   (B) implement
   (C) improvise   (D) impetuous

2. His _____ manners impressed everyone at the formal dinner.

   (A) impeccable   (B) impetuous
   (C) inadvertent   (D) inadequate

3. With no time to prepare, the speaker had to _____ a speech on the spot.

   (A) improvise   (B) illuminate
   (C) implement   (D) impulse

4. The error was an _____ mistake, but it still caused significant delays in the process.

   (A) impeccable   (B) inadvertent
   (C) impetuous   (D) inadequate

5. The professor used examples to _____ the complex concept for the students.

   (A) impulse   (B) impassive
   (C) illuminate   (D) impeccable

MIDDLE 1 2 3 4 5 6 7 8 9 10

UPPER 1 2 3 4 5 6 7 8 9 10

291 inaugurate   296 industrious

292 incentive   297 inept

293 incident   298 initiate

294 incognito   299 inquire

295 indomitable   300 insanity

Cogito, ergo sum.
(I think, therefore I am.)
나는 생각한다, 고로 존재한다.

SSATKOREA.com

inaugurate
[in-**aw**-gyuh-reyt]

v. to formally begin or introduce something, especially a system, policy, or period
(공식적으로) 시작하다, 취임하다

*The school **inaugurated** a new lunch program to provide healthier meals for students.*

syn. launch, commence, initiate

incentive
[in-**sen**-tiv]

n. something that incites or tends to incite to action or greater effort
(어떤 행동을 장려하기 위한) 유도책, 유인책

*Tax-refund **incentives** encourage tourist to buy more products.*

syn. inducement, lure

incident
[**in**-si-d*uh*nt]

n. an individual occurrence or event
(특이하거나 불쾌한) 일, 사건

*An error in the translation nearly caused a diplomatic **incident**.*

syn. event, accident, occurrence

incognito
[in-kog-**nee**-toh]

adj. having one's identity concealed
자기 신분을 숨기고, 가명으로

*The film star is **incognito** using a false name to make a reservation.*

syn. anonymous, disguised, concealed

indomitable
[in-**dom**-i-tuh-b*uh*l]

adj. that cannot be subdued or overcome, as person's will or courage
불굴의, 절대 굴복하지 않는

*She has an **indomitable** spirit, never giving up.*

syn. invincible, unconquerable, unbeatable

industrious
[in-**duhs**-tree-*uh*s]

adj. working energetically and devotedly
근면한, 부지런한

*He was an **industrious** worker working very hard.*

syn. diligent, assiduous, conscientious

inept
[in-**ept**]

adj. without skill or aptitude for a particular task or assignment

솜씨 없는, 서투른

*The green politician was **inept** at dealing with people.*

syn.   unskilled, clumsy, ungainly

initiate
[ih-**nish**-ee-eyt]

v. to begin, set going, or originate

시작하다, 착수하다

*The school has **initiated** a program of higher education.*

syn.   commence, launch, inaugurate

inquire
[in-**kwahy**uhr]

v. to seek information by questioning

묻다, 알아보다

*The detective kept **inquiring** about a neighbor.*

syn.   ask, investigate, probe

insanity
[in-**san**-i-tee]

n. a foolish or senseless action, policy, statement, etc.

정신이상, 무모한 짓

*The crimes against humanity are so primitive that to allow such **insanity** to happen at this turn of the century is incomprehensible.*

syn.   lunacy, frenzy, foolishness

ISEE Sentence Completion 6-5

Directions : Fill in the blanks to complete the sentences.

1. The journalist called to _____ about details of the upcoming press conference.

   (A) inquire   (B) incident
   (C) indomitable   (D) inept

2. The company offered a generous financial _____ to employees who met their sales targets.

   (A) initiate   (B) inquire
   (C) incentive   (D) industrious

3. The spy decided to go _____ during the mission to avoid being recognized.

   (A) industrious   (B) incognito
   (C) inquire   (D) initiate

4. Her _____ spirit allowed her to overcome every challenge she faced with courage.

   (A) indomitable   (B) inept
   (C) insanity   (D) incentive

5. The president will _____ a new policy to improve education across the country.

   (A) industrious   (B) inaugurate
   (C) incognito   (D) inquire

⚑ **Answers**
1. (A) 2. (C) 3. (B) 4. (A) 5. (B)

Analogy 6. Part & Whole

전체와 부분 간의 관계도 꼭 알아야 할 유형이죠? 이 때 포인트는 부분의 위치도 같은 것이 더 가까운 관계가 된다는 것입니다. 문제가 전체에서 앞쪽을 가리키면, 답도 전체의 앞쪽 부분에 있는 것이 된다는 것이죠.

A는 B의 Front 앞 부분

preface : book
서문 : 책

Preamble : Constitution
헌법 서문 : 헌법

overture : opera
서곡 : 오페라

prologue : novel
프롤로그 : 소설

A는 B의 Ending 끝 부분

finale : opera
피날레 : 오페라

epilogue : novel
에필로그 : 소설

dessert : meal
디저트 : 식사

postscript : letter
추신 : 편지

같은 기능이나, 같은 위치를 하는 것을 연결한 관계

candle : wick
양초 : 심지

bulb : filament
전구 : 필라멘트

pinnacle : mountain
산봉우리 : 산

crest : wave
물마루 : 파도

POP
QUIZ

1. Preamble is to Constitution as
(A) overture is to opera
(B) epilogue is to novel
(C) frigid is to algid
(D) intermission is to play
(E) recess is to school

2. Postscript is to letter as
(A) salutation is to greeting
(B) finale is to class
(C) appetizer is to banquet
(D) epilogue is to novel
(E) caliber is to gun

3. Gill is to fish as
(A) shark is to fish
(B) talon is to eagle
(C) poem is to stanza
(D) chapter is to book
(E) lung is to man

4. Bulb is to filament as
(A) candle is to wick
(B) bear is to claw
(C) harpsichord is to piano
(D) sentence is to paragraph
(E) rind is to watermelon

Check-up 6-1

Directions   Each of the following questions consists of one word followed by five words or phrases.
You are to select the one word or phrase whose meaning is closest to the word in capital letters.

1. GIMMICK
(A) finesse
(B) cadence
(C) lull
(D) platoon
(E) helix

2. GLARE
(A) appall
(B) stare
(C) resist
(D) quiver
(E) submit

3. GLOOMY
(A) lively
(B) careless
(C) dim
(D) bright
(E) energetic

4. GOSSIP
(A) trophy
(B) barrier
(C) fortress
(D) advantage
(E) rumor

5. GRACEFUL
(A) fascinating
(B) immense
(C) gracious
(D) skilled
(E) available

6. GRACIOUS
(A) sensational
(B) unwieldy
(C) courteous
(D) prosperous
(E) remote

7. GREEDY
(A) grim
(B) gluttonous
(C) gigantic
(D) heroic
(E) elegant

8. GROTESQUE
(A) malformed
(B) exultant
(C) former
(D) urban
(E) exasperating

9. GUARDED
(A) terse
(B) cautious
(C) reluctant
(D) celebrated
(E) obedient

10. GUILE
(A) delicate
(B) confident
(C) cunning
(D) barren
(E) durable

Answer 1.A 2.B 3.C 4.E 5.D 6.C 7.B 8.A 9.B 10.C

Check-up 6-2

Directions   Each of the following questions consists of one word followed by five words or phrases. You are to select the one word or phrase whose meaning is closest to the word in capital letters.

1. HARASS
(A) liberate
(B) revive
(C) badger
(D) slither
(E) decrease

2. HARBOR
(A) taper
(B) pledge
(C) transform
(D) shelter
(E) convalesce

3. HAZARD
(A) blossom
(B) limb
(C) frontier
(D) fringe
(E) danger

4. HEAVE
(A) celebrate
(B) bask
(C) raise
(D) prosper
(E) pardon

5. HECTIC
(A) massive
(B) stationary
(C) frantic
(D) benevolent
(E) deft

6. HEED
(A) taper
(B) care
(C) elevate
(D) glisten
(E) adore

7. HERCUELEAN
(A) minute
(B) unruly
(C) resourceful
(D) competitive
(E) arduous

8. HERITAGE
(A) progeny
(B) legacy
(C) culture
(D) heirloom
(E) harbinger

9. HIERARCHY
(A) ranking
(B) proportion
(C) excess
(D) dearth
(E) hibernation

10. HINDRANCE
(A) bough
(B) request
(C) prospect
(D) obstruction
(E) tower

Check-up 6-3

Directions Each of the following questions consists of one word followed by five words or phrases. You are to select the one word or phrase whose meaning is closest to the word in capital letters.

1. HOLLOW
(A) pretentious
(B) doleful
(C) engrossing
(D) empty
(E) squalid

2. HONORABLE
(A) elaborate
(B) straightforward
(C) colossal
(D) fantastic
(E) reputable

3. HORDE
(A) refuge
(B) mob
(C) portrait
(D) shade
(E) hostility

4. HOSPITABLE
(A) awesome
(B) exhilarating
(C) cordial
(D) open
(E) famine

5. HOSTILE
(A) antagonistic
(B) elusive
(C) splendid
(D) constant
(E) brief

6. HUE
(A) color
(B) frivolity
(C) mural
(D) freight
(E) cargo

7. HUMILITY
(A) edict
(B) cadence
(C) modesty
(D) prose
(E) arrogance

8. HURL
(A) envelop
(B) diminish
(C) substitute
(D) fling
(E) boycott

9. HYPNOTIC
(A) unique
(B) outmoded
(C) discreet
(D) complicated
(E) spellbinding

10. HYPOCRITICAL
(A) elated
(B) insincere
(C) continuous
(D) leisurely
(E) tentative

115

Check-up 6-4

1. ILLUMINATE
(A) brighten
(B) wonder
(C) assemble
(D) disguise
(E) intimidate

2. ILLUSTRIOUS
(A) reckless
(B) renowned
(C) defective
(D) squalid
(E) pathetic

3. IMPASSIVE
(A) brisk
(B) ravenous
(C) unemotional
(D) indolent
(E) relentless

4. IMPECCABLE
(A) resolute
(B) flawless
(C) controversial
(D) tranquil
(E) insolent

5. IMPETUOUS
(A) bankrupt
(B) invaluable
(C) rigorous
(D) insolvent
(E) impulsive

6. IMPLEMENT
(A) pierce
(B) falter
(C) quiver
(D) execute
(E) purge

7. IMPROVISE
(A) extemporize
(B) originate
(C) relocate
(D) beget
(E) exasperate

8. IMPULSE
(A) remedy
(B) expansion
(C) impetus
(D) riot
(E) blizzard

9. INADEQUATE
(A) insufficient
(B) placid
(C) ecstatic
(D) genuine
(E) realistic

10. INADVERTENT
(A) intended
(B) solitary
(C) unwitting
(D) fruitful
(E) futile

Check-up 6-5

Directions   Each of the following questions consists of one word followed by five words or phrases.
You are to select the one word or phrase whose meaning is closest to the word in capital letters.

1. INAUGURATE
(A) launch
(B) terminate
(C) hesitate
(D) peep
(E) abort

2. INCENTIVE
(A) dictator
(B) disaster
(C) inducement
(D) concept
(E) upbringing

3. INCIDENT
(A) affliction
(B) fume
(C) lumber
(D) event
(E) rebel

4. INCOGNITO
(A) lethal
(B) effective
(C) acrid
(D) muddled
(E) anonymous

5. INDOMITABLE
(A) futile
(B) invincible
(C) treacherous
(D) hectic
(E) distinct

6. INDUSTRIOUS
(A) mortal
(B) aghast
(C) alleged
(D) diligent
(E) blatant

7. INEPT
(A) unskilled
(B) adept
(C) apathetic
(D) deft
(E) alternative

8. INITIATE
(A) commence
(B) infest
(C) declare
(D) bluster
(E) emerge

9. INQUIRE
(A) posture
(B) restraint
(C) breach
(D) ask
(E) transport

10. INSANITY
(A) sage
(B) lunacy
(C) procrastination
(D) filibuster
(E) veto

117

301	inspect	306	inundate
302	inspire	307	invade
303	integrate	308	invert
304	intellectual	309	irrelevant
305	intense	310	jabber

Quid pro quo.
(Something for something)
대가성 교환

SSATKOREA.com

integrate
[**in**-ti-greyt]

v. to bring together or incorporate into a whole

통합시키다, 합치다

*The wanderers **integrated** into a social group and became a major part of this society.*

syn. combine, amalgamate, merge

intellectual
[in-tl-**ek**-choo-*uhl*]

adj. appealing to or engaging the intellect

지적인, 높은 지능과 지식을 가진

*Companies should protect their **intellectual** property with patents and trademarks.*

syn. cerebral, smart, brainy

inspect
[in-**spekt**]

v. to look carefully at or over

점검하다, 조사하다

*He **inspected** every detail, looking at every part of it carefully.*

syn. examine, check, scrutinize

intense
[in-**tens**]

adj. occurring in a high or extreme degree

극심한, 강렬한

*The principal is under **intense** pressure to resign.*

syn. acute, forceful, severe

inspire
[in-**spahy***uhr*]

v. to fill with an amazing, quickening, or exalting influence

격려하다, 고무하다

*His performance **inspired** the young boy to do something new or unusual.*

syn. stimulate, encourage, influence

inundate
[**in**-*uh*n-deyt]

v. to fill completely, usually with water

범람하다, 침수시키다

*Flood waters typically **inundate** farmland, making the land unworkable.*

syn. flood, overwhelm, deluge

invade
[in-**veyd**]

v. to enter forcefully as an enemy

침입하다, 침략히다

*I don't want to **invade** your private life unnecessarily.*

syn. intrude, raid, occupy

invert
[in-**vurt**]

v. to turn upside down

(아래 위를) 뒤집다

*Place a plate over the pancake and **invert** it.*

syn. reverse, upturn, transpose

irrelevant
[ih-**rel**-uh-v*u*/nt]

adj. having no connection with the subject

무관한, 상관없는

*She considered politics **irrelevant** to her life.*

syn. immaterial, impertinent, inappropriate

jabber
[**jab**-er]

v. to talk rapidly, indistinctively or nonsensically

(흥분해서 알아듣기 힘들게) 지껄이다

*The kids were **jabbering** very quickly, and I could not understand them.*

syn. babble, prattle, chatter

ISEE Sentence Completion 7-1

Directions : Fill in the blanks to complete the sentences.

1. Her passion for art was able to
   _____ creativity in her students.

   (A) inspire   (B) invade
   (C) invert   (D) integrate

2. The engineer needed to _____
   the machinery thoroughly before
   approving its use.

   (A) jabber   (B) inundated
   (C) invert   (D) inspect

3. She felt completely _____
   with work and struggled to meet
   deadlines.

   (A) intellectual   (B) irrelevant
   (C) invade   (D) inundated

4. Installing security cameras can
   sometimes _____ people's
   privacy if not handled carefully.

   (A) intense   (B) invade
   (C) invert   (D) irrelevant

5. The designer decided to _____
   the image for a fresh perspective
   on the layout.

   (A) invert   (B) inundate
   (C) jabber   (D) inspect

Answers

1. (A) 2. (D) 3. (D) 4. (B) 5. (A)

011	jostle	316	lapse
312	jubilant	317	literal
313	jumble	318	litigate
314	juvenile	319	lore
315	labyrinth	320	magnanimous

Labor omnia vincit.
(Work conquers all.)
노력은 모든 것을 이긴다.

SSATKOREA.com

jostle
[**jos**-*uhl*]

v. to bump, push, or elbow roughly or rudely

(많은 사람들 사이에서) 거칠게 밀치다

*People were **jostling** in a crowd, and they were trying to get past me.*

syn. bump, shove, push

jubilant
[**joo**-buh-l*uh*nt]

adj. showing great joy, satisfaction, or triumph

승리감에 넘치는, 득의 만면한, 의기양양한

*She was **jubilant** after making an impressive comeback.*

syn. triumphant, overjoyed, exultant

jumble
[**juhm**-b*uh*l]

v. to mix in a confused mass

뒤섞다

*Toys, books, and blocks were **jumbled** together on the floor.*

syn. muddle, disorganize, clutter

juvenile
[**joo**-vuh-nl]

adj. of, pertaining to, characteristics of, or suitable or intended for young persons

청소년의

*A **juvenile** delinquent is a young person who is guilty of committing crimes.*

syn. young, childish, immature, puerile

labyrinth
[**lab**-uh-rinth]

n. an intricate combination of paths or passages in which it is difficult to find one's way or to reach the exit

미로

*The **labyrinth** was made up of a complicated series of paths or passages.*

syn. maze, warren, tangle, web

lapse
[laps]

n. a slip or error, often of a trivial sort

실수, 과실

*A momentary **lapse** of concentration in the final round cost her the match.*

syn. mistake, blunder, blooper

literal
[lit-er-*uhl*]

adj. in accordance with, involving, or being the primary or strict meaning of the word

문자 그대로의

*Doesn't it feel like a **literal** translation?*

syn. exact, factual, word for word

litigate
[**lit**-i-geyt]

v. to make the subject of a lawsuit

소송하다, 고소하다

*The majority of lawsuits can be very complicated to **litigate**.*

syn. sue, prosecute, file a lawsuit

lore
[lawr]

n. traditional wisdom

민간 전승, 전해 내려오는 이야기

*According to local **lore**, this hot spring has healing properties.*

syn. information, knowledge, wisdom

magnanimous
[mag-**nan**-uh-m*uh*s]

adj. generous in forgiving an insult or injury

관대한, 마음이 넓은

*The **magnanimous** ruler behaved generously towards his enemy.*

syn. generous, forgiving, noble

ISEE Sentence Completion 7-2

Directions : Fill in the blanks to complete the sentences.

1. The lawyer worked tirelessly to _____ a case on behalf of her client.

   (A) lapse   (B) magnanimous
   (C) jostle   (D) litigate

2. Commuters often _____ for space on crowded trains during rush hour.

   (A) lore   (B) jubilant
   (C) jostle   (D) litigate

3. They got lost in the _____ of streets in the old city, struggling to find their destination.

   (A) literal   (B) jumble
   (C) labyrinth   (D) lore

4. His temporary _____ in judgment caused him to make a costly mistake at work.

   (A) lapse   (B) literal
   (C) juvenile   (D) jubilant

5. The document was a _____ translation, losing much of its poetic meaning in the process.

   (A) literal   (B) jostle
   (C) jumble   (D) labyrinth

Answers
1. (D) 2. (C) 3. (C) 4. (A) 5. (A)

321 malleable   326 medley

322 massive   327 mend

323 mayhem   328 migrate

324 meager   329 miraculous

325 meandering   330 miserable

Semper fortis.
(Always strong.)
항상 용감하게.

SSATKOREA.com

malleable
[**mal**-ee-uh-b*uh*l]

adj. easily influenced, trained, or controlled

영향을 잘 받는, 잘 변하는

Malleable materials can be formed cold using stamping or pressing.

syn.   pliable, flexible, amenable

massive
[**mas**-iv]

adj. consisting of or forming a large mass

거대한, 엄청나게 큰

Eight massive stone pillars supported the roof.

syn.   huge, enormous, tremendous

mayhem
[**mey**-hem]

n. the crime of willfully inflicting a bodily injury

신체 상해, 파괴 행위, 대혼란

Their arrival caused mayhem as crowds of fans rushed towards them.

syn.   violence, chaos, destruction

meager
[**mee**-ger]

adj. deficient in quantity or quality

메마른, 빈약한, 결핍된

His meager wage is not enough to support his family.

syn.   scanty, sparse, inadequate

meandering
[mee-**an**-dering]

adj. winding or indirect

구불구불한

Meandering paths lead into a small town.

syn.   winding, twisting, curving

medley
[**med**-lee]

n. a mixture of different things, especially tunes put together

여러 가지 뒤섞인 것

The jazz band played a medley of Beatles songs.

syn.   mixture, blend, assortment

mend

[mend]

v. to make whole, sound, or usable by repairing

수리하다, 고치다

*Never try to **mend** a broken machine without disconnecting it from the electricity supply.*

syn.   alter, fix, amend

migrate

[**mahy**-greyt]

v. to travel to another place

(새나 동물이) 계절에 따라 이동하다

*These birds **migrate** to Europe in the summer season.*

syn.   travel, relocate, move

miraculous

[mi-**rak**-yuh-l*uhs*]

adj. surprisingly wonderful

기적적인

*She made a **miraculous** recovery from her fatal injuries.*

syn.   incredible, supernatural, amazing

miserable

[**miz**-er-uh-b*uhl*]

adj. wretchedly unhappy

비참한, 우울한

*Why do you make yourself **miserable** by taking on too much work?*

syn.   wretched, gloomy, depressed

ISEE Sentence Completion 7-3

Directions : Fill in the blanks to complete the sentences.

1. The _____ river wound its way through the valley, creating a picturesque scene.

   (A) meandering   (B) massive
   (C) malleable   (D) mayhem

2. The protest turned into complete _____ when the crowd began to scatter and disrupt traffic.

   (A) medley   (B) mayhem
   (C) miraculous   (D) miserable

3. Gold is a highly _____ material, making it easy to shape into various designs.

   (A) malleable   (B) massive
   (C) meager   (D) mend

4. She struggled to make ends meet on her _____ salary, despite working long hours.

   (A) massive   (B) meager
   (C) mend   (D) migrate

5. The _____ weather ruined their picnic plans, forcing everyone to stay indoors.

   (A) miserable   (B) meager
   (C) mend   (D) mayhem

Answers

1. (A)   2. (B)   3. (A)   4. (B)   5. (A)

331 mislead   336 motive

332 moderate   337 multitude

333 modify   338 mumble

334 mollify   339 murky

335 motif   340 mutiny

Explorare, Discere, Invenire.
(Explore, Learn, Discover)
탐험하고, 배우고, 발견하라.

SSATKOREA.com

mislead
[mis-**leed**]

v. to lead someone in the wrong direction
속이다, 잘못된 방향으로 이끌다

*It is prohibited to provide false information to **mislead** consumers.*

syn. deceive, defraud, misinform

moderate
[**mod**-er-it]

adj. keeping within reasonable or proper limits
보통의, 중간의

*He was an easygoing man of very **moderate** views.*

syn. mild, temperate, average

modify
[**mod**-uh-fahy]

v. to change somewhat the form or qualities of
수정하다, 바꾸다

*Established habits are difficult to **modify**.*

syn. change, alter, adjust

mollify
[**mol**-uh-fahy]

v. to soften in feeling or temper
(사람을) 달래다, 진정시키다

*Please say something to **mollify** his anger.*

syn. pacify, appease, soothe

motif
[moh-**teef**]

n. a recurring subject, theme, or idea
(문학이나 음악 작품 속에서 반복되는) 주제, 모티프

*The theme of creation is a recurrent **motif** in Celtic mythology.*

syn. theme, idea, design

motive
[**moh**-tiv]

n. something that causes a person to act in a certain way
동기, 이유

*There seemed to be no clear **motive** for the attack.*

syn. reason, purpose, aim

multitude

[m**uh**l-ti-tood]

n. a great number

아주 많은 수, 다수, 대중

*Success covers a **multitude** of blunders.*

syn. crowd, horde, legion

mumble

[muhm-b*uhl*]

v. to speak in a low indistinct manner

웅얼거리듯 말하다, 중얼거리다

*I wish you wouldn't **mumble**; I can't hear you clearly.*

syn. mutter, whisper, murmur

murky

[**mur**-kee]

adj. dark, gloomy, obscure with mist

(연기나 안개 등으로 불쾌하게) 어두컴컴한, 흐린

*The light was too **murky** to continue playing.*

syn. gloomy, obscure, dark

mutiny

[**myoot**-n-ee]

n. rebellion against any authority

반역, 반란

*Mark led a military **mutiny** against the commanders.*

syn. revolt, riot, uprising

ISEE Sentence Completion 7-4

Directions : Fill in the blanks to complete the sentences.

1. The architect had to _____ the design to meet the client's changing requirements.

   (A) mislead   (B) modify
   (C) murky   (D) mumble

2. He began to _____ under his breath, making it difficult for anyone to hear him.

   (A) mumble   (B) mollify
   (C) moderate   (D) murky

3. The politician attempted to _____ the angry crowd with promises of immediate action.

   (A) mollify   (B) mutiny
   (C) murky   (D) mislead

4. The runner maintained a _____ pace throughout the race to conserve energy.

   (A) mutiny   (B) murky
   (C) motive   (D) moderate

5. The water in the pond was so _____ that it was impossible to see what lay beneath the surface.

   (A) mislead   (B) motif
   (C) murky   (D) multitude

Answers
1. (B)   2. (A)   3. (A)   4. (D)   5. (C)

341 nimble   346 objection

342 nomad   347 objective

343 novel   348 obscure

344 novice   349 obvious

345 nudge   350 offend

Nihil novi sub sole.
(Nothing new under the sun.)
태양 아래 새로운 것은 없다.

———————————— SSATKOREA.com

nimble
[**nim**-b*uh*l]

adj. quick and light in movement
(동작이) 빠른, 날렵한

Her nimble fingers undid the knot in seconds.

syn.   agile, quick, lively

nomad
[**noh**-mad]

n. a person or tribe that has no adj. of a new and unusual kind
유목민

He is a nomad moving from place to place to find pasture and food.

syn.   itinerant, traveler, migrant

novel
[**nov**-uhl]

adj. of a new and unusual kind
새로운, 독창적인

Rachel has suggested a novel approach to the problem.

syn.   new, original, innovative

novice
[**nov**-is]

n. a person who is new to the circumstances
초보자

I'm a novice at these things, but you're the professional.

syn.   beginner, tyro, newcomer

nudge
[nuhj]

v. to push slightly or gently
(팔꿈치로 살짝) 쿡 찌르다

She nudged gently in my ribs to tell me to shut up.

syn.   poke, elbow, push

objection
[*uh*b-**jek**-sh*uh*n]

n. a reason or argument offered in disagreement
이의, 반대

The Congress overrode the President's objection and passed the law.

syn.   protest, protestation, demur

objective

[*uhb*-**jek**-tiv]

n. something that one's efforts or actions are intended to attain

목적, 목표

*Winning is not the prime **objective** in this sport.*

syn. goal, target, aim

obscure

[*uhb*-**skyoor**]

adj. not clear or plain

잘 알려져 있지 않는, 불명확한

*Her poetry is full of **obscure** literary allusions.*

syn. unclear, ambiguous, nebulous

obvious

[**ob**-vee-*uhs*]

adj. easily seen, recognized, or understood

분명한, 확실한

*Lack of qualifications is an **obvious** disadvantage.*

syn. clear, plain, evident, apparent

offend

[uh-**fend**]

v. to affect disagreeably

기분 상하게 하다, 불쾌하게 하다

*I didn't mean to **offend** you.*

syn. affront, displease, upset, distress

ISEE Sentence Completion 7-5

Directions : Fill in the blanks to complete the sentences.

1. The jeweler's _____ fingers skillfully shaped the delicate gold ring.

   (A) nimble   (B) novel
   (C) nudge   (D) obscure

2. Because he never stayed in one place for too long and traveled constantly, he was considered a _____.

   (A) obscure   (B) nomad
   (C) offend   (D) novel

3. He gave his friend a gentle _____ to remind them to pay attention.

   (A) obvious   (B) objection
   (C) nudge   (D) offend

4. The new student was a _____ at writing essays, so the teacher provided extra guidance.

   (A) obscure   (B) nimble
   (C) nudge   (D) novice

5. The poem's _____ meaning left the readers puzzled and intrigued.

   (A) obscure   (B) obvious
   (C) offend   (D) nudge

Analogy 7. Kinds of

종류와 그 중 하나를 연결짓는 관계입니다. 다른 곳에서 보기 힘든 다양한 명사가 등장하! | 이 유형의 질 나오는 어휘들은 꼭 기억해두세요.

hammock : bed 그물침대, 해먹 : 침대	stool : chair 등받이 없는 의자, 스툴 : 의자
coal : mineral 석탄 : 광물	gold : metal 금 : 금속
cave : dwelling 동굴 : 거주지	cactus : plant 선인장 : 식물
elm : tree 느릅나무 : 나무	tendril : vine 덩굴손 : 덩굴식물
violin : string 바이올린 : 현악기	flute : woodwind 플루트 : 목관악기
cymbals : percussion 심벌즈 : 타악기	trombone : brass 트롬본 : 금관악기
ebony : wood 흑단 : 목재	sable : fur 흑담비 : 모피
gauntlet : glove 갑옷용 장갑 : 장갑	beret : hat 베레모 : 모자
moccasin : shoes 모카신 : 신발	pullover : sweater 풀오버 : 스웨터
diamond : gemstone 다이아몬드 : 보석	velvet : textile 벨벳 : 직물

POP
QUIZ

1. Cello is to string as

(A) flute is to woodwind
(B) cymbals is to brass
(C) grand is to piano
(D) conductor is to orchestra
(E) trombone is to percussion

2. Hammock is to bed as

(A) painter is to exhibit
(B) recital is to musician
(C) fleet is to ships
(D) tent is to house
(E) panoply is collection

Check-up 7-1

Directions   Each of the following questions consists of one word followed by five words or phrases.
You are to select the one word or phrase whose meaning is closest to the word in capital letters.

1. INSPECT
(A) examine
(B) hatch
(C) interpret
(D) moor
(E) baffle

2. INSPIRE
(A) stimulate
(B) sear
(C) loom
(D) hoax
(E) complicate

3. INTEGRATE
(A) contaminate
(B) combine
(C) shroud
(D) pierce
(E) analyze

4. INTELLECTUAL
(A) lethargic
(B) cerebral
(C) pretentious
(D) momentous
(E) scanty

5. INTENSE
(A) unbiased
(B) esteemed
(C) acute
(D) indifferent
(E) buoyant

6. INUNDATE
(A) suspend
(B) cultivate
(C) flood
(D) expel
(E) preserve

7. INVADE
(A) topple
(B) accommodate
(C) assume
(D) abdicate
(E) intrude

8. INVERT
(A) betray
(B) cultivate
(C) lean
(D) reverse
(E) excavate

9. IRRELEVANT
(A) immaterial
(B) sacred
(C) legendary
(D) inevitable
(F) lucrative

10. JABBER
(A) accelerate
(B) babble
(C) hop
(D) narrate
(E) demolish

129

Check-up 7-2

Each of the following questions consists of one word followed by five words or phrases. You are to select the one word or phrase whose meaning is closest to the word in capital letters.

1. JOSTLE
- (A) betray
- (B) cultivate
- (C) decline
- (D) bump
- (E) excavate

2. JUBILANT
- (A) rustic
- (B) parochial
- (C) proficient
- (D) sleek
- (E) triumphant

3. JUMBLE
- (A) dictate
- (B) employ
- (C) muddle
- (D) burden
- (E) provoke

4. JUVENILE
- (A) privileged
- (B) wary
- (C) unwitting
- (D) trifling
- (E) young

5. LABYRINTH
- (A) sermon
- (B) maze
- (C) fragment
- (D) amulet
- (E) priority

6. LAPSE
- (A) mistake
- (B) charm
- (C) lullaby
- (D) pause
- (E) companion

7. LITERAL
- (A) robust
- (B) far-fetched
- (C) exact
- (D) impractical
- (E) receptive

8. LITIGATE
- (A) allege
- (B) negotiate
- (C) annihilate
- (D) fascinate
- (E) sue

9. LORE
- (A) distinction
- (B) era
- (C) abyss
- (D) information
- (E) apathy

10. MAGNANIMOUS
- (A) ruthless
- (B) generous
- (C) scrupulous
- (D) tedious
- (E) ungainly

Check-up 7-3

Each of the following questions consists of one word followed by five words or phrases. You are to select the one word or phrase whose meaning is closest to the word in capital letters.

1. MALLEABLE
(A) urgent
(B) toxic
(C) pliable
(D) wrathful
(E) climactic

2. MASSIVE
(A) vigilant
(B) subtle
(C) tiny
(D) bounty
(E) huge

3. MAYHEM
(A) theme
(B) violence
(C) climax
(D) casualty
(E) authority

4. MEAGER
(A) unscathed
(B) stringent
(C) ponderous
(D) scanty
(E) vulnerable

5. MEANDERING
(A) staunch
(B) obnoxious
(C) plausible
(D) strenuous
(E) winding

6. MEDLEY
(A) mixture
(B) citrus
(C) abode
(D) bigot
(E) authority

7. MEND
(A) alter
(B) comply
(C) teem
(D) oppose
(E) consist

8. MIGRATE
(A) concur
(B) resemble
(C) travel
(D) antagonize
(E) petrify

9. MIRACULOUS
(A) nomadic
(B) ominous
(C) incredible
(D) murky
(F) personable

10. MISERABLE
(A) permanent
(B) wretched
(C) precise
(D) negligent
(E) naive

131

MIDDLE 1 2 3 4 5 6 7 8 9 10

UPPER 1 2 3 4 5 6 7 8 9 10

Check-up 7-4

Each of the following questions consists of one word followed by five words or phrases. You are to select the one word or phrase whose meaning is closest to the word in capital letters.

1. MISLEAD
(A) suspend
(B) topple
(C) deceive
(D) present
(E) idle

2. MODERATE
(A) fanciful
(B) mild
(C) humid
(D) supreme
(E) hardy

3. MODIFY
(A) resume
(B) change
(C) retain
(D) retire
(E) preserve

4. MOLLIFY
(A) sever
(B) afflict
(C) pacify
(D) aggravate
(E) terminate

5. MOTIF
(A) quarry
(B) victim
(C) theme
(D) symptom
(E) hail

6. MOTIVE
(A) century
(B) capital
(C) grace
(D) reason
(E) talon

7. MULTITUDE
(A) crowd
(B) peer
(C) livelihood
(D) portion
(E) vision

8. MUMBLE
(A) assume
(B) mutter
(C) reign
(D) expel
(E) suspend

9. MURKY
(A) gloomy
(B) progress
(C) outrage
(D) practice
(E) threat

10. MUTINY
(A) rabble
(B) altercation
(C) retrospection
(D) novelty
(E) revolt

Check-up 7-5

Directions   Each of the following questions consists of one word followed by five words or phrases.
              You are to select the one word or phrase whose meaning is closest to the word in capital letters.

1. NIMBLE
(A) preliminary
(B) agile
(C) casual
(D) extravagant
(E) versatile

2. NOMAD
(A) maestro
(B) surrogate
(C) itinerant
(D) contributor
(E) deputy

3. NOVEL
(A) frugal
(B) convenient
(C) brisk
(D) new
(E) apprehensive

4. NOVICE
(A) scoundrel
(B) authority
(C) veteran
(D) connoisseur
(E) beginner

5. NUDGE
(A) coincide
(B) poke
(C) exist
(D) fuse
(E) esteem

6. OBJECTION
(A) priority
(B) siege
(C) woe
(D) protest
(E) elation

7. OBJECTIVE
(A) onset
(B) controversy
(C) goal
(D) peril
(E) rigor

8. OBSCURE
(A) cheerful
(B) monotonous
(C) mediocre
(D) prominent
(E) unclear

9. OBVIOUS
(A) clear
(B) appropriate
(C) inept
(D) mobile
(F) oblivious

10. OFFEND
(A) exclude
(B) compete
(C) affront
(D) corrode
(E) rejoice

133

351 opponent   356 overwhelm

352 option   357 pamper

353 organize   358 paragon

354 original   359 partial

355 overlap   360 perceive

Per capita.
(Per person)
1인당

SSATKOREA.com

organize
[**awr**-guh-nahyz]

v. to form into a coherent unity

조직하다, 정리하다

*We rely heavily on computers to **organize** our work.*

syn. arrange, sort, coordinate

original
[uh-**rij**-uh-nl]

adj. created, undertaken, or presented for the first time

독창적인

*He has a highly **original** mind.*

syn. creative, inventive, fresh, novel

opponent
[uh-**poh**-nuhnt]

n. a person who is on an opposing side in a game

경쟁 상대, 적수

*In a debate, she was a formidable **opponent**.*

syn. adversary, foe, antagonist

overlap
[oh-ver-**lap**]

v. to cover and extend beyond

겹치다, 포개지다

***Overlap** the slices carefully, so there are no gaps.*

syn. overlay, overlie, extend over

option
[op-shuhn]

n. the power or right of choosing

선택, 선택권, 선택사항

*She had no **option** but to ask him to leave.*

syn. choice, alternative, recourse

overwhelm
[oh-ver-**hwelm**]

v. to overcome completely in mind or feeling

(격한 감정이) 휩싸다, 압도하다

*Napoleon's army was strong enough to **overwhelm** nearly any potential enemy.*

syn. flood, crush, inundate

pamper

[pam-per]

v. to treat or gratify with extreme indulgence, kindness, or care

소중히 보살피다, 애지중지하다

Why not pamper yourself after a hard day with a hot bath with aroma oils?

syn. indulge, coddle, whim

paragon

[par-uh-gon]

n. a model or pattern of excellence

좋은 예, 귀감, 모범

The professor is a paragon of virtue and learning.

syn. exemplar, outstanding example, epitome

partial

[pahr-shuhl]

adj. biased or prejudiced in favor of a person or side

편파적인, 편견을 가진

The information we have is somewhat partial and biased.

syn. biased, prejudiced, unfair

perceive

[per-seev]

v. to become aware of, know, or identify by means of the senses

감지하다, 인지하다

Voters perceive him as a decisive and resolute international leader.

syn. discern, recognize, distinguish

ISEE Sentence Completion 8-1

Directions : Fill in the blanks to complete the sentences.

1. The teacher was careful not to appear _____ when grading the essays, treating every student's work equally.

   (A) overlap   (B) overwhelm
   (C) partial   (D) original

2. Her idea for the story was completely _____ and unlike anything the teacher had ever read before.

   (A) partial   (B) original
   (C) paragon   (D) organize

3. The chess player studied her _____ carefully, anticipating every move to gain an advantage.

   (A) option   (B) overlap
   (C) paragon   (D) opponent

4. The sudden influx of orders began to _____ the small bakery, which struggled to keep up with demand.

   (A) perceive   (B) overwhelm
   (C) pamper   (D) paragon

5. The hero in the story was portrayed as a _____ of virtue, always doing what was right and setting an example for others.

   (A) paragon   (B) option
   (C) organize (D) partial

361 permanent 366 pertinent

362 perpetual 367 pester

363 persevere 368 phenomenal

364 persistent 369 piquant

365 perspective 370 placate

Amat victoria curam.
(Victory loves preparation.)
승리는 준비하는 자를 사랑한다.

permanent
[**pur**-muh-n*uh*nt]

adj. long-lasting or nonfading
영원한, 영구적인

*Heavy drinking can cause **permanent** damage to the brain.*

syn. unending, eternal, perpetual

perpetual
[per-**pech**-oo-*uh*l]

adj. continuing or enduring forever
(오래 동안) 끊임없이 계속되는

*A contented mind is a **perpetual** feast.*

syn. everlasting, eternal, permanent

persevere
[pur-suh-**veer**]

v. to persist in anything undertaken
인내하며 계속하다

*You'll need to **persevere** if you want to succeed.*

syn. persist, endure, continue

persistent
[per-**sis**-t*uh*nt]

adj. persisting, especially in spite of opposition, obstacles, discouragement
끈질긴, 집요한

*They were removed from the school for **persistent** bad behavior.*

syn. unyielding, tenacious, relentless

perspective
[per-**spek**-tiv]

n. a mental view or prospect
관점, 시각

*His experience abroad provides a wider **perspective**.*

syn. view, outlook, aspect

pertinent
[**pur**-tn-*uh*nt]

adj. relating directly and significantly to the matter
(특정한 상황에) 적절한, 관련 있는

*Please keep your comments **pertinent** to the topic under discussion.*

syn. relevant, apposite, appropriate

pester
[**pes**-ter]

v. to bother persistently

괴롭히다

*She used to **pester** her father until she got exactly what she wanted.*

syn.   bother, annoy, badger

phenomenal
[**fi**-nom-uh-nl]

adj. highly extraordinary or exceptional

놀랄만한, 보통이 아닌, 엄청난

*The space shuttle travels at **phenomenal** speed.*

syn.   exceptional, extraordinary, prodigious

piquant
[**pee**-ku*h*nt]

adj. agreeably pungent or sharp in taste

톡 쏘는 듯한, 짜릿한

*Bland vegetables are often served with a **piquant** sauce.*

syn.   spicy, intriguing, stimulating

placate
[**pley**-keyt]

v. to appease or pacify

달래다, 진정시키다

*She smiled, trying to **placate** me.*

syn.   pacify, calm, appease

ISEE Sentence Completion 8-2

Directions : Fill in the blanks to complete the sentences.

1. During the meeting, she asked a _____ question that shifted the focus to the main issue.

   (A) pertinent   (B) placate
   (C) perpetual   (D) perspective

2. She was thrilled to finally land a _____ position after years of contract work.

   (A) pester   (B) perpetual
   (C) permanent   (D) phenomenal

3. The scientist explained the concept of _____ motion, where an object continues indefinitely.

   (A) perpetual   (B) placate
   (C) piquant   (D) persistent

4. Unlike the bland soup, the new recipe had a _____ taste that made it much more enjoyable.

   (A) pertinent   (B) perpetual
   (C) piquant   (D) placate

5. His _____ efforts to improve his skills eventually paid off with a major promotion.

   (A) persistent   (B) permanent
   (C) piquant   (D) pertinent

Answers

1. (A)   2. (C)   3. (A)   4. (C)   5. (A)

371 plead	376 portion
372 plight	377 precarious
373 pluck	378 precipitate
374 poise	379 predominant
375 ponderous	380 prestige

Homo homini lupus.
(Man is a wolf to man.)
인간은 인간에게 늑대이다.

———— SSATKOREA.com

plead
[pleed]

v. to appeal or entreat earnestly

애원하다

*He had a good lawyer to **plead** his case.*

syn. beg, implore, entreat

plight
[plahyt]

n. an unfavorable condition

역경, 곤경

*The **plight** of the refugees arouses our compassion.*

syn. predicament, quandary, trouble

pluck
[pluhk]

v. to pull off or out from the place of growth

(털을) 뽑다

*The falcons **pluck** the feathers and strip the flesh off their bird prey.*

syn. pull out, pick, pull off

poise
[poiz]

n. a state of balance or equilibrium

침착, 균형, 평형

*The queen's **poise** expressed both dignity and grace.*

syn. calmness, aplomb, self-composure

ponderous
[**pon**-der-*uhs*]

adj. of great weight, awkward or unwieldy

육중한, 크고 무거워 움직임이 둔한

*His steps were heavy and **ponderous**.*

syn. heavy, cumbersome, labored

portion
[**pawr**-sh*uhn*]

n. a part of any whole

부분, 일부, 1인분

*She only eats a small **portion** of food.*

syn. part, piece, share, slice

precarious

[pri-**kair**-ee-*uh*s]

adj. not securely held or in a stable position

불안정한, 위태로운

*The climber balanced on a **precarious** ledge, fearing it might crumble under his weight.*

syn. insecure, unstable, hazardous

precipitate

[pri-**sip**-i-teyt]

v. to hasten the occurrence of

(나쁜 일을) 빨리 일어나게 하다, 진척시키다

*An invasion would certainly **precipitate** a political crisis.*

syn. hurry, speed, accelerate

predominant

[pri-**dom**-uh-n*uh*nt]

adj. most common or frequent

두드러진, 뚜렷한

*Which country is the **predominant** member of the alliance?*

syn. prevalent, dominant, principal

prestige

[pre-**steezh**]

n. reputation arising from success, achievement, or rank

위신, 명망, 명성

*As the king's **prestige** continues to fall, people consider him a liability.*

syn. status, stature, reputation

ISEE Sentence Completion 8-3

Directions : Fill in the blanks to complete the sentences.

1. She leaned over to _____ a flower from the garden and place it in her hair.

   (A) predominant   (B) plead
   (C) poise   (D) pluck

2. The ancient gate was said to be a _____ to another world, shrouded in mystery.

   (A) pluck   (B) portion
   (C) prestige   (D) plight

3. Standing on the edge of the cliff was a _____ position that made everyone uneasy.

   (A) precarious   (B) poise
   (C) portal   (D) plight

4. Rushing to _____ a decision without proper information often leads to regret.

   (A) precarious   (B) precipitate
   (C) plead   (D) predominant

5. The university is known for its academic _____, attracting students from all over the world.

   (A) prestige   (B) portion
   (C) poise   (D) pluck

Answers

1. (D)   2. (A)   3. (A)   4. (B)   5. (A)

381	presume	386	provisional
382	prodigal	387	prowl
383	proficient	388	purge
384	profound	389	pursue
385	proponent	390	quiver

Tempus fugit.
(Time flies.)
시간은 날아간다

SSATKOREA.com

proficient
[pruh-**fish**-*uh*nt]

adj. well-advanced or competent in any art, science, or subject

능숙한, 솜씨 좋은

*With practice, you should become **proficient** within a year.*

syn.   skilled, skillful, expert

profound
[pruh-**found**]

adj. penetrating deeply into subjects of thought

매우 깊은, 심오한

*Meditation made a **profound** man.*

syn.   deep, intense, thoughtful

presume
[pri-**zoom**]

v. to suppose or assume something

추정하다, 추측하다

*I **presume** that an agreement will eventually be reached.*

syn.   assume, suppose, guess

proponent
[pruh-**poh**-n*uh*nt]

n. a person who puts forward a proposition or proposal

지지자, 옹호자

*She is a **proponent** of alternative medicine that uses a holistic approach.*

syn.   advocate, champion, supporter

prodigal
[**prod**-i-g*uh*l]

adj. wastefully extravagant, giving profusely

낭비하는, 돈을 펑펑 쓰는

*A miserly father makes a **prodigal** son.*

syn.   wasteful, extravagant, profligate

provisional
[pruh-**vizh**-uh-nl]

adj. providing or serving for the time being only

임시의, 일시적인

*We accept **provisional** bookings by phone.*

syn.   temporary, tentative, interim

prowl
[proul]

v. to rove over in search of what may be found

(동물이) 돌아다니다, 어슬렁대다

Several wolves prowled earlier.

syn.   lurk, stroll, roam

purge
[purj]

v. to rid of whatever is impure or undesirable

제거하다, 정화하다

His first act as leader was to purge the party of extremists.

syn.   cleanse, clear, purify

pursue
[per-**soo**]

v. to follow in order to overtake, to strive to gain

추구하다, 밀고 나가다

If you are passionate about something, pursue it.

syn.   chase, follow, strive

quiver
[**kwiv**-er]

v. to shake or tremble slightly

떨다, 흔들리다

She could feel her hands quiver as she stepped onto the stage.

syn.   shake, shiver, tremble

ISEE Sentence Completion 8-4

Directions : Fill in the blanks to complete the sentences.

1. His _____ lifestyle led to financial ruin despite his substantial inheritance.

   (A) purge   (B) proficient
   (C) provisional   (D) prodigal

2. She is _____ in several languages, which makes her a valuable asset to the international team.

   (A) proficient   (B) prodigal
   (C) profound   (D) presume

3. The new policy had a _____ impact on the education system, changing it for the better.

   (A) proficient   (B) provisional
   (C) profound   (D) prowl

4. The two countries reached a _____ agreement to avoid immediate conflict while negotiating further.

   (A) prowl   (B) provisional
   (C) quiver   (D) prodigal

5. The court instructed the jury to _____ innocence until proven guilty.

   (A) presume   (B) pursue
   (C) quiver   (D) purge

091	quote	
392	radiant	
393	rambling	
394	rash	
395	ratio	
396	reasonable	
397	rebellion	
398	recede	
399	reckless	
400	redundant	

Eureka!
(I have found it!)
찾았다!

rambling
[**ram**-bling]

adj. straying from one subject to another
횡설수설하는, 장황하고 두서 없는

*Be not careless in deeds, nor confused in words, nor **rambling** in thought.*

syn. digressive, straggling, desultory

rash
[rash]

adj. acting or tending to act too hastily
무분별한, 무모한

*He made a **rash** decision, and now he is suffering for it.*

syn. foolhardy, impulsive, impetuous

quote
[kwoht]

v. to use a brief excerpt from
인용하다, (남의 말을 그대로) 전달하다

*I can **quote** you several instances of her being deliberately rude.*

syn. cite, repeat, recall

ratio
[**rey**-shoh]

n. proportional relation or rate
비율, 비례

*The **ratio** of boys to girls was two to one.*

syn. proportion, quota, fraction

radiant
[**rey**-dee-*uh*nt]

adj. emitting rays of light, bright with joy
(행복감이나 건강 등으로) 빛나는, 환한

*She was **radiant** with joy at her wedding.*

syn. shinning, bright, illuminated

reasonable
[**ree**-zuh-nuh-b*uh*l]

adj. agreeable to reason or sound judgement
타당한, 논리적인, 이치에 맞는

*The **reasonable** man adapts himself to the world.*

syn. sensible, rational, logical

rebellion
[ri-**bel**-y*uh*n]

n. resistance to one's government or ruler

반란, 모반

*Oppression provoked the people to start the **rebellion**.*

syn. uprising, revolt, defiance

recede
[ri-**seed**]

v. to go or move away

(서서히) 물러나다, 약해지다

*Once a viral trend, the dance challenge quickly **receded** from social media.*

syn. retreat, withdraw, diminish

reckless
[rek-lis]

adj. careless about danger or risk

무모한, 신중하지 못한

***Reckless** driving can lead to serious accidents and injuries.*

syn. careless, foolhardy, rash

redundant
[ri-**duhn**-d*uh*nt]

adj. relating to unnecessary repetition in expressing ideas

(글이나 말에서) 불필요하게 반복되는

*Your writing has too much **redundant** detail.*

syn. repetitive, unnecessary, superfluous

ISEE Sentence Completion 8-5

Directions : Fill in the blanks to complete the sentences.

1. The writer removed the second paragraph from her essay because it was _____ and repeated the same idea as the first.

   (A) rash   (B) reasonable
   (C) radiant   (D) redundant

2. Acting in a _____ manner, the young athlete joined the game without stretching, which led to an injury.

   (A) reasonable   (B) rash
   (C) radiant   (D) rambling

3. The garden was filled with _____ flowers that seemed to glow under the sunlight.

   (A) radiant   (B) recede
   (C) rambling   (D) ratio

4. The teacher explained that the _____ of boys to girls in the class was 3:2, showing a slight imbalance.

   (A) rebellion   (B) ratio
   (C) redundant   (D) recede

5. His answer was so _____ that it went on for several minutes without ever addressing the main question.

   (A) radiant   (B) rash
   (C) rambling   (D) rebellion

1. (D) 2. (B) 3. (A) 4. (B) 5. (C)

 Answers

Analogy 8. Shells

물체와 그 외피를 연결시키는 문제도 자주 출제됩니다.

A는 B의 껍질

corn : husk 옥수수 : 옥수수 껍질	**tree : bark** 나무 : 나무 껍질
potato : skin 감자 : 감자 껍질	**apple : peel** 사과 : 사과 껍질
grapefruit : rind 자몽 : 두꺼운 껍질	**oyster : shell** 굴 : 굴 껍질
engine : housing 엔진 : 엔진 커버	**watch : case** 시계 : 시계 프레임
horse : hide 말 : 말 가죽	**bird : plumage** 새 : 깃털
goose : down 거위: 거위털	**sheep : wool** 양 : 양털
head : scalp 머리 : 두피	**body : skin** 몸 : 피부
rabbit : angora 토끼 : 토끼털	**bread : crust** 빵 : 빵 껍질
snake : scales 뱀 : 비늘	**egg : shell** 달걀 : 달걀 껍질
fish : scales 물고기 : 비늘	**walnut : shell** 호두 : 호두 껍질

POP
QUIZ

1. Goose is to down as
- (A) bird is to wing
- (B) horse is to mane
- (C) potato is to peel
- (D) sheep is to wool
- (E) flax is to linen

2. Scalp is to head as
- (A) cherry is to pit
- (B) bark is to tree
- (C) grapefruit is to skin
- (D) rind is to orange
- (E) apple is to crate

Check-up 8-1

Directions   Each of the following questions consists of one word followed by five words or phrases.
You are to select the one word or phrase whose meaning is closest to the word in capital letters.

1. OPPONENT
(A) adversary
(B) velocity
(C) exploit
(D) stench
(E) loom

2. OPTION
(A) splendor
(B) choice
(C) sanctuary
(D) tyrant
(E) leeway

3. ORGANIZE
(A) elaborate
(B) scoff
(C) arrange
(D) hover
(E) contribute

4. ORIGINAL
(A) creative
(B) err
(C) wend
(D) inflate
(E) exhibit

5. OVERLAP
(A) exhaust
(B) conserve
(C) overlie
(D) exterminate
(E) abbreviate

6. OVERWHELM
(A) sheathe
(B) inhabit
(C) inhibit
(D) flood
(E) dissent

7. PAMPER
(A) inscribe
(B) quench
(C) swivel
(D) retrieve
(E) indulge

8. PARAGON
(A) trace
(B) victor
(C) awe
(D) majority
(E) exemplar

9. PARTIAL
(A) grudging
(B) drastic
(C) paltry
(D) biased
(E) skeptical

10. PERCEIVE
(A) segregate
(B) discern
(C) ooze
(D) swarm
(E) jeopardize

Check-up 8-2

1. PERMANENT
- (A) rash
- (B) abundant
- (C) unending
- (D) conspicuous
- (E) skeptical

2. PERPETUAL
- (A) marvelous
- (B) everlasting
- (C) innate
- (D) arid
- (E) vital

3. PERSEVERE
- (A) fathom
- (B) evict
- (C) persist
- (D) foster
- (E) enroll

4. PERSISTENT
- (A) nimble
- (B) ultimate
- (C) unyielding
- (D) principal
- (E) naive

5. PERSPECTIVE
- (A) complement
- (B) authority
- (C) makeshift
- (D) view
- (E) counterpart

6. PERTINENT
- (A) impartial
- (B) bashful
- (C) aboveboard
- (D) sheepish
- (E) relevant

7. PESTER
- (A) bother
- (B) assent
- (C) dwindle
- (D) bestow
- (E) loathe

8. PHENOMENAL
- (A) ultimate
- (B) exceptional
- (C) mediocre
- (D) absolute
- (E) cursory

9. PIQUANT
- (A) detrimental
- (B) impromptu
- (C) spicy
- (D) mythical
- (E) predatory

10. PLACATE
- (A) aspire
- (B) beseech
- (C) dumbfound
- (D) enlighten
- (E) pacify

146

Check-up 8-3

Directions   Each of the following questions consists of one word followed by five words or phrases.
You are to select the one word or phrase whose meaning is closest to the word in capital letters.

1. PLEAD
(A) ebb
(B) beg
(C) abduct
(D) wax
(E) acclaim

2. PLIGHT
(A) figment
(B) garrison
(C) homage
(D) agent
(E) predicament

3. PLUCK
(A) pull out
(B) take in
(C) get over
(D) push down
(E) let out

4. POISE
(A) acquisition
(B) debut
(C) calmness
(D) garland
(E) bias

5. PONDEROUS
(A) illiterate
(B) lush
(C) mottled
(D) heavy
(E) inanimate

6. PORTION
(A) maneuver
(B) revelry
(C) part
(D) obsession
(E) nomad

7. PRECARIOUS
(A) insecure
(B) elusive
(C) compelling
(D) engaging
(E) accommodating

8. PRECIPITATE
(A) devour
(B) emphasize
(C) hurry
(D) gobble
(E) emit

9. PREDOMINANT
(A) exotic
(B) incredulous
(C) devoid
(D) prevalent
(E) indifferent

10. PRESTIGE
(A) status
(B) hovel
(C) omen
(D) mentor
(E) plight

147

Check-up 8-4

1. PRESUME
(A) detach
(B) forage
(C) insulate
(D) assume
(E) haggle

2. PRODIGAL
(A) capricious
(B) distraught
(C) formidable
(D) haughty
(E) wasteful

3. PROFICIENT
(A) atypical
(B) skilled
(C) congested
(D) headlong
(E) dismal

4. PROFOUND
(A) docile
(B) uneasy
(C) deep
(D) vain
(E) widespread

5. PROPONENT
(A) anchor
(B) bliss
(C) benefit
(D) advocate
(E) ordeal

6. PROVISIONAL
(A) suitable
(B) threadbare
(C) transparent
(D) valiant
(E) temporary

7. PROWL
(A) inundate
(B) lurk
(C) devastate
(D) smolder
(E) adopt

8. PURGE
(A) dissuade
(B) endure
(C) cleanse
(D) flourish
(E) kindle

9. PURSUE
(A) monitor
(B) sustain
(C) oblige
(D) chase
(E) perturb

10. QUIVER
(A) shake
(B) replenish
(C) ponder
(D) dispatch
(E) extend

148

Check-up 8-5

Directions   Each of the following questions consists of one word followed by five words or phrases.
You are to select the one word or phrase whose meaning is closest to the word in capital letters.

1. QUOTE
(A) cite
(B) scavenge
(C) adopt
(D) affect
(E) ban

2. RADIANT
(A) impetuous
(B) shinning
(C) heedful
(D) grievous
(E) dumbfounded

3. RAMBLING
(A) exceptional
(B) finicky
(C) digressive
(D) fragile
(E) humble

4. RASH
(A) intelligent
(B) keen
(C) marine
(D) foolhardy
(E) precious

5. RATIO
(A) brig
(B) mutiny
(C) talent
(D) proportion
(E) source

6. REASONABLE
(A) recent
(B) petty
(C) novel
(D) mature
(E) sensible

7. REBELLION
(A) token
(B) spine
(C) uprising
(D) bough
(E) terror

8. RECEDE
(A) snub
(B) retreat
(C) mystify
(D) hibernate
(E) invade

9. RECKLESS
(A) benevolent
(B) ignorant
(C) acute
(D) careless
(E) dim

10. REDUNDANT
(A) severe
(B) sullen
(C) spacious
(D) temporary
(E) repetitive

149

401	refined	406	remedy
402	refrain	407	rendezvous
403	reject	408	reserved
404	relocate	409	reside
405	reluctant	410	resource

Errare humanum est.
(To err is human.)
실수하는 것은 인간적인 일이다

SSATKOREA.com

refined
[ri-**fahynd**]

adj. showing well-bred feeling or taste
교양 있는, 세련된, 고상한

He was a boy of a refined nature, an avid reader and an eager student.

syn. cultured, civilized, cultivated

refrain
[ri-**freyn**]

v. to stop oneself from doing something
삼가다, 자제하다

He had to refrain from eating sweets while on a diet.

syn. hold back, avoid, resist

reject
[ri-**jekt**]

v. to refuse to have or take
거절하다, 거부하다

Never reject an idea, dream or goal because it will be hard work.

syn. rebuff, dismiss, snub

relocate
[ree-**loh**-keyt]

v. to move to a new place, especially to live or work
이주하다, 이전하다

Her family decided to relocate to a different city for a better job opportunity.

syn. move, transfer, resettle

reluctant
[ri-**luhk**-t*uh*nt]

adj. disinclined to become involved
꺼리는, 마지못한

People are very reluctant to talk about their private lives.

syn. unwilling, grudging, disinclined

remedy
[**rem**-i-dee]

n. something that cures a disease
치료약, 처리방안, 해결책

Danger itself is the best remedy for danger.

syn. cure, solution, antidote

rendezvous

[**rahn**-duh-voo]

n. an agreement between two or more persons to meet

만남, 만날 약속

*I have a **rendezvous** with Ben at a restaurant.*

syn. meeting, appointment, assignation

reserved

[ri-**zurvd**]

adj. quiet and not openly expressing emotions or opinions

내성적인, 말수가 적은

*She was **reserved** in social settings and preferred to listen rather than talk.*

syn. Introverted, reticent, withdrawn

reside

[ri-**zahyd**]

v. to dwell permanently

(특정한 곳에) 살다, 거주하다

*She **resides** in a small town by the beach.*

syn. inhabit, dwell, occupy

resource

[**ree**-sawrs]

n. a source of supply, support, or aid

(목적을 이루는 데 도움이 되는) 재료, 재원

*The company's greatest **resource** is the dedication of its workers.*

syn. supply, ability, property

ISEE Sentence Completion 9-1

Directions : Fill in the blanks to complete the sentences.

1. The treaty was signed with a _____ agreement from both parties, despite their initial hesitations.

   (A) reluctant   (B) refined
   (C) remedy   (D) reserved

2. She used a natural _____ to alleviate her cold symptoms without taking medication.

   (A) remedy   (B) resource
   (C) rendezvous   (D) relieve

3. The two spies arranged a secret _____ to exchange classified information.

   (A) reside   (B) rendezvous
   (C) refined   (D) remedy

4. The critic was known for his _____ taste in art and fine dining.

   (A) refined   (B) refrain
   (C) reject   (D) resource

5. She was quiet and _____, rarely sharing her thoughts in large groups.

   (A) reside   (B) refined
   (C) rendezvous   (D) reserved

Answers

1. (A) 2. (A) 3. (B) 4. (A) 5. (D)

411	retain	416	sanctuary
412	reverse	417	sapient
413	revise	418	savage
414	rigorous	419	scarce
415	rummage	420	scheme

Deus ex machina
(God from the machine)
기계에서 나온 신

SSATKOREA.com

retain
[ri-**teyn**]

v. to keep possession of
(계속) 유지하다

*She **retains** a clear memory of those days.*

syn. hold, contain, possess

reverse
[ri-**vurs**]

v. to turn something the other way around or up or inside out
(정반대로) 뒤바꾸다, 뒤집다

*Can anything be done to **reverse** this trend?*

syn. undo, invert, overturn

revise
[ri-**vahyz**]

v. to rewrite or reorganize something
(책을) 개정하다, 변경하다

*You must **revise** your first draft.*

syn. correct, alter, amend

rigorous
[**rig**-er-uhs]

adj. rigidly severe or harsh, as people, rules, or discipline
엄격한, 철저한

*The school has a **rigorous** academic program that challenges students.*

syn. strict, thorough, severe

rummage
[**ruhm**-ij]

v. to search thoroughly
뒤지다, 샅샅이 찾다

*He **rummaged** through piles of second-hand clothes for something that fits.*

syn. search, hunt, explore

sanctuary
[**sangk**-choo-er-ee]

n. a place of safety, protection, or refuge
성소, 피난처, 보호구역

*After the storm, the family found **sanctuary** in a nearby community center.*

syn. refuge, haven, shelter

sapient

[**sey**-pee-*uh*nt]

adj. having or showing great wisdom, intelligence, or discernment

지혜로운, 총명한

*The **sapient** old man shared stories that taught valuable life lessons to the children.*

syn. wise, judicious, intelligent

savage

[**sav**-ij]

adj. fierce, violent, or hostile

야만적인, 잔인한

*The article was a **savage** attack on her past actions.*

syn. brutal, ferocious, barbaric

scarce

[skairs]

adj. insufficient to satisfy the need

부족한, 드문

*Food was often **scarce** in the winter.*

syn. scanty, meager, rare, sparse

scheme

[skeem]

n. a plan, design, or program of action to be followed

계획, 책략, 제도

*The **scheme** was criticized as too idealistic and impracticable.*

syn. plot, project, strategy

ISEE Sentence Completion 9-2

Directions : Fill in the blanks to complete the sentences.

1. The villagers were horrified by the _____ attack on their peaceful community.

   (A) sapient   (B) savage
   (C) scheme   (D) sanctuary

2. The thief came up with a clever _____ to steal the valuable painting without being noticed.

   (A) rigorous   (B) savage
   (C) revise   (D) scheme

3. The council voted to _____ a previous decision due to new evidence presented.

   (A) scarce   (B) scheme
   (C) reverse   (D) retain

4. He began to _____ through the drawer, searching for his misplaced keys.

   (A) savage   (B) rummage
   (C) revise   (D) sanctuary

5. The national park was established as a _____ to protect endangered species.

   (A) scheme   (B) scarce
   (C) sanctuary   (D) savage

Answers

1. (B) 2. (D) 3. (C) 4. (B) 5. (C)

421	secure	426	shorten
422	seize	427	shove
423	senior	428	significant
424	sentiment	429	simulate
425	serene	430	sink

Ad hoc
(For this purpose)
즉석에서, 특별한 목적을 위한

SSATKOREA.com

senior
[si:niə(r)]

n. someone who holds a higher rank, position, or age

선배, 고령자

*As a **senior** in high school, she is busy preparing for her college applications.*

syn. elder, upperclassman, superior

sentiment
[**sen**-tuh-m*u*hnt]

n. an attitude toward something, a mental feeling

정서, 감정

*His speech was encouraging nationalistic **sentiment**.*

syn. feeling, attitude, sentimentality

secure
[si-**kyoor**]

adj. free from or not exposed to danger or harm

안전한, 확보된

*She doesn't feel **secure** when she is alone in the house.*

syn. safe, protected, defended

serene
[suh-**reen**]

adj. calm, peaceful, or tranquil

고요한, 평화로운, 조용한

*She looked as calm and **serene** as she always did.*

syn. calm, composed, tranquil

seize
[seez]

v. to take hold of suddenly

꽉 붙잡다, 움켜잡다

***Seize** the opportunity when it comes up.*

syn. grasp, capture, clutch

shorten
[**shawr**-tn]

v. to make short or shorter

짧게 하다, 단축하다

*When the days **shorten** in winter, some people suffer depression.*

syn. abbreviate, abridge, condense

shove

[shuhv]

v. to move along by force from behind

(거칠게) 밀치다

*Help me **shove** this furniture aside.*

syn. push, thrust, propel

significant

[sig-**nif**-i-k*uh*nt]

adj. expressing a meaning

중요한, 의미 있는

*His most **significant** achievement was the abolition of slavery.*

syn. notable, important, meaningful

simulate

[**sim**-yuh-leyt]

v. to imitate the appearance or condition

…한 척하다, 가장하다

*Computer software can be used to **simulate** conditions.*

syn. pretend, imitate, affect

sink

[singk]

v. to go beneath the surface of a liquid

(물에) 가라앉다

*The boat started to **sink** into the sea.*

syn. founder, go under, capsize

ISEE Sentence Completion 9-3

Directions : Fill in the blanks to complete the sentences.

1. Without proper repairs, the old boat began to _____ as water leaked through the damaged hull.

   (A) sink   (B) sentiment
   (C) significant   (D) serene

2. He encouraged his students to _____ the opportunity to present their ideas at the conference.

   (A) sentiment   (B) sink
   (C) seize   (D) serene

3. Choosing a career path is a _____ decision that requires careful thought and planning.

   (A) sensible   (B) significant
   (C) secure   (D) simulate

4. He had to _____ the door open when it got stuck during the storm.

   (A) simulate   (B) secure
   (C) shove   (D) seize

5. Despite the failure of her project, she remained _____, calmly reflecting on how to improve.

   (A) sink   (B) serene
   (C) shove   (D) seize

431 skeptical	436 splendor
432 slothful	437 sporadic
433 sociable	438 spontaneous
434 specific	439 squander
435 spirited	440 steadfast

Citius, Altius, Fortius.
(Faster, Higher, Stronger.)
더 빠르게, 더 높이, 더 강하게.

SSATKOREA.com

skeptical
[**skep**-ti-k*uh*l]

adj. doubtful about a particular thing
의심 많은, 회의적인

*He is **skeptical** about how much will*
be accomplished by legislation.

syn. dubious, doubtful, suspicious

slothful
[**slawth**-f*uh*l]

adj. disinclined to work or exertion
나태한, 게으른

*Fatigue had made him **slothful**.*

syn. lazy, idle, inactive

sociable
[**soh**-shuh-b*uh*l]

adj. inclined to associate with others
사람들과 어울리기 좋아하는, 사교적인

*Dogs show a very **sociable***
disposition.

syn. outgoing, friendly, gregarious

specific
[spi-**sif**-ik]

adj. stated explicitly or in detail
구체적인, 명확한, 분명한

Massage may help to increase blood
*flow to **specific** areas of the body.*

syn. particular, specified, detailed

spirited
[**spir**-i-tid]

adj. having courage, vigor, liveliness, etc.
명랑한, 활발한

*She was by nature a **spirited** little girl.*

syn. lively, vivacious, vibrant

splendor
[**splen**-der]

n. a brilliant or gorgeous appearance
화려함, 웅장함

*All the **splendor** in the world is not*
worth a good friend.

syn. magnificence, radiance, grandeur

spontaneous

[spon-tey-nee-uhs]

adj. happening naturally or without prior planning

자발적인, 즉흥적인, 자연스러운

The class burst into spontaneous applause when the teacher announced there would be no homework.

syn. unplanned, impulsive, natural

sporadic

[spuh-**rad**-ik]

adj. happening at irregular intervals in time

산발적인, 이따금 발생하는

*There was rioting and **sporadic** fighting in the city, as rival gangs clashed.*

syn. intermittent, occasional, infrequent

squander

[**skwon**-der]

v. to waste something (money, time, resources) in a careless or foolish way

낭비하다, 허비하다

*He **squandered** his inheritance on luxury cars and parties*

syn. waste, misuse, lavish

steadfast

[**sted**-fast]

adj. firm and unwavering in belief, loyalty, or purpose

확고한, 흔들리지 않는

*She remained **steadfast** in her decision despite criticism.*

syn. determined, loyal, unwavering

ISEE Sentence Completion 9-4

Directions : Fill in the blanks to complete the sentences.

1. His _____ attitude towards work often frustrated his more hardworking colleagues.

   (A) slothful   (B) sociable
   (C) sporadic   (D) squander

2. The region experiences _____ rainfall, with dry spells followed by sudden downpours.

   (A) sporadic   (B) steady
   (C) specific   (D) spirited

3. A _____ person is always at ease in social gatherings and enjoys meeting new people.

   (A) sociable   (B) skeptical
   (C) specific   (D) spirited

4. The crowd broke into _____ applause after the amazing performance.

   (A) steadfast   (B) slothful
   (C) spontaneous   (D) sporadic

5. Instead of saving for the future, he chose to _____ his money on unnecessary luxuries.

   (A) splendor   (B) skeptical
   (C) spirited   (D) squander

Answers

1. (A) 2. (D) 3. (A) 4. (C) 5. (D)

441 steer	446 strive
442 stifle	447 subdue
443 stoic	448 subside
444 strategy	449 substantial
445 strenuous	450 substitute

Non desistas, non exieris.
(Never give up, never surrender.)
절대 포기하지 말라, 절대 물러서지 말라.

SSATKOREA.com

stoic
[**stoh**-ik]

adj. showing no emotion, especially in hardship or pain
감정을 드러내지 않는, 무표정한

*He remained **stoic** during the crisis, showing no fear or panic.*

syn. unemotional, calm, impassive

strategy
[**strat**-i-jee]

n. a careful plan for achieving a goal
전략, 계획

*Tactics win battles; **strategy** wins wars.*

syn. plan, scheme, method

steer
[steer]

v. to guide the course of by a rudder
(보트나 배 등을) 조종하다, 몰다

*Try to **steer** the lifeboat towards the big ship so that we can pick it up.*

syn. navigate, direct, guide

strenuous
[**stren**-yoo-*uhs*]

adj. characterized by vigorous exertion
힘이 많이 드는, 몹시 힘든, 격렬한

*The doctor advised Jay to avoid **strenuous** exercise.*

syn. arduous, herculean, onerous

stifle
[**stahy**-*fuhl*]

v. to quell, crush, or end by force
(감정 등을) 억누르다, 억압하다, 숨막히게 하다

*How can the government **stifle** debate on such a crucial issue?*

syn. suffocate, suppress, constrain

strive
[strahyv]

v. to exert oneself vigorously
분투하다, 힘들게 노력하다

*Two dogs **strive** for a bone, the third runs away with it.*

syn. endeavor, attempt, struggle

subdue
[suhb-**doo**]

v. to overpower by superior force

진압하다, 억누르다

*The police **subdued** the protest.*

syn.   repress, quell, suppress

subside
[su*h*b-**sahyd**]

v. to become quiet or less active

가라앉다, 진정되다

*King's rage was beginning
to **subside**.*

syn.   diminish, abate, decrease

substantial
[su*h*b-**stan**-shu*h*l]

adj. of considerable amount, quantity,
size, etc.

(양이나 가치, 중요성 등이) 상당한

*The findings show a **substantial**
difference between the two parties.*

syn.   significant, material, consequential

substitute
[**suhb**-sti-toot]

n. someone or something that takes the
place of another for a period of time

대리인, 대체물

*Butter can be a **substitute** for olive oil
in this recipe.*

syn.   surrogate, backup, replacement

ISEE Sentence Completion 9-5

Directions : Fill in the blanks to
complete the sentences.

1. Micromanaging can _____
   creativity and prevent employees
   from reaching their full potential.

   (A) strive   (B) steer
   (C) substantial   (D) stifle

2. He remained calm under pressure,
   showing a _____ demeanor.

   (A) subside   (B) strenuous
   (C) stoic   (D) stifle

3. The team developed an effective
   _____ to win the game against
   their strongest opponents.

   (A) substantial   (B) strategy
   (C) steer   (D) substitute

4. She always encourages her
   students to _____ for
   excellence in all that they do.

   (A) subdue   (B) stifle
   (C) substitute   (D) strive

5. Firefighters worked tirelessly to
   _____ the fire before it could
   spread further.

   (A) subdue   (B) subside
   (C) steer   (D) strategy

1. (D) 2. (C) 3. (B) 4. (D) 5. (A)

♦ Answers

Analogy 9. Unit & Measure

여러가지 기본 단위, 재는 도구와 대상을 연결짓는 관계입니다. 특히 아래 수학 단위 세 가지는 가장 기본이니 꼭 알아두어야 합니다.

MATH UNIT

Distance
1 yard (yd) = 3 feet (ft) = 36 inches (in)
1 mile (mi) = 1,760 yards (yd) = 5,280 feet (ft)

Volume
1 gallon (gal) = 4 quarts (qt) = 8 pints (pt) = 16 cups (c)

Weight
1 pound (lb) = 16 ounces (oz)
1 ton (t) = 2,000 pounds (lbs)

A는 B의 단위

carat : diamond
캐럿 : 다이아몬드

fathom : depth
패덤 (물의 깊이 측정 단위, 6피트) : 깊이

acre : farmland
에이커 : 농지

decibel : sound
데시벨 : 소리

foot : distance
피트 : 거리

calorie : heat
칼로리 : 열량

A는 B를 재는 도구

altimeter : height
고도계 : 높이

speedometer : velocity
속도계 : 속도

odometer : mileage
주행기록계 : 주행거리, 마일 수

thermometer : temperature
온도계 : 온도

scale : weight
저울 : 무게

compass : direction
나침반 : 방향

1. Odometer is to mileage as
- (A) thermometer is to height
- (B) altimeter is to population
- (C) pedometer is to circumference
- (D) thermometer is to temperature
- (E) compass is to distance

2. Diamond is to carat as
- (A) farmland is to acre
- (B) yard is to foot
- (C) pint is to quart
- (D) milk is to inch
- (E) dozen is to egg

Check-up 9-1

Directions   Each of the following questions consists of one word followed by five words or phrases.
              You are to select the one word or phrase whose meaning is closest to the word in capital letters.

1. REFINED
(A) scarce
(B) cultured
(C) uneasy
(D) parallel
(E) opposite

6. REMEDY
(A) pessimist
(B) phase
(C) cure
(D) scoundrel
(E) depth

2. REFRAIN
(A) bring up
(B) come across
(C) hold back
(D) break down
(E) call off

7. RENDEZVOUS
(A) endeavor
(B) meeting
(C) climate
(D) dusk
(E) merit

3. REJECT
(A) blend
(B) appall
(C) bustle
(D) rebuff
(E) contain

8. RESERVED
(A) vociferous
(B) arduous
(C) boisterous
(D) introverted
(E) tempestuous

4. RELOCATE
(A) confirm
(B) deprive
(C) forbid
(D) embrace
(E) move

9. RESIDE
(A) soil
(B) extinguish
(C) inhabit
(D) kindle
(E) ascend

5. RELUCTANT
(A) unwilling
(B) petty
(C) stout
(D) responsible
(E) positive

10. RESOURCE
(A) supply
(B) contrast
(C) contempt
(D) misgiving
(E) impact

Check-up 9-2

Each of the following questions consists of one word followed by five words or phrases. You are to select the one word or phrase whose meaning is closest to the word in capital letters.

1. RETAIN
(A) intrude
(B) invade
(C) jeer
(D) hold
(E) isolate

2. REVERSE
(A) mystify
(B) undo
(C) launch
(D) limp
(E) memorize

3. REVISE
(A) locate
(B) master
(C) starve
(D) torch
(E) correct

4. RIGOROUS
(A) furious
(B) strict
(C) active
(D) dreary
(E) exceptional

5. RUMMAGE
(A) migrate
(B) waft
(C) yield
(D) search
(E) mock

6. SANCTUARY
(A) wisdom
(B) meadow
(C) foliage
(D) scapegoat
(E) refuge

7. SAPIENT
(A) drab
(B) wise
(C) sanitary
(D) audacious
(E) hygienic

8. SAVAGE
(A) crafty
(B) amiable
(C) brutal
(D) drowsy
(E) feeble

9. SCARCE
(A) external
(B) familiar
(C) hearty
(D) scanty
(E) excessive

10. SCHEME
(A) plot
(B) breadth
(C) surface
(D) peasant
(E) grove

162

Check-up 9-3

Directions   Each of the following questions consists of one word followed by five words or phrases.
You are to select the one word or phrase whose meaning is closest to the word in capital letters.

1. SECURE
(A) individual
(B) gradual
(C) forlorn
(D) safe
(E) mammoth

2. SEIZE
(A) dissolve
(B) reinforce
(C) plummet
(D) grasp
(E) improvise

3. SENIOR
(A) channel
(B) lack
(C) elder
(D) interval
(E) jet

4. SENTIMENT
(A) hue
(B) feeling
(C) shelter
(D) hamlet
(E) chamber

5. SERENE
(A) calm
(B) instant
(C) parallel
(D) recent
(E) quaint

6. SHORTEN
(A) abbreviate
(B) glare
(C) domesticate
(D) evolve
(E) vanquish

7. SHOVE
(A) restrain
(B) push
(C) abandon
(D) persevere
(E) captivate

8. SIGNIFICANT
(A) sensitive
(B) doleful
(C) notable
(D) restless
(E) reckless

9. SIMULATE
(A) glimpse
(B) hone
(C) exaggerate
(D) pretend
(E) swarm

10. SINK
(A) gripe
(B) possess
(C) extend
(D) originate
(E) founder

163

Check-up 9-4

1. SKEPTICAL
- (A) dubious
- (B) merciful
- (C) conciliatory
- (D) allaying
- (E) vengeful

2. SLOTHFUL
- (A) rash
- (B) grateful
- (C) weary
- (D) insightful
- (E) lazy

3. SOCIABLE
- (A) cunning
- (B) euphonious
- (C) outgoing
- (D) unforgiving
- (E) querulous

4. SPECIFIC
- (A) contemptuous
- (B) particular
- (C) aspirant
- (D) redoubtable
- (E) grandiose

5. SPIRITED
- (A) accumulated
- (B) relevant
- (C) brutal
- (D) lively
- (E) rancorous

6. SPLENDOR
- (A) albino
- (B) magnificence
- (C) garment
- (D) oblivion
- (E) miniature

7. SPONTANEOUS
- (A) unplanned
- (B) vacant
- (C) reusable
- (D) logical
- (E) preoccupied

8. SPORADIC
- (A) intermittent
- (B) favored
- (C) adaptable
- (D) limited
- (E) praised

9. SQUANDER
- (A) shed
- (B) linger
- (C) recount
- (D) waste
- (E) persecute

10. STEADFAST
- (A) restive
- (B) admirable
- (C) remorseful
- (D) frail
- (E) determined

Check-up 9-5

Directions   Each of the following questions consists of one word followed by five words or phrases.
              You are to select the one word or phrase whose meaning is closest to the word in capital letters.

1. STEER
(A) direct
(B) imprison
(C) stare
(D) reign
(E) emancipate

2. STIFLE
(A) veto
(B) suffocate
(C) determine
(D) enfranchise
(E) detect

3. STOIC
(A) refined
(B) prodigal
(C) unemotional
(D) incognito
(E) emaciated

4. STRATEGY
(A) caliber
(B) plan
(C) depth
(D) nobility
(E) etiquette

5. STRENUOUS
(A) arduous
(B) barbarian
(C) cultivated
(D) haggard
(E) smug

6. STRIVE
(A) torture
(B) transform
(C) coerce
(D) endeavor
(E) summit

7. SUBDUE
(A) splice
(B) capsize
(C) vanquish
(D) sink
(E) repress

8. SUBSIDE
(A) convert
(B) fling
(C) wax
(D) diminish
(E) alter

9. SUBSTANTIAL
(A) lackluster
(B) scintillating
(C) drab
(D) significant
(E) sizeable

10. SUBSTITUTE
(A) glut
(B) term
(C) investigation
(D) entourage
(E) surrogate

165

451 suffering   456 suspend

452 summon   457 sustain

453 suppress   458 sympathy

454 supreme   459 systematic

455 surrender   460 tangle

Magnum opus
(Masterpiece)
대작

SSATKOREA.com

suffering
[**suhf**-er-ing]

n. feelings of mental or physical pain

고통, 괴로움

*The famine caused great **suffering** of the people.*

syn. agony, pain, distress

summon
[**suhm**-*uhn*]

v. to call upon to do something specified

소환하다, 호출하다, 부르다

*The event **summoned** up old memories.*

syn. call, request, convene

suppress
[suh-**pres**]

v. to keep down by unjust use of one's authority

진압하다, 억누르다

*She tried to **suppress** a smile but felt the corner of her mouth twitch.*

syn. restrain, hold in check, abolish

supreme
[suh-**preem**]

adj. highest in rank or authority

(계급이나 위치 면에서) 최고의

*The Pope is the **supreme** leader of the Roman Catholic Church.*

syn. absolute, foremost, perfect

surrender
[suh-**ren**-der]

v. to give up one's power or possessions

항복하다, 굴복하다, 투항하다

*The terrorists were given ten minutes to **surrender**.*

syn. give up, resign, abandon

suspend
[suh-**spend**]

v. to hold or keep undetermined

(결정을) 미루다, 유예하다

*The government has decided to **suspend** production at the country's biggest plant.*

syn. hang, postpone, adjourn

sustain

[suh-**steyn**]

v. to support, hold, or bear up from below

(힘, 생명 등을) 버티다, 지속하다

*These four pillars **sustain** the entire structure.*

syn. keep up, maintain, support

sympathy

[**sim**-puh-thee]

n. harmony of or agreement in feeling

동정, 연민

*His remorse is just an artifice to gain **sympathy**.*

syn. compassion, affinity, rapport

systematic

[sis-tuh-**mat**-ik]

adj. having a system, method, or plan

체계적인, 조직적인

*Science is the **systematic** classification of experience.*

syn. methodical, orderly, organized

tangle

[**tang**-guhl]

v. to bring together into a mass of confusedly interlaced threads

헝클어뜨리다, 헝클어지다

*The broom somehow got **tangled** up in my long skirt.*

syn. entangle, snarl, entwine

ISEE Sentence Completion 10-1

Directions : Fill in the blanks to complete the sentences.

1. The storm's intensity began to
   _____ off as it moved away
   from the coastline.

   (A) summon   (B) suppress
   (C) suspend   (D) taper

2. He had to _____ the courage
   to confront his fears and speak in
   public.

   (A) sympathy   (B) suspend
   (C) summon   (D) sustain

3. She tried to _____ her emotions
   during the argument to avoid
   making the situation worse.

   (A) suppress   (B) surrender
   (C) taper   (D) sympathy

4. The soldiers were forced to
   _____ to the enemy after their
   supplies ran out.

   (A) tangle   (B) summon
   (C) surrender   (D) suppress

5. The scientist used a _____
   approach to ensure accuracy in
   her experiments.

   (A) systematic   (B) suffering
   (C) supreme   (D) sustain

1. (D)   2. (C)   3. (A)   4. (C)   5. (A)

Answers

461 tedious   466 terminate

462 temperate   467 timid

463 tempo   468 tolerant

464 tenable   469 torrent

465 tentative   470 torture

Ex nihilo nihil fit.
(Nothing comes from nothing.)
무에서 무가 나올 수 없다.

SSATKOREA.com

tempo
[tem-poh]

n. characteristic rate, rhythm, or pattern of work or activity
(음악 작품의) 박자, 템포

*This tune has a fast **tempo**.*

syn. pace, speed, cadence

tenable
[ten-*uh*-b*uh*l]

adj. able to be defended or held, especially in an argument
(이론 · 주장 등이) 방어될 수 있는, 유지될 수 있는

*Her argument was logically **tenable**, as it was supported by strong evidence.*

syn. defensible, sustainable, justifiable

tedious
[tee-dee-*uhs*]

adj. marked by monotony or tedium
지루한, 싫증나는

*He was bored by the speaker's **tedious** talk.*

syn. boring, dull, monotonous

tentative
[ten-t*uh*-tiv]

adj. not certain or fixed; subject to change
잠정적인, 불확실한

*We made a **tentative** plan to meet next week.*

syn. uncertain, indefinite, hesitant

temperate
[tem-per-it]

adj. moderate or self-restrained
온화한

*Please be more **temperate** in your language.*

syn. mild, clement, moderate

terminate
[tur-muh-neyt]

v. to bring to an end
끝나다, 종료되다

*He had no right to **terminate** the contract.*

syn. end, abort, finish

timid

[**tim**-id]

adj. lacking in self-assurance, courage, or bravery

소심한, 용기가 없는, 자신감이 없는

*She was a rather **timid** and meek child.*

syn. apprehensive, fearful, timorous

tolerant

[**tol**-er-*uh*nt]

adj. inclined or disposed to tolerate

관대한, 아량 있는

*People need to be **tolerant** of different points of view.*

syn. open-minded, forbearing, liberal

torrent

[tawr-u*hn*t]

n. a strong and fast-moving stream of water or another liquid.

급류, 거센 흐름

*After the heavy rain, a **torrent** of water rushed down the hillside, flooding the streets.*

syn. flood, deluge, rush

torture

[**tawr**-cher]

n. the act of inflicting excruciating pain

고문, 심한 고통

*Half of the prisoners died after **torture** and starvation.*

syn. torment, persecution, suffering

ISEE Sentence Completion 10-2

Directions : Fill in the blanks to complete the sentences.

1. The date for the school field trip is still _____ because the teachers need to check the weather forecast before confirming it.

    (A) timid   (B) torrent
    (C) temperate   (D) tentative

2. The soldier's actions during the rescue mission were so brave that even the most _____ member of the team felt inspired.

    (A) temperate   (B) terminate
    (C) timid   (D) torrent

3. As soon as the famous singer walked onto the stage, a _____ of cheers and applause filled the stadium.

    (A) terminate   (B) timid
    (C) temperate   (D) torrent

4. The climbers found the weather in the mountains to be surprisingly _____ and perfect for their hike.

    (A) tentative   (B) temperate
    (C) tedious   (D) tolerant

5. The musician increased the _____ of the song, making it faster and more exciting for the audience.

    (A) tempo   (B) torture
    (C) terminate   (D) temperate

Answers

1. (D)   2. (C)   3. (D)   4. (B)   5. (A)

471 toxic	476 ungainly
472 trickery	477 unique
473 trim	478 unwavering
474 ultimate	479 urge
475 uncouth	480 valiant

Verba volant, scripta manent.
(Spoken words fly away,
written words remain.)
말은 날아가고, 글은 남는다.

━━━━━━━ SSATKOREA.com

trim
[trim]

v. to put into a neat by clipping,
to remove by cutting

다듬다, 손질하다

*We should **trim** off the unnecessary*
parts of our spending.

syn. prune, shear, clip

ultimate
[**uhl**-tuh-mit]

adj. last or ending a process or series

궁극적인, 최후의

*The **ultimate** decision lies with*
the parents.

syn. final, eventual, last

toxic
[**tok**-sik]

adj. of, pertaining to, affected with or
caused by a toxin or poison

독이 있는, 유독성의

*These factories are releasing **toxic***
gases into the atmosphere.

syn. poisonous, virulent, noxious

uncouth
[uhn-**kooth**]

adj. strange and ungraceful in appearance

무례한, 상스러운

He may embarrass you with his
***uncouth** behavior.*

syn. crude, boorish, vulgar

trickery
[**trik**-uh-ree]

n. the use or practice of tricks

사기, 속임수

*The impostor resorted to **trickery** to*
get what he wanted.

syn. deception, deceit, artifice

ungainly
[uhn-**geyn**-lee]

adj. not graceful

어색한, 솜씨없는

*On land the turtle is **ungainly**,*
but in the water, it is very agile.

syn. clumsy, awkward, ungraceful

unique
[yoo-**neek**]

adj. existing as the only one

유일한, 하나만 존재하는

*Each person's genetic code is **unique** except in the case of identical twins.*

syn. singular, distinctive, remarkable

unwavering
[un-**wey**-ver-ing]

adj. marked by firm determination

변함없는, 확고한

*She has been encouraged by the **unwavering** support of her family.*

syn. steadfast, resolute, firm

urge
[urj]

v. to push or force along

충고하다, 설득하려 하다

*She **urged** to shout at him.*

syn. encourage, exhort, spur

valiant
[**val**-yuhnt]

adj. boldly courageous

용맹한, 용감한

*The prince was handsome and **valiant** like all princes in stories.*

syn. brave, courageous, valorous

ISEE Sentence Completion 10-3

Directions : **Fill in the blanks to complete the sentences.**

1. Her _____ support during the crisis gave everyone hope and strength.

   (A) unwavering　　(B) trickery
   (C) urge　　　　　(D) ungainly

2. Working in a _____ environment can negatively affect an employee's mental health.

   (A) valiant　　　(B) ultimate
   (C) unique　　　(D) toxic

3. The magician was known for his skillful use of _____ to entertain the audience.

   (A) trickery　　　(B) toxic
   (C) unwavering　(D) ungainly

4. She decided to _____ the edges of the fabric to make it look neat and professional.

   (A) urge　　　(B) urge
   (C) trim　　　(D) toxic

5. His _____ behavior at the dinner party embarrassed his friends.

   (A) uncouth　　(B) toxic
   (C) trickery　　(D) unwavering

Answers
1. (A)　2. (D)　3. (A)　4. (C)　5. (A)

481 vanity	486 vigor
482 verdict	487 vintage
483 versatile	488 vital
484 veto	489 void
485 vibrant	490 voracious

Ars longa, vita brevis.
(Art is long, life is short.)
예술은 길고 인생은 짧다.

SSATKOREA.com

vanity
[**van**-i-tee]

n. excessive pride in one's appearance, abilities, or achievements

자만심, 허영심

*Her **vanity** was evident when she refused to go to the party because she thought her outfit wasn't perfect.*

syn. conceit, arrogance, self-importance

verdict
[**vur**-dikt]

n. the decision reached by a judge or jury

(배심원단의) 평결, (숙고 뒤 내린) 결정

*The jury reached a unanimous **verdict** of 'not guilty.'*

syn. judgment, adjudication, decision

versatile
[**vur**-*suh*-tlor]

adj. capable of turning easily from one to another of various tasks

다재다능한, 다용도의

*The smartphone is so **versatile** that you can use it for gaming, studying, and taking photos.*

syn. adaptable, resourceful, flexible

veto
[**vee**-toh]

n. the power vested in one branch of a government to cancel or postpone the decisions

거부권, 금지

*The President has the **veto** over new legislation.*

syn. rejection, refusal, ban

vibrant
[**vahy**-bru*h*nt]

adj. pulsating with vigor and energy

활기찬

*Seoul is a **vibrant**, dynamic and fascinating city.*

syn. spirited, vivid, lively

vigor
[**vig**-er]

n. good health

생기, 활력

*A brief rest restored the traveler's **vigor**.*

syn. energy, strength, vitality

vintage
[**vin**-tij]

n. something classic, high-quality, and often from a past era

고풍스러운, 특정 연도에 생산된 (특히 와인 관련)

*My mom loves collecting **vintage** dresses because they have unique designs that you can't find in stores today.*

syn.   classic, antique, retro

vital
[**vahyt**-l]

adj. so important that it is required

필수적인, (생명 유지에) 꼭 필요한

*Police have found a **vital** clue to solve the mystery.*

syn.   critical, crucial, essential

void
[void]

adj. having no legal force or effect

무효의, 법적으로 효력이 없는

*The contract was declared **void** because it was not signed properly.*

syn.   invalid, null, worthless

voracious
[vaw-rey-sh*uh*s]

adj. having a desire to eat large amounts of food

게걸스러운, 탐욕스러운

*He was a **voracious** antique collector.*

syn.   greedy, gluttonous, insatiable

ISEE Sentence Completion 10-4

Directions : Fill in the blanks to complete the sentences.

1. The jury delivered its _____ after hours of deliberation in the courtroom.

    (A) verdict   (B) veto
    (C) void   (D) versatile

2. Despite his age, he tackled the job with energy and _____, surprising his colleagues.

    (A) vital   (B) vintage
    (C) vigor   (D) veto

3. After the hike, he ate with a _____ appetite, devouring everything on his plate.

    (A) voracious   (B) vibrant
    (C) vintage   (D) versatile

4. As a _____ performer, he excelled in acting, singing, and dancing.

    (A) void   (B) versatile
    (C) voracious   (D) vintage

5. The president decided to _____ the bill, citing concerns about its implications.

    (A) vanity   (B) verdict
    (C) veto   (D) vibrant

1. (A) 2. (C) 3. (A) 4. (B) 5. (C)

Answers

491 vulgar   496 whet

492 wander   497 whimsical

493 wane   498 wicked

494 watchful   499 wily

495 wax   500 withdrawn

Bellum omnium contra omnes.
(The war of all against all.)
만인의 만인에 대한 전쟁

SSATKOREA.com

vulgar
[**vuhl**-ger]

adj. lacking good manners or taste
저속한, 천박한

*I think that is the most **vulgar** and tasteless remark I ever heard in my life.*

syn.   rude, indecent, indelicate

wander
[**won**-der]

v. to ramble without a definite purpose
거닐다, 돌아다니다, 헤매다

*The cattle are allowed to **wander** freely.*

syn.   stroll, stray, depart

wane
[weyn]

v. to decrease in strength
약해지다, 줄어들다

*The leaders' influence had begun to **wane** by this time.*

syn.   diminish, decrease, decline

watchful
[**woch**-*fuhl*]

adj. vigilant or alert
지켜보는, 경계하는

*My dad was both a **watchful** parent and an affectionate friend.*

syn.   observant, alert, vigilant

wax
[waks]

v. to increase in extent, quantity, intensity or power
점점 커지다

*The moon **waxes** and wanes; it first increases and then decreases.*

syn.   increase, enlarge, augment

whet
[hwet]

v. to make keen or eager
(욕구나 흥미를) 돋우다

*The book will **whet** your appetite for more of her work.*

syn.   sharpen, stimulate, excite

whimsical
[**whim**-si-cal]

adj. erratic or unpredictable

엉뚱한, 기발한, 변덕스러운

*She has a **whimsical** sense of humor.*

syn. capricious, fanciful, quirky

wicked
[**wik**-id]

adj. very mean or evil

못된, 사악한

*The **wicked** fairy bewitched the princess and made her fall into a long sleep.*

syn. vicious, sinful, immoral

wily
[**wahy**-lee]

adj. clever, sneaky, and skilled at using tricks to achieve goals

교활한, 약삭빠른, 꾀가 많은

*The **wily** fox escaped from the hunters by hiding in a burrow.*

syn. crafty, cunning, sly

withdrawn
[with-**drawn**]

adj. shy or reticent

내성적인, 내향적인

*She became **withdrawn** and pensive, hardly speaking to anyone.*

syn. introverted, reserved, inhibited

ISEE Sentence Completion 10-5

Directions : Fill in the blanks to complete the sentences.

1. He was reprimanded for using _____ language during the meeting.

   (A) vulgar   (B) whimsical
   (C) withdrawn   (D) wicked

2. After hours of battle, their strength began to _____, and they retreated.

   (A) watchful   (B) wane
   (C) vulgar   (D) whimsical

3. His energy seemed to _____ and wane depending on his mood and environment.

   (A) wax   (B) wander
   (C) wicked   (D) vulgar

4. The artist's work featured a _____ design that delighted and puzzled viewers alike.

   (A) withdrawn   (B) wicked
   (C) whimsical   (D) watchful

5. The _____ child sat quietly in the corner, avoiding interaction with the other students.

   (A) withdrawn   (B) watchful
   (C) wicked   (D) wax

Analogy 10. Animals

동물 관련 Analogy는 언제나 사랑받는 유형이죠. 특히 Middle Level을 준비하는 학생이라면 더욱 꼼꼼하게 봐야합니다. 흔히 외웠던 단어들이 아닌 고유명사와 명칭이 많으니 따로 꼭 기억해주세요.

동물 : 동물 분류	
beaver : rodent 비버 : 설치류	kangaroo : marsupial 캥거루 : 유대류
shark : fish 상어 : 물고기	frog : amphibian 개구리 : 양서류

암컷 : 수컷	
ewe : ram 암양 : 숫양	doe : stag 암사슴 : 수사슴
hen : rooster 암탉 : 수탉	lioness : lion 암사자 : 숫사자

동물 : 사는 곳 (사람이 만든 곳)	
bee : apiary 벌 : 양봉장	bird : aviary 새 : 새장
horse : stable 말 : 마구간	cow : barn 소 : 외양간

동물 : 동물 새끼	
cow : calf 소 : 송아지	kangaroo : joey 캥거루 : 아기캥거루
pig : piglet 돼지 : 새끼 돼지	goat : kid 염소 : 새끼 염소

동물 : 무리	
lion : pride 사자 : 사자 떼	wolf : pack 늑대 : 늑대 떼
fish : school 물고기 : 물고기 떼	bird : flock 새 : 새 떼

동물 : 내는 소리	
owl : hoot 올빼미 : 올빼미가 우는 소리	snake : hiss 뱀 : 뱀이 쉿하고 내는 소리
dog : bark 개 : 짖는 소리	cat : meow 고양이 : 야옹 소리

1. Snake is to hiss as

   (A) bellow is to bird
   (B) chirp is to donkey
   (C) bray is to raven
   (D) crow is to tiger
   (E) owl is to hoot

2. Goat is to kid as

   (A) bear is to eaglet
   (B) eagle is to calf
   (C) dog is to kitten
   (D) elephant is to herd
   (E) kangaroo is to joey

Check-up 10-1

Directions   Each of the following questions consists of one word followed by five words or phrases. You are to select the one word or phrase whose meaning is closest to the word in capital letters.

1. SUFFERING
- (A) unanimity
- (B) friendliness
- (C) agony
- (D) impartiality
- (E) bias

2. SUMMON
- (A) call
- (B) prefer
- (C) evacuate
- (D) ascertain
- (E) coerce

3. SUPPRESS
- (A) extenuate
- (B) restrain
- (C) fabricate
- (D) debunk
- (E) linger

4. SUPREME
- (A) absolute
- (B) feasible
- (C) dubious
- (D) equitable
- (E) facile

5. SURRENDER
- (A) go on
- (B) come up with
- (C) set up
- (D) give up
- (E) take on

6. SUSPEND
- (A) founder
- (B) imitate
- (C) hang
- (D) loathe
- (E) sway

7. SUSTAIN
- (A) break in
- (B) keep up
- (C) catch up
- (D) fall out
- (E) come apart

8. SYMPATHY
- (A) impediment
- (B) hyperbole
- (C) homage
- (D) implement
- (E) compassion

9. SYSTEMATIC
- (A) beaming
- (B) lax
- (C) radiant
- (D) tardy
- (E) methodical

10. TANGLE
- (A) lament
- (B) entangle
- (C) inhabit
- (D) moan
- (E) inhibit

177

Check-up 10-2

Each of the following questions consists of one word followed by five words or phrases. You are to select the one word or phrase whose meaning is closest to the word in capital letters.

1. TEDIOUS
(A) evanescent
(B) radical
(C) boring
(D) downtrodden
(E) gradual

2. TEMPERATE
(A) ignoble
(B) famished
(C) mild
(D) haughty
(E) reverent

3. TEMPO
(A) pace
(B) abode
(C) fair
(D) domicile
(E) era

4. TENABLE
(A) eternal
(B) naïve
(C) cunning
(D) defensible
(E) erratic

5. TENTATIVE
(A) rash
(B) uncertain
(C) vacant
(D) indefatigable
(E) indispensable

6. TERMINATE
(A) initiate
(B) hinder
(C) commence
(D) end
(E) deter

7. TIMID
(A) ghastly
(B) soiled
(C) fierce
(D) sacred
(E) apprehensive

8. TOLERANT
(A) open-minded
(B) level-headed
(C) well-mannered
(D) self-centered
(E) old-fashioned

9. TORRENT
(A) famine
(B) avalanche
(C) flood
(D) tremor
(E) drought

10. TORTURE
(A) malice
(B) liaison
(C) replica
(D) lexicon
(E) torment

Check-up 10-3

Directions   Each of the following questions consists of one word followed by five words or phrases.
You are to select the one word or phrase whose meaning is closest to the word in capital letters.

1. TOXIC
(A) poisonous
(B) innocuous
(C) indolent
(D) meritorious
(E) misconstrued

2. TRICKERY
(A) deception
(B) jubilee
(C) kiln
(D) satire
(E) epic

3. TRIM
(A) grieve
(B) prune
(C) contrive
(D) devise
(E) narrate

4. ULTIMATE
(A) nonchalant
(B) diurnal
(C) final
(D) invidious
(E) jovial

5. UNCOUTH
(A) sophisticated
(B) indifferent
(C) crude
(D) kinetic
(E) leery

6. UNGAINLY
(A) nocturnal
(B) nosy
(C) obvious
(D) clumsy
(E) meddlesome

7. UNIQUE
(A) paltry
(B) xenophobic
(C) officious
(D) singular
(E) ostentatious

8. UNWAVERING
(A) onerous
(B) steadfast
(C) sumptuous
(D) pliable
(E) opinionated

9. URGE
(A) quell
(B) mollify
(C) appease
(D) raze
(E) encourage

10. VALIANT
(A) prejudiced
(B) presumptuous
(C) brave
(D) opulent
(E) proficient

179

Check-up 10-4

Directions Each of the following questions consists of one word followed by five words or phrases. You are to select the one word or phrase whose meaning is closest to the word in capital letters.

1. VANITY
(A) inquiry
(B) diction
(C) aspiration
(D) composure
(E) conceit

2. VERDICT
(A) judgement
(B) loom
(C) pier
(D) synopsis
(E) knack

3. VERSATILE
(A) adaptable
(B) opinionated
(C) pungent
(D) luminous
(E) reasonable

4. VETO
(A) ruse
(B) rejection
(C) patron
(D) sequence
(E) pinnacle

5. VIBRANT
(A) penitent
(B) insolvent
(C) spirited
(D) prominent
(E) reclusive

6. VIGOR
(A) ovation
(B) portal
(C) plight
(D) energy
(E) predicament

7. VINTAGE
(A) winery
(B) classic
(C) postscript
(D) courtyard
(E) avant-garde

8. VITAL
(A) refractory
(B) superfluous
(C) reputable
(D) refutable
(E) critical

9. VOID
(A) unwilling
(B) tenuous
(C) unyielding
(D) boisterous
(E) invalid

10. VORACIOUS
(A) greedy
(B) skeptical
(C) acute
(D) obtuse
(E) sluggish

180

Check-up 10-5

Directions Each of the following questions consists of one word followed by five words or phrases. You are to select the one word or phrase whose meaning is closest to the word in capital letters.

1. VULGAR
(A) serene
(B) subservient
(C) rude
(D) tacit
(E) disenchanted

2. WANDER
(A) repudiate
(B) stroll
(C) purify
(D) agitate
(E) relinquish

3. WANE
(A) diminish
(B) rectify
(C) siege
(D) petrify
(E) sojourn

4. WATCHFUL
(A) uniform
(B) toxic
(C) succinct
(D) observant
(E) solitary

5. WAX
(A) lunge
(B) increase
(C) smite
(D) thwart
(E) writhe

6. WHET
(A) transgress
(B) sully
(C) wily
(D) sharpen
(E) terminate

7. WHIMSICAL
(A) smeared
(B) tenacious
(C) capricious
(D) unscrupulous
(E) sullen

8. WICKED
(A) lengthy
(B) verbose
(C) untimely
(D) vicious
(E) therapeutic

9. WILY
(A) crafty
(B) wordy
(C) competent
(D) tenuous
(E) vivacious

10. WITHDRAWN
(A) gregarious
(B) woeful
(C) introverted
(D) doleful
(E) wanton

181

UPPER

한세희의 SSAT HIT VOCABULARY

LEVEL

1 abbreviate	6 acclaim
2 abdicate	7 accost
3 abscond	8 acquiesce
4 abstain	9 acquit
5 accentuate	10 adamant

School Motto

"Aspirando et Perseverando"

(Aspiring and Persevering)

- Avon Old Farms School

SSATKOREA.com

abbreviate
[uh-**bree**-vee-eyt]

v. to shorten a word or phrase

축약하다, 줄여서 쓰다

*You can **abbreviate** the word, "page" to "p."*

syn.   shorten, abridge, reduce

abdicate
[**ab**-di-keyt]

v. to give up or renounce authority, duties or an office

(왕위나 권리를) 포기하다, 버리다

*Edward VIII **abdicated** the British throne to marry the woman he loved.*

syn.   resign, repudiate, quit

abscond
[ab-**skond**]

v. to depart secretly

몰래 도주하다, 무단 이탈하다

*Detained patients **absconded** from the hospital.*

syn.   run away, disappear, depart secretly

abstain
[ab-**steyn**]

v. to hold oneself back voluntarily from an action

자제하다, 삼가다

*After reading the article on the effect of meat on blood pressure, she decided to **abstain** from eating meat.*

syn.   refrain, avoid, renounce

accentuate
[ak-**sen**-choo-eyt]

v. to put stress on

강조하다, 두드러지게 하다

*Delete the negative; **accentuate** the positive!*

syn.   emphasize, highlight, underline

acclaim
[uh-**kleym**]

v. to announce with great approval

칭송하다, 환호를 보내다

*She was **acclaimed** as Sportscaster of the Year in 1978.*

syn.   applaud, laud, praise

accost
[uh-**kost**]

v. to speak to someone

다가가 말 걸다

*He **accosted** me with excessive kindness, for he had been drinking much.*

syn. address, come up to, approach

acquiesce
[ak-wee-**es**]

v. to comply silently without protest

마지못해 조용히 따르다, 순순히 따르다

*Alex **acquiesced** to his brother's request to join the party.*

syn. comply, consent, agree

acquit
[uh-**kwit**]

v. declare not guilty

무죄를 선고하다

*The jury **acquitted** John, but he still thinks he's guilty.*

syn. exonerate, absolve, vindicate

adamant
[**ad**-uh-m*uh*nt]

adj. stubbornly refusing to change one's mind

요지부동의, 단호한

*Ellen was **adamant** that she would not go.*

syn. unyielding, determined, insistent

ISEE Sentence Completion 1-1

Directions : Fill in the blanks to complete the sentences.

1. The king chose to _____ the throne, allowing his younger brother to rule.

    (A) abdicate   (B) abscond
    (C) acclaim   (D) accost

2. The employee was caught trying to _____ with company funds after embezzling money.

    (A) acquiesce   (B) abscond
    (C) abbreviate   (D) abstain

3. The editor decided to _____ the lengthy word to fit it into the headline.

    (A) abbreviate   (B) abdicate
    (C) acquiesce   (D) adamant

4. Some voters decided to _____ from voting in the controversial election.

    (A) acclaim   (B) accost
    (C) abstain   (D) adamant

5. Under pressure, the government decided to _____ to the protesters' demands.

    (A) adamant   (B) abbreviate
    (C) acclaim   (D) acquiesce

1. (A)   2. (B)   3. (A)   4. (C)   5. (D)

 Answers

11 adhere   16 advocate

12 admonish   17 aesthetic

13 adroit   18 affected

14 adversary   19 affiliate

15 adversity   20 affinity

School Motto

"Amat Victoria Curam"

(Victory Loves Care)

- Baylor School

SSATKOREA.com

adhere
[ad-**heer**]

v. to stick fast

달라붙다, 지지하다

*Her wet clothes **adhere** to the skin.*

syn.   stick, cling, attach

admonish
[ad-**mon**-ish]

v. to caution, advise, or counsel

부드럽게 타이르다, 훈계하다

*The teacher **admonished** the students not to forget the homework.*

syn.   warn, criticize gently, advise

adroit
[uh-**droit**]

adj. expert or nimble in the use of the hands or body

솜씨 좋은, 노련한

*The **adroit** basketball player scored forty points and twenty assists.*

syn.   dexterous. skillful, clever

adversary
[ad-ver-ser-ee]

n. someone who fights against

적, 적대자

*He will take vengeance on his **adversaries**.*

syn.   foe, enemy, opponent

adversity
[ad-**vur**-si-tee]

n. adverse fortune or fate

역경, 고난

*By facing **adversity**, people learn how to handle difficult situations.*

syn.   hardship, mishap, trouble

advocate
[**ad**-vuh-keyt]

n. a supporter

지지자, 옹호자

*Nancy got a powerful **advocate** to defend her.*

syn.   backer, proponent, supporter

aesthetic

[es-**thet**-ik]

adj. having a sense of beauty

아름다움의, 심미적인, 미적인

*The colors she uses in her paintings create a lively **aesthetic** sense.*

syn. artistic, visual, tasteful

affected

[uh-**fek**-tid]

adj. assumed artificially or pretending

~ 한 척하는, 가장된, 꾸민

*Her **affected** laugh shows her indifference.*

syn. theatrical , pretentious, artificial

affiliate

[uh-**fil**-ee-eyt]

v. to associate with a larger organization

제휴하다, 연계하다

*The research center is **affiliated** with the university.*

syn. associate, ally, partner

affinity

[uh-**fin**-i-tee]

n. a natural liking for or attraction to a person, thing, or idea

친밀감

*Henry has always had an **affinity** and a passion for cars.*

syn. attraction, connection, similarity

ISEE Sentence Completion 1-2

Directions : **Fill in the blanks to complete the sentences.**

1. The architect's design was praised for its _____ appeal and modern elegance.

   (A) aesthetic   (B) affinity
   (C) adhere   (D) advocate

2. His _____ tone during the speech made it hard to tell if he was being sincere.

   (A) affinity   (B) adversary
   (C) aesthetic   (D) affected

3. All members of the organization are expected to _____ to the established rules and regulations.

   (A) adhere   (B) advocate
   (C) affiliate   (D) adversity

4. The teacher had to _____ the student for disrupting the class repeatedly.

   (A) advocate   (B) aesthetic
   (C) admonish   (D) affected

5. Despite facing severe _____, she remained optimistic and continued to pursue her dreams.

   (A) aesthetic   (B) adversity
   (C) adroit   (D) affected

1. (A) 2. (D) 3. (A) 4. (C) 5. (B)

Answers

21 aftermath

22 akin

23 allege

24 allocate

25 aloof

26 altercation

27 ambivalent

28 amend

29 amicable

30 amnesty

School Motto

"Pro Vita Non Pro Schola Discimus"

(Learning - Not just for School, but for Life)

- Berkshire School

SSATKOREA.com

aftermath
[**af**-ter-math]

n. the consequences of an event

결과, 여파, 후유증

The United Nations was founded in the aftermath of World War II.

syn. consequence, result, chain reaction

akin
[uh-**kin**]

adj. related by blood

비슷한, 관련 있는

This game is closely akin to football.

syn. related, connected, blood-related

allege
[uh-**lej**]

v. to assert without proof

혐의클 제기하나, 수창하다

The police allege that the man was murdered, but they have given no proof.

syn. assert, claim, charge

allocate
[**al**-*uh*-keyt]

v. to assign or distribute resources or tasks

할당하다, 분배하다

The city decided to allocate more money for building new parks.

syn. distribute, assign, apportion

aloof
[uh-**loof**]

adj. remote in manner

냉담한, 무관심한

They always stood aloof from their classmates.

syn. detached, distant, apathetic

altercation
[awl-ter-**key**-sh*uh*n]

n. a heated or angry dispute

심한 논쟁, 언쟁, 말싸움

He became involved in an altercation with a police officer over a parking ticket.

syn. dispute, argument, quarrel

ambivalent

[am-**biv**-uh-l*uh*nt]

adj. having mixed feelings about someone or something

반대 감정이 공존하는

*She felt **ambivalent** about her new school.*

syn. conflicting, contradictory, mixed

amend

[uh-**mend**]

v. to make better

고치다, 더 좋게 바꾸다

*Congress has the right to **amend** the Constitution.*

syn. change, alter, mend

amicable

[**am**-i-kuh-b*uh*l]

adj. friendly and peaceful

우호적인, 원만한

*The **amicable** relations between the two countries helped them quickly agree to reduce the tariff.*

syn. friendly, peaceful, harmonious

amnesty

[**am**-n*uh*-stee]

n. an official pardon granted by a government

사면, 공식적으로 죄를 용서함

*The government declared an **amnesty** for all political prisoners.*

syn. pardon, forgiveness, reprieve

ISEE Sentence Completion 1-3

Directions : Fill in the blanks to complete the sentences.

1. His ideas are _____ to those expressed by earlier philosophers in their writings.

   (A) akin   (B) aloof
   (C) amicable   (D) allocate

2. The government announced plans to _____ resources to improve education and healthcare.

   (A) amicable   (B) akin
   (C) aloof   (D) allocate

3. The employee was dismissed after the company decided to _____ misconduct in his behavior.

   (A) amend   (B) aftermath
   (C) allege   (D) ambivalent

4. The committee worked hard to _____ the document to reflect the recent changes in policy.

   (A) aloof   (B) allege
   (C) akin   (D) amend

5. In the _____ of the disaster, the community came together to rebuild and support each other.

   (A) aftermath   (B) amend
   (C) allocate   (D) amnesty

31 analogous   36 anonymous

32 anguish   37 anthology

33 animosity   38 antithesis

34 annihilate   39 apathy

35 annotation   40 aplomb

School Motto

"Venite, Studete, Discite"
(Come, Study, Learn)
- Blair Academy

SSATKOREA.com

analogous
[uh-**nal**-uh-g*uh*s]

adj. corresponding in some particular
유사한, 비슷한

The director is analogous to the conductor of a symphony orchestra.

syn. similar, corresponding, agreeing

anguish
[**ang**-gwish]

n. severe suffering or pain
고통, 괴로움, 고민

He felt not the physical pain but mental anguish.

syn. agony, suffering, pain

animosity
[an-uh-**mos**-i-tee]

n. a feeling of strong dislike
적대감, 적개심

Life appears to me too short to be spent in nursing animosity.

syn. hatred, hostility, antipathy

annihilate
[uh-**nahy**-uh-leyt]

v. to destroy utterly
전멸시키다, 완패시키다

The massive attack almost annihilated the city.

syn. pulverize, demolish, decimate

annotation
[an-uh-**tey**-sh*uh*n]

n. a critical or explanatory note
주석, 낱말이나 문장의 뜻을 쉽게 풀이하는 설명

You can provide instant feedback from anywhere, adding an annotation.

syn. footnote, comment, note

anonymous
[uh-**non**-uh-m*uh*s]

adj. without any name acknowledged
익명으로, 존재를 알리지 않고

Coincidence is God's way of remaining anonymous.

syn. nameless, unknown, unidentified

anthology
[an-**thol**-uh-jee]

adj. a collection of selected writings

시 선집, 문집, 작품 모음집

*A well-chosen **anthology** is a medicine for the mental distress.*

syn. collection, compilation, selection

antithesis
[an-**tith**-uh-sis]

n. opposition or contrast

정반대

*The writer's life has been the **antithesis** of his famous book.*

syn. opposite, reverse, contrast

apathy
[**ap**-uh-thee]

n. absence of passion or emotion

냉담, 무관심

*Hate is not the opposite of love; **apathy** is.*

syn. indifference, aloofness, detachment

aplomb
[uh-**plom**]

n. great calmness and composure

침착함, 태연함

*The manager could handle angry customers with **aplomb**.*

syn. poise, assurance, calmness

ISEE Sentence Completion 1-4

Directions **: Fill in the blanks to complete the sentences.**

1. The teacher explained that the new concept was _______ to what we had learned earlier.

   (A) apathy (B) anonymous
   (C) anthology (D) analogous

2. The hospital received a large donation from an _______ donor who wished to remain unnamed.

   (A) anonymous (B) anthology
   (C) apathy (D) annihilate

3. The poetry _______ included works from both classic and modern poets.

   (A) anguish (B) antithesis
   (C) anthology (D) analogous

4. Many citizens expressed _______ towards the election, choosing not to vote.

   (A) annihilate (B) animosity
   (C) anthology (D) apathy

5. She walked into the meeting with complete _______, handling every question with confidence.

   (A) aplomb (B) anguish
   (C) apathy (D) anonymous

Answers

1. (D) 2. (A) 3. (C) 4. (D) 5. (A)

41 apprehensive 46 assess

42 archaic 47 assiduous

43 ardent 48 atrocity

44 articulate 49 atone

45 ascertain 50 audacious

School Motto

"Victuri te Salutamus"

(we greet thee, we, about to live)

- Brooks School

SSATKOREA.com

apprehensive
[ap-ri-**hen**-siv]

adj. uneasy or fearful about something that might happen

걱정되는, 두려워하는, 불안한

*He was **apprehensive** about telling anyone he really liked her.*

syn. anxious, fearful, afraid

archaic
[ahr-**key**-ik]

adj. primitive or old

오래된, 구식의, 고대의

*You can see a wonderful **archaic** Greek marble object in this museum.*

syn. ancient, antiquated, obsolete

ardent
[**ahr**-dnt]

adj. eager or enthusiastic

열렬한, 열성적인

*James is an **ardent** supporter of the national soccer team.*

syn. passionate, zealous, eager

articulate
[ahr-**tik**-yuh-lit]

v. to express and pronounce clearly

또박또박 말하다, 분명히 표현하다

*Good business leaders create a vision and **articulate** the vision.*

syn. clarify, explain, explicate

ascertain
[as-er-**teyn**]

v. to find out

알아내다, 확인하다

*The police are trying to **ascertain** what happened.*

syn. determine, certify, conclude

assess
[uh-**ses**]

v. to estimate officially the value

평가하다, 측정하다

*The government needs to **assess** the value of your home before they set the property tax.*

syn. appraise, estimate, measure

assiduous

[uh-**sij**-oo-*uhs*]

adj. working diligently at a task

근면한, 성실한

She was assiduous in her attendance at church.

syn. industrious, laborious, diligent

atrocity

[*uh*-**tros**-i-tee]

n. a shocking or cruel act

잔혹 행위, 악행

The soldiers' actions during the war were considered atrocities by the international community.

syn. cruelty, outrage, horror

atone

[uh-**tohn**]

v. to make up for

뉘우치다, 회개하다, 속죄하다

How can I atone for hurting your feelings?

syn. recompense, compensate, repent

audacious

[aw-**dey**-sh*uhs*]

adj. extremely bold or daring

대담한, 뻔뻔한

Fortune favors the audacious.

syn. bold, daring, brazen

ISEE Sentence Completion 1-5

Directions : Fill in the blanks to complete the sentences.

1. The novel used _____ language, making it difficult for modern readers to understand.

   (A) archaic   (B) ardent
   (C) assess   (D) atone

2. The professor was known as an _____ speaker, capable of explaining even the most complex topics clearly.

   (A) ascertain   (B) audacious
   (C) apprehensive   (D) articulate

3. Investigators worked to _____ the facts surrounding the mysterious disappearance.

   (A) atone   (B) archaic
   (C) ascertain   (D) assess

4. The _____ student spent hours reviewing every detail of her notes before the exam.

   (A) ardent   (B) assiduous
   (C) audacious   (D) apprehensive

5. The documentary highlighted the _____ of war, showing its devastating impact on civilians.

   (A) atrocity   (B) audacious
   (C) assess   (D) atone

Answers

1. (A)   2. (D)   3. (C)   4. (B)   5. (A)

Analogy 11. Group : Member

전체와 그 구성원을 연결하는 문제 입니다. 매번 빠지지 않고 등장하는 출제 빈도가 높은 유형이죠.

A는 B로 구성되어 있는 것	
constellation : star 별자리: 별	archipelago : island 군도 : 섬
faculty : teacher 강사진 : 선생님	jury : juror 배심원단 : 배심원
orchestra : instrumentalist 오케스트라 : 연주자	choir : singer 합창단 : 가수
mosaic : tile 모자이크 : 타일	bouquet : flower 꽃다발 : 꽃
team : player 팀 : 선수	congregation : worshipper (예배보러 모인) 신도들 : 신도
mob : insurgent 군중 : 반역자	regiment : soldier (군대의) 연대 : 군인
city : precinct 도시 : 구역	company : division 회사 : 부서
paragraph : sentence 문단 : 문장	sentence : word 문장 : 단어
poem : stanza 시 : 연	book : chapter 책 : 장
play : act 연극 : 막	symphony : movement 교향곡 : 악장

POP QUIZ

1. Mob is to insurgent as
- (A) sentence is to paragraph
- (B) regiment is to soldier
- (C) city is to municipal
- (D) line is to stanza
- (E) faculty is to caliber

2. Movement is to symphony as
- (A) play is to act
- (B) flower is to bouquet
- (C) chapter is to book
- (D) aria is to singer
- (E) company is to division

Check-up 1-1

Directions   Each of the following questions consists of one word followed by five words or phrases.
You are to select the one word or phrase whose meaning is closest to the word in capital letters.

1. ABBREVIATE
(A) retire
(B) forsake
(C) shorten
(D) mimic
(E) liberate

2. ABDICATE
(A) captivate
(B) imbibe
(C) prohibit
(D) resign
(E) illuminate

3. ABSCOND
(A) run away
(B) listen secretly
(C) watch secretly
(D) save secretly
(E) tell secretly

4. ABSTAIN
(A) obtain
(B) refrain
(C) pertain
(D) attain
(F) sustain

5. ACCENTUATE
(A) recount
(B) abate
(C) perplex
(D) emphasize
(E) beckon

6. ACCLAIM
(A) confer
(B) abridge
(C) counsel
(D) edify
(E) applaud

7. ACCOST
(A) inquire
(B) obtain
(C) address
(D) insinuate
(E) praise

8. ACQUIESCE
(A) comply
(B) inspire
(C) yearn
(D) dwindle
(E) associate

9. ACQUIT
(A) extend
(B) confine
(C) acquire
(D) summon
(E) exonerate

10. ADAMANT
(A) aesthetic
(B) unyielding
(C) bewildered
(D) insane
(E) adjoining

195

Check-up 1-2

Directions Each of the following questions consists of one word followed by five words or phrases.
You are to select the one word or phrase whose meaning is closest to the word in capital letters.

1. ADHERE
- (A) stick
- (B) detach
- (C) contact
- (D) retain
- (E) adjust

2. ADMONISH
- (A) amuse
- (B) warn
- (C) predict
- (D) activate
- (E) require

3. ADROIT
- (A) remote
- (B) placid
- (C) lofty
- (D) treacherous
- (E) dexterous

4. ADVERSARY
- (A) wilderness
- (B) taunt
- (C) foe
- (D) debris
- (E) mischief

5. ADVERSITY
- (A) corrosion
- (B) hoist
- (C) hardship
- (D) tremor
- (E) route

6. ADVOCATE
- (A) miniature
- (B) backer
- (C) scale
- (D) expedition
- (E) affliction

7. AESTHETIC
- (A) artistic
- (B) solitary
- (C) immense
- (D) meddlesome
- (E) vital

8. AFFECTED
- (A) theatrical
- (B) splendid
- (C) natural
- (D) dreadful
- (E) apprehensive

9. AFFILIATE
- (A) dwell
- (B) associate
- (C) shroud
- (D) esteem
- (E) soothe

10. AFFINITY
- (A) originality
- (B) embarrassment
- (C) attraction
- (D) consequence
- (E) affectation

Check-up 1-3

Directions   Each of the following questions consists of one word followed by five words or phrases.
You are to select the one word or phrase whose meaning is closest to the word in capital letters.

1. AFTERMATH
(A) consequence
(B) replica
(C) prejudice
(D) fusion
(E) recipient

2. AKIN
(A) related
(B) prominent
(C) unattainable
(D) humid
(E) distant

3. ALLEGE
(A) furnish
(B) shake
(C) hoard
(D) ooze
(E) assert

4. ALLOCATE
(A) scoff
(B) lessen
(C) require
(D) distribute
(E) diminish

5. ALOOF
(A) approximate
(B) detached
(C) archaic
(D) obsolete
(E) vulnerable

6. ALTERCATION
(A) competition
(B) trauma
(C) dispute
(D) volition
(E) tome

7. AMBIVALENT
(A) conflicting
(B) sumptuous
(C) blended
(D) astute
(E) succinct

8. AMEND
(A) supersede
(B) transfer
(C) shed
(D) repel
(E) change

9. AMICABLE
(A) peculiar
(B) beneficial
(C) friendly
(D) stupendous
(E) querulous

10. AMNESTY
(A) pardon
(B) ban
(C) diversion
(D) sanction
(E) amusement

197

Check-up 1-4

Each of the following questions consists of one word followed by five words or phrases. You are to select the one word or phrase whose meaning is closest to the word in capital letters.

1. ANALOGOUS
(A) severe
(B) similar
(C) exacting
(D) versatile
(E) resourceful

2. ANGUISH
(A) jubilee
(B) voyage
(C) rash
(D) agony
(E) fatigue

3. ANIMOSITY
(A) brawl
(B) prelude
(C) supplement
(D) fracture
(E) hatred

4. ANNIHILATE
(A) investigate
(B) pulverize
(C) abolish
(D) afflict
(E) smite

5. ANNOTATION
(A) harbinger
(B) outskirts
(C) rodent
(D) perseverance
(E) footnote

6. ANONYMOUS
(A) prodigious
(B) compassionate
(C) titular
(D) nameless
(E) mere

7. ANTHOLOGY
(A) motive
(B) plight
(C) precedent
(D) collection
(E) hazard

8. ANTITHESIS
(A) fad
(B) nomad
(C) labyrinth
(D) pedestal
(E) opposite

9. APATHY
(A) skirmish
(B) indifference
(C) controversy
(D) objective
(E) likeness

10. APLOMB
(A) anxiety
(B) poise
(C) novelty
(D) atlas
(E) bondage

Check-up 1-5

Directions   Each of the following questions consists of one word followed by five words or phrases.
             You are to select the one word or phrase whose meaning is closest to the word in capital letters.

1. APPREHENSIVE
(A) unwieldy
(B) bold
(C) vertical
(D) anxious
(E) numerous

2. ARCHAIC
(A) subsequent
(B) fanciful
(C) innate
(D) minute
(E) ancient

3. ARDENT
(A) passionate
(B) aloft
(C) sinister
(D) exhilarating
(E) nostalgic

4. ARTICULATE
(A) pursue
(B) revive
(C) decelerate
(D) clarify
(E) accelerate

5. ASCERTAIN
(A) slither
(B) determine
(C) accustom
(D) translate
(E) segregate

6. ASSESS
(A) appraise
(B) inscribe
(C) envelop
(D) diminish
(E) possess

7. ASSIDUOUS
(A) industrious
(B) fruitful
(C) monotonous
(D) auspicious
(E) inattentive

8. ATROCITY
(A) cruelty
(B) honor
(C) affirmation
(D) humanity
(E) label

9. ATONE
(A) detain
(B) terminate
(C) insist
(D) glare
(E) recompense

10. AUDACIOUS
(A) fair
(B) bold
(C) indifferent
(D) laudable
(E) deficient

199

51 augment 56 banal

52 auspicious 57 belittle

53 austere 58 belligerent

54 avert 59 benediction

55 badger 60 benevolent

School Motto

"Servons"

(Let Us Serve)

- Cate School

SSATKOREA.com

augment
[awg-**ment**]

v. to add to

증가시키다, 늘리다

She wants to find work to augment her income.

syn. amplify, enlarge, expand

auspicious
[aw-**spish**-uhs]

adj. favored by fortune

상서로운, 길조의

Getting an A on your first quiz is an auspicious way to start the semester.

syn. favorable, fortunate, prosperous

austere
[aw-**steer**]

adj. severe in manner or appearance

꾸밈없는, 엄격한

The courtroom was a large dark chamber, an austere place.

syn. harsh, severe, strict

avert
[uh-**vurt**]

v. to turn away or aside

외면하다, 피하다

We averted getting stuck in traffic by leaving early in the morning.

syn. prevent, avoid, preclude

badger
[**baj**-er]

v. to harass or urge persistently

귀찮게 하다, 괴롭히다

The boys badgered their mother for candy.

syn. annoy, pester, vex

banal
[buh-**nal**]

adj. devoid of freshness or originality

진부한, 평범한

It was just another banal gossip.

syn. hackneyed, trite, insipid

belittle
[bih-**lit**-l]

v. to regard or portray as less impressive or important

우습게 알다, 하찮게 여기다

She felt her boss belittled her achievements.

syn. depreciate, disparage, put down

belligerent
[buh-**lij**-er-uhnt]

adj. combative, pugnacious, aggressive

호전적인, 적대적인

The belligerent student was always starting fights.

syn. aggressive, hostile, bellicose

benediction
[ben-i-**dik**-shuhn]

n. an utterance of good wishes

축복, 축복의 기도

The pastor pronounced a benediction before the big football game.

syn. blessing, prayer, invocation

benevolent
[buh-**nev**-uh-luhnt]

adj. expressing goodwill or kindly feelings

친절한, 자애로운

Donating her bone marrow to her cousin was a benevolent act.

syn. kind, generous, charitable

ISEE Sentence Completion 2-1

Directions : **Fill in the blanks to complete the sentences.**

1. He worked overtime to _____ his income and save for his family's vacation.

   (A) avert
   (B) augment
   (C) belittle
   (D) badger

2. The couple believed their wedding on New Year's Day marked an _____ beginning for their marriage.

   (A) belligerent
   (B) austere
   (C) benevolent
   (D) auspicious

3. Living an _____ lifestyle, the monk owned only a few possessions and focused on meditation.

   (A) belligerent
   (B) banal
   (C) austere
   (D) badger

4. The pilot's quick thinking helped to _____ a disaster during the emergency landing.

   (A) augment
   (B) avert
   (C) banal
   (D) belittle

5. The child's constant questions began to _____ his older brother, who was trying to study.

   (A) badger
   (B) belittle
   (C) benevolent
   (D) benediction

Answers
1. (B) 2. (D) 3. (C) 4. (B) 5. (A)

MIDDLE 1 2 3 4 5 6 7 8 9 10
UPPER 1 2 3 4 5 6 7 8 9 10

SSAT UPPER LEVEL 201

61	berate	66	bravado
62	bias	67	bulwark
63	bilk	68	caliber
64	blend	69	callous
65	bondage	70	candid

School Motto

"Fidelitas et Integritas"

(Fidelity and Integrity)

- Choate Rosemary Hall

SSATKOREA.com

berate
[bih-**reyt**]

v. to scold

질책하다, 심하게 꾸짖다

John's mother berated him for not studying more for the test.

syn. reproach, rebuke, reprimand

bias
[**bahy**-uhs]

n. a particular tendency or inclination

편견

Some institutions still have a strong bias against women.

syn. prejudice, partiality, predilection

bilk
[bilk]

v. to cheat or defraud someone

속이나, 속여서 돈을 빼았다.

The scammer tried to bilk the elderly woman, but she caught on in time.

syn. defraud, cheat, swindle

blend
[blend]

v. to mix smoothly and inseparably together

섞다, 혼합하다

To make a milkshake, blend ice cream and milk.

syn. mix, mingle, amalgamate

bondage
[**bon**-dij]

n. slavery or involuntary servitude

노예제, 구속, 속박

Abraham Lincoln freed the slaves from their bondage.

syn. slavery, subjugation, enslavement

bravado
[br*uh*-**vah**-doh]

n. a bold or confident manner

허세, 겉으로만 용감한 척함

The villain's bravado crumbled when the hero confronted him.

syn. swagger, boldness, boastfulness

bulwark
[**bool**-werk]

n. a wall of earth or other material
protection for defense

방어물, 성채, 요새

*The king ordered the construction of
defensive **bulwarks** around the castle.*

syn. fort, fortress, citadel

caliber
[**kal**-uh-ber]

n. degree of capacity or competence

도량, 재간, 능력

*She needs a lawyer of high **caliber**
to ensure she doesn't go to jail.*

syn. ability, quality, capability

callous
[**kal**-uhs]

adj. insensitive or emotionally hardened

냉담한, 감정이 없는

*The tyrant showed a **callous**
indifference to human suffering.*

syn. insensitive, indifferent, apathetic

candid
[**kan**-did]

adj. open and sincere

솔직한, 숨김 없는

*Let me be quite **candid** with you.*

syn. frank, open, ingenuous

ISEE Sentence Completion 2-2

Directions : **Fill in the blanks to
complete the sentences.**

1. Implicit _____ can influence
   decisions without people even
   realizing it.

   (A) bias   (B) bravado
   (C) bulwark   (D) bondage

2. The dish was praised for its
   unique _____ of flavors, which
   delighted the diners.

   (A) bias   (B) bondage
   (C) caliber   (D) blend

3. The school is known for attracting
   students of high academic
   _____, ensuring quality
   education.

   (A) bias   (B) bravado
   (C) caliber   (D) bondage

4. Her _____ attitude during the
   discussion hurt others' feelings,
   as she seemed indifferent to their
   concerns.

   (A) callous   (B) candid
   (C) bilk   (D) berate

5. He appreciated her _____
   opinion, as it provided honest and
   constructive feedback.

   (A) callous   (B) blend
   (C) candid   (D) bulwark

Answers

1. (A) 2. (D) 3. (C) 4. (A) 5. (C)

MIDDLE 1 2 3 4 5 6 7 8 9 10

UPPER 1 2 3 4 5 6 7 8 9 10

SSAT UPPER LEVEL 203

71 capricious 76 chagrin

72 catastrophe 77 chide

73 cease 78 chronic

74 celestial 79 circumvent

75 censure 80 cite

School Motto

"Aim High"

- Cranbrook Schools

SSATKOREA.com

capricious
[kuh-**prish**-uhs]

adj. impulsive and unpredictable

변덕스러운, 잘 변하는

The capricious spring weather is unpredictable.

syn. fickle, whimsical, erratic

catastrophe
[kuh-**tas**-truh-fee]

n. a sudden and widespread disaster

대참사, 대재앙

The expansion of the business was a catastrophe for the firm.

syn. calamity, disaster, misfortune

cease
[sees]

v. to stop or end

중단되다, 그치다

All chattering ceases every time my gym teacher blows her whistle.

syn. discontinue, quit, stop, halt

celestial
[suh-**les**-ch*uh*l]

adj. pertaining to the sky or visible heaven

하늘의, 천상의, 천체의

Planets, stars, and comets are all celestial objects.

syn. heavenly, ethereal, divine

censure
[**sen**-sher]

v. to criticize or reproach in a harsh or vehement manner

비난, 질책하다

The teacher censured Luke for talking in class.

syn. blame, chide, reprove

chagrin
[shuh-**grin**]

n. a feeling of vexation, disappointment or humiliation

원통함, 분함

The severe racism was a source of chagrin for Tiara.

syn. embarrassment, humiliation, disappointment

chide

[chahyd]

v. to express disapproval of

꾸짖다, 야단치다

*Tania's mother **chided** her for not eating her vegetables.*

syn. reprimand, scold, reprove

chronic

[**kron**-ik]

adj. continuing over a long period

만성적인, 고질적인

*Ray's **chronic** lateness frustrated his teacher.*

syn. persistent, stubborn, constant

circumvent

[sur-kuhm-**vent**]

v. to avoid fulfilling, answering, or performing

피하다

*The fugitive **circumvented** capture by anticipating the movements of the police.*

syn. avoid, bypass, evade

cite

[sahyt]

v. to quote a passage, book, author

이유나 예를 들다, 인용하다

*An effective essay will **cite** several authorities' sources.*

syn. quote, mention, indicate

ISEE Sentence Completion 2-3

Directions : Fill in the blanks to complete the sentences.

1. His _____ nature made it difficult for others to predict his decisions.

   (A) chide   (B) celestial
   (C) chronic   (D) capricious

2. The region was struck by a natural _____ that left thousands homeless.

   (A) catastrophe   (B) chagrin
   (C) censure   (D) circumvent

3. He had been suffering from a _____ condition that required constant medical care.

   (A) censure   (B) capricious
   (C) chronic   (D) chagrin

4. Some individuals attempt to _____ the rules rather than follow them.

   (A) capricious   (B) cite
   (C) cease   (D) circumvent

5. The professor asked the student to _____ an example to support their argument.

   (A) cite   (B) chide
   (C) cease   (D) catastrophe

Answers

1. (D) 2. (A) 3. (C) 4. (D) 5. (A)

01 clamor   86 cogent

82 clandestine   87 collaborate

83 clot   88 commend

84 clutch   89 compassion

85 coerce   90 compelling

School Motto

"Amor Caritas"

(love charity)

- Dana Hall School

SSATKOREA.com

clamor
[**klam**-er]

n. a loud uproar, as from a crowd of people

아우성, 소란, 외침, 떠들썩함

The students rushed out of the school to and the source of the clamor.

syn. uproar, outcry, commotion

clandestine
[klan-**des**-tin]

adj. done in or executed with secrecy or concealment

은밀한, 남몰래 하는

Romeo and Juliet had to arrange clandestine meetings.

syn. surreptitious, stealthy, furtive

clot
[klot]

n. a solid lump or mass

피가 응고된 덩어리

Some clots that occur inside blood vessels can be harmful.

syn. lump, cluster, coagulation

clutch
[kluhch]

v. to seize with or as with the hands or claws, snatch

꽉 움켜잡다

The little girl clutched the money her mother gave her to buy bread.

syn. clench, grasp, grip

coerce
[koh-**urs**]

v. to compel by force, intimidation, or authority

강요하다, 강제로 시키다

Linda was coerced into signing the contract.

syn. force, compel, impel

cogent
[**koh**-juhnt]

adj. powerfully persuasive

설득력 있는

The teacher praised Jane for the cogent arguments in her essay.

syn. convincing, telling, influential

collaborate

[kuh-**lab**-uh-reyt]

v. to work together with someone to produce or achieve something

협력하다, 공동으로 일하다

*Scientists from different countries **collaborated** on the research project.*

syn.   cooperate, work together, team up

commend

[kuh-**mend**]

v. to express a good opinion of

칭찬하다

*We should **commend** his good deeds.*

syn.   praise, recommend, applaud

compassion

[kuhm-**pash**-uhn]

n. a feeling of deep sympathy and sorrow for another

동정심, 연민

*I was hoping she might show a little **compassion**.*

syn.   sympathy, commiseration, empathy

compelling

[kum-pel-ing]

adj. grabbing attention, convincing, and very interesting

눈을 뗄 수 없는, 매우 설득력 있는

*The movie was so **compelling** that I couldn't take my eyes off the screen until the very end.*

syn.   persuasive, engaging, convincing

ISEE Sentence Completion 2-4

Directions : Fill in the blanks to complete the sentences.

1. The children's loud _____ made it difficult to concentrate on the task at hand.

   (A) clamor   (B) clot
   (C) coerce   (D) compassion

2. The doctor discovered a _____ in the patient's leg that required immediate attention.

   (A) clutch   (B) clamor
   (C) clot   (D) collaborate

3. The lawyer presented a _____ argument that left no room for doubt in the jury's mind.

   (A) cogent   (B) clamor
   (C) collaborate   (D) commend

4. Her _____ for others was evident in the way she volunteered at the shelter every weekend.

   (A) clot   (B) cogent
   (C) clamor   (D) compassion

5. The prosecutor presented _____ evidence that convinced the jury of the defendant's guilt.

   (A) clandestine   (B) compelling
   (C) commend   (D) collaborate

1. (A)   2. (C)   3. (A)   4. (D)   5. (B)
 Answers

SSAT UPPER LEVEL   **207**

91 compensate   96 confer

92 complacent   97 conscientious

93 conciliatory   98 consecutive

94 concoct   99 contention

95 condone   100 contiguous

School Motto

"Worthy of Your Heritage"

- Deerfield Academy

SSATKOREA.com

compensate
[**kom**-puhn-seyt]

v. give (someone) something, typically money, in recognition of loss, suffering, or injury
보상하다, 보상금을 주다

The food company gave her a hundred dollars to compensate her for her trouble.

syn. reimburse, pay, recompense

complacent
[kuhm-**pley**-suhnt]

adj. satisfied with oneself
현실에 안주하는, 자기 만족적인

If a student becomes complacent about his studies, his grades might drop.

syn. content, contented, self-satisfied

conciliatory
[kuhn-**sil**-ee-uh-tawr-ee]

adj. making or willing to make concessions
달래는, 회유하는

If you want to end the fight with your friends, you should make a conciliatory gesture.

syn. mollifying, appeasing, pacifying

concoct
[kon-**kokt**]

v. to create or devise something, especially a story, plan, or mixture
(여러 가지를) 섞어서 만들어내다, (이야기를) 꾸며내다

She concocted a delicious soup by mixing different ingredients.

syn. invent, fabricate, devise

condone
[kuhn-**dohn**]

v. to pardon or forgive
용납하다, 봐주다

We cannot condone violence of any sort.

syn. excuse, forgive, pardon

confer
[kuhn-**fur**]

v. to compare views
상의하다, 협의하다

I must confer with my lawyer before I decide.

syn. consult, deliberate, parley

conscientious

[kon-shee-**en**-shuhs]

adj. characterized by extreme care and great effort

양심적인, 성실한

He was a conscientious doctor who did everything possible to help a patient.

syn. diligent, hardworking, ethical

consecutive

[k*uh*n-**sek**-y*uh*-tiv]

adj. happening one after another without interruption or break

연속적인, 연이은

The team won three consecutive games and advanced to the finals.

syn. successive, sequential, uninterrupted

contention

[kuhn-**ten**-shuhn]

n. the disagreement that results from opposing arguments

논쟁, 언쟁, 주장

Contention arose about how to take care of their ill mother.

syn. argument, dispute, competition

contiguous

[kuhn-**tig**-yoo-uhs]

adj. in close proximity without actually touching

인접한, 근접한

France is contiguous with Spain.

syn. bordering, neighboring, tangential

ISEE Sentence Completion 2-5

Directions : **Fill in the blanks to complete the sentences.**

1. His _____ attitude towards his work led him to miss key deadlines and lose opportunities.

   (A) consecutive   (B) conciliatory
   (C) complacent   (D) contiguous

2. The company promised to _____ its customers for losses caused by the delayed shipment.

   (A) compensate   (B) condone
   (C) confer   (D) contention

3. In an effort to ease tensions, she made a _____ gesture by offering to compromise.

   (A) conscientious   (B) conciliatory
   (C) consecutive   (D) contiguous

4. To avoid getting in trouble for being late, Jake decided to _____ a story about rescuing a lost puppy.

   (A) consecutive   (B) compensate
   (C) contention   (D) concoct

5. Their team celebrated three _____ wins in the championship, securing their place in history.

   (A) consecutive   (B) conciliatory
   (C) contiguous   (D) condone

Analogy 12. Without

[A는 B가 없는] 것의 without 관계 문제는 B 부분이 형용사 adjective 일수도 있고, 명사 noun 형태로 나올 수도 있습니다. 매우 자주 출제되는 유형 중 하나이니 관계를 확실히 이해 해두는 것이 필요합니다.

A는 B가 없는 (Adj : Noun)

slack : tension 느슨한 : 긴장	brash : discretion 경솔한 : 신중함
impeccable : flaw 흠 없는 : 결점	frivolous : solemnness 경박한 : 진지함
numb : sensation 마비된 : 감각	unrehearsed : rehearsal 리허설을 하지 않은 : 리허설(예행 연습)
brazen : tact 뻔뻔한 : 재치, 요령	Impromptu : plan 즉흥적인 : 계획
Ignorant : knowledge 무식한 : 지식	inattentive : attention 주의를 기울이지 않는 : 집중
indecisive : determination 우유부단한 : 결단력	vacant : occupancy 비어 있는 : 점유
opaque : clarity 불투명한 : 투명함	impulsive : forethought 충동적인 : 사전 고려

A는 B가 없는 것 (Noun : Noun)

dehydration : water 탈수 : 물	starvation : food 기근 : 식량
Insomnia : sleep 불면증 : 잠	amnesia : memory 기억상실 : 기억
void : substance 텅 빈 공간 : 물질	exhaustion : energy 탈진 : 에너지
chaos : order 혼돈 : 질서	arrogance : humility 거만 : 겸손

POP QUIZ

1. Brazen is to tact as

(A) impromptu is to impetus
(B) famine is to water
(C) dehydrated is to food
(D) ignorant is to knowledge
(E) inattentive is to ambition

2. Insomnia is to sleep as

(A) disillusion is to vision
(B) disenchantment is to coma
(C) amnesia is to memory
(D) souvenir is to keepsake
(E) numbness is to anesthesia

Check-up 2-1

Directions   Each of the following questions consists of one word followed by five words or phrases.
You are to select the one word or phrase whose meaning is closest to the word in capital letters.

1. AUGMENT
(A) amplify
(B) betray
(C) debunk
(D) concur
(E) reassure

2. AUSPICIOUS
(A) terse
(B) hardy
(C) tranquil
(D) favorable
(E) earnest

3. AUSTERE
(A) stout
(B) dormant
(C) foolhardy
(D) diligent
(E) harsh

4. AVERT
(A) manipulate
(B) prevent
(C) abdicate
(D) convert
(E) swivel

5. BADGER
(A) concord
(B) annoy
(C) unveil
(D) violate
(E) interpret

6. BANAL
(A) mobile
(B) aloft
(C) hackneyed
(D) elegant
(E) gigantic

7. BELITTLE
(A) depreciate
(B) encounter
(C) petrify
(D) improve
(E) corrode

8. BELLIGERENT
(A) perpetual
(B) brittle
(C) vital
(D) paltry
(E) aggressive

9. BENEDICTION
(A) colony
(B) majority
(C) blessing
(D) predicament
(E) fee

10. BENEVOLENT
(A) apprehensive
(B) woeful
(C) scalding
(D) kind
(E) heroic

Check-up 2-2

Each of the following questions consists of one word followed by five words or phrases. You are to select the one word or phrase whose meaning is closest to the word in capital letters.

1. BERATE
(A) reproach
(B) stall
(C) distress
(D) evade
(E) budge

2. BIAS
(A) campaign
(B) hue
(C) prejudice
(D) restraint
(E) abode

3. BILK
(A) compliment
(B) pardon
(C) defraud
(D) relate
(E) overlap

4. BLEND
(A) fume
(B) shed
(C) detect
(D) rejoice
(E) mix

5. BONDAGE
(A) blizzard
(B) avalanche
(C) task
(D) poverty
(E) slavery

6. BRAVADO
(A) integrity
(B) swagger
(C) prowess
(D) affection
(E) humbleness

7. BULWARK
(A) oblivion
(B) revenge
(C) crusade
(D) fort
(E) lineage

8. CALIBER
(A) ability
(B) option
(C) prairie
(D) pension
(E) scabbard

9. CALLOUS
(A) conspicuous
(B) abashed
(C) insensitive
(D) numerous
(E) arrogant

10. CANDID
(A) unanimous
(B) brittle
(C) slovenly
(D) frank
(E) confident

212

Check-up 2-3

Directions   Each of the following questions consists of one word followed by five words or phrases.
You are to select the one word or phrase whose meaning is closest to the word in capital letters.

1. CAPRICIOUS
(A) cumbersome
(B) fickle
(C) edible
(D) substantial
(E) engrossing

2. CATASTROPHE
(A) breach
(B) calamity
(C) quest
(D) tremor
(E) refuge

3. CEASE
(A) yearn
(B) vow
(C) discontinue
(D) attain
(E) collide

4. CELESTIAL
(A) brief
(B) apt
(C) cordial
(D) peculiar
(E) heavenly

5. CENSURE
(A) blame
(B) establish
(C) soar
(D) plunge
(E) applaud

6. CHAGRIN
(A) immigrant
(B) eclipse
(C) marvel
(D) embarrassment
(E) famine

7. CHIDE
(A) shove
(B) nudge
(C) reprimand
(D) blunder
(E) accustom

8. CHRONIC
(A) flimsy
(B) ridiculous
(C) previous
(D) ingenious
(E) persistent

9. CIRCUMVENT
(A) assign
(B) negotiate
(C) revive
(D) analyze
(E) avoid

10. CITE
(A) quote
(B) challenge
(C) boast
(D) provoke
(E) beseech

Check-up 2-4

1. CLAMOR

(A) outskirts
(B) mob
(C) uproar
(D) pedestal
(E) stem

2. CLANDESTINE

(A) surreptitious
(B) puny
(C) distinct
(D) remote
(E) prominent

3. CLOT

(A) game
(B) lump
(C) domicile
(D) motion
(E) haven

4. CLUTCH

(A) accelerate
(B) burden
(C) oppose
(D) clench
(E) abandon

5. COERCE

(A) allude
(B) meddle
(C) force
(D) clasp
(E) grasp

6. COGENT

(A) versatile
(B) evident
(C) ferocious
(D) overdue
(E) convincing

7. COLLABORATE

(A) wage
(B) portray
(C) diverge
(D) cooperate
(E) distill

8. COMMEND

(A) translate
(B) deteriorate
(C) command
(D) praise
(E) mimic

9. COMPASSION

(A) oblivion
(B) sympathy
(C) keepsake
(D) priority
(E) skirmish

10. COMPELLING

(A) ecumenical
(B) invincible
(C) persuasive
(D) belated
(E) wandering

Check-up 2-5

Directions   Each of the following questions consists of one word followed by five words or phrases.
You are to select the one word or phrase whose meaning is closest to the word in capital letters.

1. COMPENSATE
(A) reimburse
(B) deprive
(C) withdraw
(D) equivocate
(E) broach

2. COMPLACENT
(A) awesome
(B) evident
(C) obedient
(D) desperate
(E) content

3. CONCILIATORY
(A) terrific
(B) commanding
(C) insecure
(D) mere
(E) mollifying

4. CONCOCT
(A) assess
(B) confess
(C) babble
(D) invent
(E) reiterate

5. CONDONE
(A) retain
(B) excuse
(C) attain
(D) coincide
(E) employ

6. CONFER
(A) consult
(B) baffle
(C) erode
(D) investigate
(E) stroll

7. CONSCIENTIOUS
(A) treacherous
(B) placid
(C) esteemed
(D) delicate
(E) diligent

8. CONSECUTIVE
(A) factual
(B) insufficient
(C) successive
(D) ill-fed
(E) engaging

9. CONTENTION
(A) revenge
(B) loom
(C) territory
(D) argument
(E) property

10. CONTIGUOUS
(A) ludicrous
(B) aboveboard
(C) neighboring
(D) reluctant
(E) inept

215

101	contradict	106	correlate
102	convalesce	107	cosmopolitan
103	convey	108	credulous
104	copious	109	creed
105	corpulent	110	crest

School Motto

"Gaudet Patientia Duris"

(Patience Rejoices in Adversity)

- Emma Willard School

SSATKOREA.com

contradict
[kon-truh-**dikt**]

v. to assert the contrary of

부정하다, 반박하다, 모순되다

She loves to quote Albert Einstein because nobody dares to contradict her.

syn.   belie, contravene, counter

convalesce
[kon-vuh-**les**]

v. to recover health and strength after illness

요양하다, 건강을 회복하다

He fell in love with the nurse while he was convalescing in a hospital.

syn.   recover, recuperate, heal

convey
[k*uh*n-**vey**]

v. to communicate or transport something

진딜하다, 진하나

The teacher used a diagram to convey the concept of photosynthesis to the class.

syn.   communicate, express, deliver

copious
[**koh**-pee-uh-s]

adj. large in quantity or number

많은, 풍부한, 풍요로운

He drank copious amounts of wine.

syn.   abundant, affluent, ample

corpulent
[**kawr**-pyuh-luh-nt]

adj. large or bulky of body

뚱뚱한, 과체중의

A "fat" man can be politely described as "corpulent" gentleman.

syn.   obese, fat, stout

correlate
[**kawr**-uh-leyt]

v. to have a mutual or reciprocal relation

연관성이 있다, 상관관계가 있다

Red is such an interesting color to correlate with emotion.

syn.   connect, relate, associate

cosmopolitan

[koz-muh-**pol**-i-tn]

adj. free from local, provincial, or national ideas

전세계적인, 국제적인

Paris is a very cosmopolitan city, with people and ideas from all over the world.

syn. universal, ecumenical, international

credulous

[**krej**-uh-luhs]

adj. willing to believe or trust too readily

잘 믿는, 잘 속는

Credulous people are easily misled by false advertisements.

syn. gullible, naive, trusting

creed

[kreed]

n. a set of beliefs or principles

신조, 신념, 교리

Many people live by the creed that honesty is the best policy.

syn. belief, principle, doctrine

crest

[krest]

n. the highest part of a hill or mountain range

꼭대기, 정상

The hiker stood on the crest of the hill, enjoying the view.

syn. summit, peak, apex

ISEE Sentence Completion 3-1

Directions : Fill in the blanks to complete the sentences.

1. As the surfer paddled, she reached the _____ of the wave and prepared for the descent.

   (A) crest (B) copious
   (C) convey (D) corpulent

2. The letter was intended to _____ a message of hope and solidarity.

   (A) crest (B) convalesce
   (C) convey (D) cosmopolitan

3. The principles of their _____ dictated how they lived their daily lives.

   (A) creed (B) correlate
   (C) crest (D) cosmopolitan

4. The painting depicted a _____ figure, dressed in lavish robes and seated on a throne.

   (A) cosmopolitan (B) creed
   (C) crest (D) corpulent

5. The scam was effective because it targeted a _____ believer who trusted everything they were told.

   (A) credulous (B) crest
   (C) copious (D) convey

1. (A) 2. (C) 3. (A) 4. (D) 5. (A)

 Answers

111	cull	116	debilitated
112	culmination	117	decimate
113	cursory	118	decree
114	curtail	119	defer
115	cynical	120	deferential

School Motto

"Fortiter, fideliter, feliciter"

(Strongly, faithfully, joyfully)

- Episcopal High School

SSATKOREA.com

cull
[k*uh*l]

v. to remove something that has been rejected

골라내다, 추리다

*Mary **culled** some of the nicest flowers in the garden for her bouquet.*

syn.   choose, select, pick

culmination
[kuhl-muh-**ney**-sh*uh*n]

n. the highest point or most important result of something

정점, 최고조, 절정

*Winning the championship was the **culmination** of months of hard work and practice by the team.*

syn.   climax, peak, apex

cursory
[**kur**-suh-ree]

adj. going rapidly over something, without noticing details

피상적인, 대충하는, 건성의

*He signed with only a **cursory** glance at the report.*

syn.   superficial, hasty, perfunctory

curtail
[ker-**teyl**]

v. to cut short

짧게 줄이다, 축소하다

*We must try to **curtail** our spending.*

syn.   shorten, abridge, reduce

cynical
[**sin**-i-k*uh*l]

adj. distrusting or disparaging the motives of others

빈정대는, 냉소적인

*His **cynical** belief was that everyone was motivated by selfish interests.*

syn.   skeptical, pessimistic, distrustful

debilitated
[dih-**bil**-i-tey-tid]

adj. weak or feeble

쇠약해진, 약해진

*Jonah was **debilitated** by severe migraine headaches.*

syn.   weakened, exhausted, impaired

decimate

[**des**-uh-meyt]

v. to destroy a great number or proportion of

대량으로 죽이다, 학살하다

The oil spill in the Caribbean Sea decimated the wildlife along the coast.

syn. destroy, devastate, annihilate

decree

[dih-**kree**]

n. a formal and authoritative order

법령, 판결

By decree of the king, all foreign visitors to the city must wear a red badge.

syn. command, mandate, order

defer

[dih-**fur**]

v. to put off action or consideration to a future time

미루다, 보류하다

The decision has been deferred by the admission committee until next week.

syn. suspend, table, procrastinate

deferential

[def-*uh*-**ren**-sh*uh*l]

adj. Showing respect and submission to someone

공손한, 존중하는, 경의를 표하는

He gave a deferential nod to the elder, showing his respect.

syn. respectful, humble, courteous

ISEE Sentence Completion 3-2

Directions : Fill in the blanks to complete the sentences.

1. The manager had to _____ the list of candidates to only five finalists for the position.

   (A) defer   (B) cull
   (C) curtail   (D) decree

2. Winning the championship was the _____ of years of hard work and dedication for the soccer team.

   (A) deferential   (B) cursory
   (C) cull   (D) culmination

3. To improve the quality of the harvest, farmers must carefully _____ the weaker plants before they spread disease to the healthy ones.

   (A) cull   (B) cursory
   (C) defer   (D) curtail

4. The government issued a _____ requiring all citizens to evacuate the area before the hurricane struck.

   (A) deferential   (B) decree
   (C) cynical   (D) cursory

5. The severe drought threatened to _____ the local crops, leaving farmers worried about their harvest.

   (A) defer   (B) cull
   (C) decimate   (D) curtail

1. (B) 2. (D) 3. (A) 4. (B) 5. (C)

Answers

121	deficient	126	despondent
122	dehydrated	127	detain
123	delectable	128	deter
124	deplore	129	detour
125	despicable	130	devastate

School Motto

"mens sana in corpore sano"
(A healthy mind in a healthy body)
- Foxcroft School

SSATKOREA.com

deficient
[dih-**fish**-uhnt]

adj. lacking some element or characteristic
부족한, 결핍된

Jenna's essay was deficient in quality citations.

syn. insufficient, inadequate, lacking

dehydrated
[dee-**hahy**-drey-tid]

adj. free from moisture for preservation
건조된, 마른, 탈수된

They brought dehydrated fruit on the hike.

syn. parched, dry, desiccated

delectable
[dih-**lek**-tuh-b*uh*l]

adj. extremely delicious or appealing
매우 맛있는, 맛있어 보이는

Delectable smells rose from the kitchen.

syn. delicious, savory, tasty

deplore
[dih-**plawr**]

v. to regret deeply or strongly
몹시 슬퍼하다, 한탄하다

My father deplores the fact that my sister and I spend so much time texting.

syn. lament, mourn, sorrow

despicable
[**des**-pi-kuh-b*uh*l]

adj. deserving to be despised, contemptible
비열한, 야비한, 못된

Posting mean rumors about her on Facebook was a despicable act.

syn. vile, contemptible, reprehensible

despondent
[dih-**spon**-duhnt]

adj. feeling profound hopelessness
기가 죽은, 의기소침한

Victor was despondent after he received a D on the test.

syn. depressed, discouraged, dejected

detain
[dih-**teyn**]

v. to keep under restraint or in custody

가두다, 억류하다

*He was **detained** by the police.*

syn. hold, keep back, confine

deter
[dih-**tur**]

v. to discourage or restrain from acting or proceeding

그만두게 하다, 단념시키다

*One goal of law is to **deter** bad behavior.*

syn. obstruct, discourage, dissuade

detour
[**dee**-toor]

n. a longer, less direct or roundabout way to get

우회로, 돌아가는 길

*A traffic accident means you have to take a **detour**.*

syn. bypass, deviation, alternate route

devastate
[**dev**-uh-steyt]

v. to lay waste or destroy

완전히 파괴하다

*The storm **devastated** his town.*

syn. demolish, ruin, ravage

ISEE Sentence Completion 3-3

Directions : Fill in the blanks to complete the sentences.

1. The environmental group worked to _____ the practice of dumping waste into the river, encouraging companies to find cleaner alternatives.

   (A) deter   (B) deplore
   (C) despondent   (D) dehydrated

2. The sudden loss of her best friend left her feeling _____ and unable to focus on her schoolwork.

   (A) deficient   (B) deplore
   (C) despondent   (D) detain

3. The hikers became dangerously _____ after several hours in the scorching sun without enough water.

   (A) deter   (B) dehydrated
   (C) deficient   (D) detour

4. The teacher warned the students that a lack of preparation would leave their essays _____ in both content and structure.

   (A) deficient   (B) deplore
   (C) delectable   (D) despondent

5. The tourists had to take a _____ when the main road was closed due to construction.

   (A) deter   (B) deficient
   (C) detour   (D) despicable

131	deviation	136	dilapidated
132	devour	137	diminutive
133	diction	138	diplomatic
134	diffuse	139	discard
135	digress	140	discerning

School Motto

"Men for Others"

- Georgetown Preparatory School

SSATKOREA.com

deviation
[dee-vee-**ey**-shuhn]

n. anything that varies from the accepted standard

일탈, 탈선, 기준에서 벗어남, 변이

When something causes a creature's DNA to change, it creates a deviation.

syn. divergence, departure, anomaly

devour
[dih-**vou**-uhr]

v. to swallow or eat up hungrily, voraciously, or ravenously

걸신들린 듯 먹다

The boys devour a meal like ravenous cowhands.

syn. gobble, consume, feast on

diction
[**dik**-shuhn]

n. style of speaking or writing

말씨, 말투

Be sure to use formal diction when writing an essay.

syn. wording, language, choice of words

diffuse
[dih-**fyooz**]

v. to spread

널리 퍼지다

Buddhism diffused from India throughout Asia.

syn. disperse, distribute, scatter

digress
[dih-**gres**]

v. to deviate from the main topic

주제에서 벗어나다

Do you mind if I digress for a moment?

syn. stray, deviate, wander

dilapidated
[dih-**lap**-i-dey-tid]

adj. fallen into partial ruin or decay as from age or neglect

다 허물어져 가는

The dilapidated building is going to need a lot of fixing up.

syn. run-down, decrepit, derelict

diminutive

[dih-**min**-yuh-tiv]

adj. very small

아주 작은

Despite its diminutive size, the car is quite comfortable.

syn. tiny, minute, infinitesimal

diplomatic

[dip-luh-**mat**-ik]

adj. skilled in dealing with sensitive matters or people

외교적 수완이 있는, 능수능란한

Politicians are usually very diplomatic.

syn. tactful, clever, astute

discard

[dih-**skahrd**]

v. to get rid of

버리다, 폐기하다

Let's discard some of these old magazines.

syn. dispose, reject, abandon

discerning

[dih-**sur**-ning]

adj. having keen insight and good judgment

안목이 있는, 통찰력이 있는

A discerning person is good at distinguishing the good from the bad.

syn. perceptive, insightful, judicious

ISEE Sentence Completion 3-4

Directions : Fill in the blanks to complete the sentences.

1. The artist preferred to use _____ light in her photographs to create a soft, even effect.

   (A) diffuse   (B) discerning
   (C) dilapidated   (D) devour

2. The student began to _____ from the topic during the presentation, losing the audience's focus.

   (A) discard   (B) diplomatic
   (C) digress   (D) diminutive

3. The teacher noticed a _____ from the norm in the student's usual writing style.

   (A) deviation   (B) dilapidated
   (C) discerning   (D) diffuse

4. The ambassador used a _____ approach to resolve the tense negotiations between the two countries.

   (A) digress   (B) discerning
   (C) diffuse   (D) diplomatic

5. The abandoned house had become a _____ building, with broken windows and peeling paint.

   (A) deviation   (B) dilapidated
   (C) discerning   (D) diffuse

1. (A)   2. (C)   3. (A)   4. (D)   5. (B)

Answers

141 discreet   146 dissect

142 disdain   147 disseminate

143 dismantle   148 dissent

144 disparage   149 distinctive

145 dispel   150 diverge

School Motto

"Cui servire est regnare"

(To serve is to rule)

- Groton school

SSATKOREA.com

discreet
[dih-**skreet**]

adj. appropriately quiet, prudent, and restrained

신중한, 조심스러운

He was wearing a discreet gray suit, so nobody noticed him.

syn. cautious, sensible, prudent

disdain
[dis-**deyn**]

n. haughty contempt

경멸, 모멸, 오만

The arrogant wrestler showed disdain for his opponents.

syn. contempt, scorn, derision

dismantle
[dis-**man**-tl]

v. to take apart

분해하다, 해체하다

The country will dismantle its nuclear program.

syn. disassemble, take apart, tear down

disparage
[dih-**spar**-ij]

v. to belittle or degrade a person or idea

얕보다, 무시하다

To pursue science is not to disparage the things of the spirit.

syn. belittle, degrade, criticize

dispel
[dih-**spel**]

v. to drive off in various directions

떨쳐버리다, 쫓아버리다

John wants to dispel the rumor that his parents got divorced.

syn. disperse, diffuse, dismiss

dissect
[dih-**sekt**]

v. to methodically cut up a body, part, or plant in order to study its internal parts

해부하다

Christine dissected a frog during biology class.

syn. anatomize, analyze, explore

disseminate

[dih-**sem**-uh-neyt]

v. to scatter or spread widely

퍼뜨리나, 유포하다

*It is important to **disseminate** helpful information.*

syn. spread, distribute, disperse

dissent

[dih-**sent**]

n. disagreement or difference

반대, 반대 의견

*These voices of **dissent** grew louder and louder.*

syn. disagreement, disapproval

distinctive

[dih-**stingk**-tiv]

adj. serving to distinguish

독특한, 다른 것과 구별되게 하는

*Her black eyes and plump lips are **distinctive** features.*

syn. characteristic, individual, one-of-a-kind

diverge

[dih-**vurj**]

v. to go in different directions

갈라지다, 나뉘지다

*Friends' lives often **diverge** after they start college.*

syn. separate, branch off, deviate

ISEE Sentence Completion 3-5

Directions : Fill in the blanks to complete the sentences.

1. The activists aimed to _____ information about the environmental crisis to a larger audience.

   (A) dispel   (B) distinctive
   (C) disseminate   (D) disparage

2. Her _____ behavior during the meeting ensured that sensitive information was not disclosed.

   (A) discreet   (B) disdain
   (C) dismantle   (D) dissent

3. The scientist worked hard to _____ the myth surrounding the new discovery.

   (A) disseminate (B) dissent
   (C) dismantle   (D) dispel

4. It took hours to carefully _____ the old barn without damaging the materials.

   (A) dismantle   (B) disseminate
   (C) diverge   (D) dissect

5. The group began to _____ from the planned route, leading to confusion about their location.

   (A) diverge   (B) disparage
   (C) disseminate (D) dispel

1. (C) 2. (A) 3. (D) 4. (A) 5. (A)

Answers

Analogy 13. Synonyms Vs. Antonym

Analogy의 유형중 동의어와 반의어를 찾는 유형도 자주 등장합니다. 그런데 관계가 쉽고 예측이 가능한 만큼 이 유형에 나오는 단어들의 난이도가 높다는 것이 포인트 이죠. 전체 문제 중 앞 쪽에 나오는 경우는 무제 유형을 받아어가 더 많고, 뒤 쪽에 나오는 경우는 동의어처럼 보이지만 Degree 인 킹우가 맋나는 것노 기억할 만한 점입니다.

A와 B는 Synonyms 관계

endeavor : attempt 노력 : 시도	debacle : catastrophe 대실패 : 파국
peril : hazard 위험 : 위험 요소	bedlam : chaos 난리, 법석 : 혼돈, 혼란
gregarious : sociable 남과 어울리기 좋아하는 : 사교적인	hang : suspend 매달다 : 걸다
passionate : fervent 열정적인 : 열렬한	malicious : spiteful 악의적인 : 앙심을 품은
mar : spoil 망치다 : 못쓰게 하다	omit : exclude 생략하다 : 제외하다
surmise : guess 추측하다 : 알아맞히다	mission : purpose 임무 : 목적

A와 B는 Antonyms 관계

originality : banality 독창성 : 진부함	benevolent : malevolent 선한, 자비로운 : 악한, 악의적인
facade : reality 외관, 겉모습 : 실제, 진실	philanthropy : greed 자선 : 탐욕
sensitive : callous 민감한 : 둔한	listless : unflagging 무기력한 : 지칠 줄 모르는
glib : sincere 겉만 번지르르한 : 진실된	garrulous : reserved 수다스러운 : 과묵한

POP QUIZ

1. Thrive is to flourish as
- (A) vex is to appease
- (B) truncate is to lengthen
- (C) hoax is to pester
- (D) endorse is to disapprove
- (E) concur is to agree

2. Debacle is to catastrophe as
- (A) specter is to spectator
- (B) surmise is to thesis
- (C) jeopardy is to security
- (D) peril is to hazard
- (E) bedlam is to composure

Check-up 3-1

Directions   Each of the following questions consists of one word followed by five words or phrases.
You are to select the one word or phrase whose meaning is closest to the word in capital letters.

1. CONTRADICT
(A) belie
(B) choose
(C) command
(D) suspend
(E) invent

2. CONVALESCE
(A) deceive
(B) preserve
(C) recover
(D) suggest
(E) separate

3. CONVEY
(A) prefer
(B) reproduce
(C) deceive
(D) communicate
(E) replace

4. COPIOUS
(A) appropriate
(B) edible
(C) audible
(D) urbane
(E) abundant

5. CORPULENT
(A) obese
(B) moral
(C) confident
(D) animated
(E) hilarious

6. CORRELATE
(A) suspend
(B) teem
(C) degrade
(D) connect
(E) quench

7. COSMOPOLITAN
(A) vertical
(B) universal
(C) squalid
(D) elusive
(E) meager

8. CREDULOUS
(A) fascinating
(B) gullible
(C) mutual
(D) obsolete
(E) carnivorous

9. CREED
(A) bias
(B) council
(C) jeopardy
(D) terrain
(E) belief

10. CREST
(A) affinity
(B) gadget
(C) compatibility
(D) summit
(E) correspondence

Check-up 3-2

Each of the following questions consists of one word followed by five words or phrases.
You are to select the one word or phrase whose meaning is closest to the word in capital letters.

1. CULL
(A) blend
(B) lap
(C) chop
(D) join
(E) choose

2. CULMINATION
(A) delight
(B) climax
(C) guile
(D) mediocrity
(E) exuberance

3. CURSORY
(A) puzzled
(B) superficial
(C) arid
(D) barren
(E) nonchalant

4. CURTAIL
(A) shorten
(B) retort
(C) sustain
(D) feed
(E) pat

5. CYNICAL
(A) leisurely
(B) cyclical
(C) fantastic
(D) skeptical
(E) grim

6. DEBILITATED
(A) superb
(B) realistic
(C) astonished
(D) weakened
(E) ravenous

7. DECIMATE
(A) sob
(B) increase
(C) transport
(D) obtain
(E) destroy

8. DECREE
(A) command
(B) awe
(C) fiber
(D) comrade
(E) occasion

9. DEFER
(A) guarantee
(B) collect
(C) conjecture
(D) suspend
(E) detach

10. DEFERENTIAL
(A) envious
(B) respectful
(C) enraged
(D) gleeful
(E) reminiscent

Check-up 3-3

Directions   Each of the following questions consists of one word followed by five words or phrases. You are to select the one word or phrase whose meaning is closest to the word in capital letters.

1. DEFICIENT
- (A) insufficient
- (B) nostalgic
- (C) unbearable
- (D) supreme
- (E) hostile

6. DESPONDENT
- (A) flimsy
- (B) prodigal
- (C) depressed
- (D) extensive
- (E) bracing

2. DEHYDRATED
- (A) severe
- (B) rigid
- (C) stark
- (D) hearty
- (E) parched

7. DETAIN
- (A) hold
- (B) advise
- (C) offend
- (D) coordinate
- (E) arrange

3. DELECTABLE
- (A) enormous
- (B) disheartened
- (C) delicious
- (D) reflective
- (E) defective

8. DETER
- (A) exult
- (B) crawl
- (C) inspire
- (D) obstruct
- (E) shed

4. DEPLORE
- (A) decline
- (B) batter
- (C) retain
- (D) lament
- (E) punctuate

9. DETOUR
- (A) idea
- (B) bypass
- (C) control
- (D) aftermath
- (E) discovery

5. DESPICABLE
- (A) outmoded
- (B) vile
- (C) innate
- (D) mediocre
- (E) rippling

10. DEVASTATE
- (A) gorge
- (B) harbor
- (C) insist
- (D) soothe
- (E) demolish

Answer 1.A 2.E 3.C 4.D 5.B 6.C 7.A 8.D 9.B 10.E

Check-up 3-4

Each of the following questions consists of one word followed by five words or phrases. You are to select the one word or phrase whose meaning is closest to the word in capital letters.

1. DEVIATION
(A) divergence
(B) poverty
(C) apparatus
(D) truce
(E) pact

2. DEVOUR
(A) share
(B) grasp
(C) leap
(D) wander
(E) gobble

3. DICTION
(A) scale
(B) breach
(C) fad
(D) aroma
(E) wording

4. DIFFUSE
(A) profuse
(B) disperse
(C) sever
(D) petrify
(E) invert

5. DIGRESS
(A) reign
(B) associate
(C) stray
(D) combine
(E) snarl

6. DILAPIDATED
(A) timid
(B) queer
(C) fierce
(D) dreadful
(E) run-down

7. DIMINUTIVE
(A) deft
(B) sedentary
(C) frivolous
(D) tiny
(E) steadfast

8. DIPLOMATIC
(A) sparse
(B) tactful
(C) jocular
(D) resolute
(E) jocose

9. DISCARD
(A) dash
(B) relieve
(C) dispose
(D) repel
(E) conquer

10. DISCERNING
(A) meddlesome
(B) numerous
(C) perceptive
(D) engrossing
(E) instinctive

230

Check-up 3-5

Directions Each of the following questions consists of one word followed by five words or phrases. You are to select the one word or phrase whose meaning is closest to the word in capital letters.

1. DISCREET
(A) fruitful
(B) cautious
(C) sensational
(D) accurate
(E) resolute

2. DISDAIN
(A) voyage
(B) contempt
(C) budget
(D) mischief
(E) cargo

3. DISMANTLE
(A) salvage
(B) extend
(C) disassemble
(D) reinforce
(E) gripe

4. DISPARAGE
(A) evaluate
(B) increase
(C) pursue
(D) belittle
(E) waddle

5. DISPEL
(A) graze
(B) furnish
(C) shroud
(D) flail
(E) disperse

6. DISSECT
(A) swallow
(B) paralyze
(C) recall
(D) tremble
(E) anatomize

7. DISSEMINATE
(A) conserve
(B) bluster
(C) emerge
(D) spread
(E) plummet

8. DISSENT
(A) disagreement
(B) acquittal
(C) euphemism
(D) connoisseur
(E) remedy

9. DISTINCTIVE
(A) convenient
(B) delicate
(C) characteristic
(D) rigorous
(E) ecstatic

10. DIVERGE
(A) sear
(B) hatch
(C) esteem
(D) separate
(E) integrate

151	divert	156	eccentric
152	divulge	157	ecumenical
153	dogmatic	158	edifice
154	dubious	159	effusive
155	eavesdrop	160	egregious

School Motto

"Whatsoever things are true"

- Hill School

SSATKOREA.com

divert
[dih-**vurt**]

v. To entertain or distract someone from their current focus or concern

(사람을) 즐겁게 하다, (주의를) 딴 데로 돌리다

*The clown **diverted** the children with funny tricks.*

syn.   entertain, amuse, recreate

divulge
[dih-**vuhlj**]

v. to make known

알려주다, 누설하다

*Journalists do not **divulge** their sources.*

syn.   debunk, disclose, reveal

dogmatic
[dawg-**mat**-ik]

adj. asserting opinions in arrogant manner

독재적인

*He was criticized by those around him for being **dogmatic**.*

syn.   opinionated, dictatorial, confident

dubious
[**doo**-bee-*uhs*]

adj. of doubtful quality or propriety

의심스러운

*I am **dubious** about what he says.*

syn.   doubtful, suspicious, uncertain

eavesdrop
[**eevz**-drop]

v. to listen secretly to a private conversation

엿듣다

*I caught him **eavesdropping** outside the window.*

syn.   snoop, spy, overhear

eccentric
[ik-**sen**-trik]

adj. deviating from the customary character or practice

별난, 기이한

*Her father is a bit of an **eccentric**.*

syn.   unconventional, quirky, odd

ecumenical

[**ek**-yoo-**men**-i-k*uhl*]

adj. general or universal

세계적인, 보편적인

They enlarge the system to more ecumenical form system and get some similar conclusion.

syn. universal, general, comprehensive

edifice

[**ed**-uh-fis]

n. a building, especially one of imposing appearance

크고 인상적인 건물

The Eiffel Tower is a great edifice of France.

syn. huge construction, monument, structure

effusive

[ih-**fyoo**-siv]

adj. extravagantly demonstrative

야단스러운, 과장되게 표현하는

He made effusive remarks about his victory.

syn. overenthusiastic, gushing, exuberant

egregious

[ih-**gree**-j*uhs*]

adj. extraordinary in some bad way

지독한, 엄청나게 나쁜

He must have had an egregious ailment.

syn. outrageous, notorious, atrocious

ISEE Sentence Completion 4-1

Directions : **Fill in the blanks to complete the sentences.**

1. She refused to _____ the secret, keeping her friend's confidence intact.

   (A) divulge   (B) divert
   (C) dubious   (D) dogmatic

2. The scientist questioned the _____ claim, as it lacked any supporting evidence.

   (A) edifice   (B) divert
   (C) eavesdrop   (D) dubious

3. Her _____ personality made her stand out in a crowd and left a lasting impression on everyone she met.

   (A) edifice   (B) eccentric
   (C) ecumenical   (D) dubious

4. The ancient city was known for its grand _____, which showcased its architectural brilliance.

   (A) edifice   (B) divert
   (C) egregious   (D) dubious

5. The lawyer pointed out the _____ mistake in the contract, which could have led to major financial losses.

   (A) dogmatic   (B) eccentric
   (C) divulge   (D) egregious

1. (A) 2. (D) 3. (B) 4. (A) 5. (D)

Answers

161	elated	166	embellish
162	eloquent	167	embezzle
163	elucidate	168	eminent
164	elusive	169	empathy
165	emancipate	170	emphatic

School Motto

"Virtus Scientia"

(Virtue through knowledge)

- Hockaday School

SSATKOREA.com

elucidate
[ih-**loo**-si-deyt]

v. to make lucid or explain clearly

명확히 해명하다, 명쾌하게 설명하다

*Please **elucidate** the reasons for your decision.*

syn. explain, clarify, illuminate

elusive
[ih-**loo**-siv]

adj. hard to express or define

규정하기 힘든, 찾기 힘든, 애매한

*The answers to these questions remain as **elusive** as ever.*

syn. evasive, mysterious, puzzling

elated
[ih-**ley**-tid]

adj. very happy or proud

기분 좋은, 신난, 행복한

*It was like waking from a beautiful dream and feeling so **elated**.*

syn. overjoyed, ecstatic, exhilarated

emancipate
[ih-**man**-suh-peyt]

v. to free from restraint, influence, or the like

풀어주다, 자유롭게 하다

*That war preserved the Union and **emancipated** the slaves.*

syn. liberate, free, release

eloquent
[**el**-uh-kw*uh*nt]

adj. exercising the power of fluent speech

웅변을 잘하는, 말솜씨가 유창한

*Ellen, in interviews, was **eloquent**, to the point, and assured.*

syn. articulate, expressive, persuasive

embellish
[em-**bel**-ish]

v. to beautify by or as if by ornamentation

장식하다, 아름답게 만들다

*You can **embellish** the front of the door with Ivy leaves.*

syn. decorate, adorn, deck

embezzle

[em-**bez**-*uhl*]

v. to appropriate fraudulently to one's own use.

횡령하다, 남의 재물을 불법으로 가지다

*He **embezzled** thousands of dollars from the charity.*

syn. misappropriate, loot, steal

eminent

[**em**-uh-n*uh*nt]

adj. high in station, rank, or repute

저명한, 유명한

*She is **eminent** both as a writer and as a painter.*

syn. renowned, distinguished, prominent

empathy

[**em**-puh-thee]

n. understanding and entering into another's feelings

공감, 감정이입

*She had a lot of **empathy** for men, and the social pressures that they go through.*

syn. understanding, insight, sympathy

emphatic

[em-**fat**-ik]

adj. forceful and definite in expression or action

단호한, 강조하는

*His response was immediate and **emphatic**.*

syn. forceful, assertive, vehement

ISEE Sentence Completion 4-2

Directions : **Fill in the blanks to complete the sentences.**

1. The politician delivered an _____ speech that captivated the audience.

   (A) elated   (B) emphatic
   (C) eloquent   (D) elusive

2. The accountant was fired after attempting to _____ company funds for personal use.

   (A) embezzle   (B) emancipate
   (C) elusive   (D) eloquent

3. The teacher took extra time to _____ the concept for students struggling to understand it.

   (A) emancipate   (B) embellish
   (C) elucidate   (D) elated

4. The answer to the mystery remained _____, no matter how hard they searched for clues.

   (A) eloquent   (B) empathy
   (C) eminent   (D) elusive

5. The coach made an _____ statement about the importance of teamwork during the game.

   (A) emphatic   (B) embellish
   (C) elusive   (D) eminent

1. (C)   2. (A)   3. (C)   4. (D)   5. (A)

Answers

171 endeavor	176 equilibrium
172 enigma	177 equitable
173 enrage	178 equivocal
174 entourage	179 evict
175 enunciate	180 exalt

School Motto

"Pro Deo et Genere Humano"

(For God and Humankind)

- Holderness School

SSATKOREA.com

endeavor
[en-**dev**-er]

v. to make an effort

노력하다, 애쓰다

*We will always **endeavor** to offer you our most favorable things.*

syn. attempt, effort, pursuit

enigma
[uh-**nig**-muh]

n. a puzzling occurrence

수수께끼

*Phoenix has always been an **enigma** to me.*

syn. mystery, puzzle, riddle

enrage
[en-**reyj**]

v. to make extremely angry

격분하다, 분노하나

*Attempting to reason with **enraged** people may only enrage them more.*

syn. infuriate, anger, irritate

entourage
[ahn-too-**rahzh**]

n. a group of attendants

(중요인물 주변의) 수행원들, 측근자들

*The president visited China with his **entourage**.*

syn. attendants, associates, staff

enunciate
[ih-**nuhn**-see-eyt]

v. to pronounce words clearly

말하다, 발음하다

*Speak out loud, and **enunciate** clearly.*

syn. articulate, speak clearly

equilibrium
[ee-kwuh-**lib**-ree-*uh*m]

n. a state of rest or balance

평형(균형) 상태

*The body's state of **equilibrium** can be disturbed by stress.*

syn. balance, poise, stability

equitable

[ek-wi-tuh-b*uhl*]

adj. fair and impartial

공정한, 공평한

*Are dental charges **equitable** and appropriate?*

syn.   fair, just, unbiased

equivocal

[ih-**kwiv**-uh-k*uhl*]

adj. allowing the possibility of several different meanings

모호한

*Dad gave mom an **equivocal** answer.*

syn.   ambiguous, uncertain, vague

evict

[ih-**vikt**]

v. to expel someone from a property

쫓아내다, 퇴거시키다

*We haven't paid the rent, and the landlord may **evict** us.*

syn.   banish, oust, expel

exalt

[ig-**zawlt**]

v. to praise highly

대단히 칭송하다, 매우 칭찬하다.

*The theater critics **exalt** the young actor.*

syn.   glorify, praise, elevate

ISEE Sentence Completion 4-3

Directions : Fill in the blanks to complete the sentences.

1. The celebrity arrived at the event with a large _____ of assistants and friends.

   (A) enigma   (B) endeavor
   (C) entourage   (D) equivocal

2. The landlord had no choice but to _____ the tenant for failing to pay rent for several months.

   (A) evict   (B) enrage
   (C) equitable   (D) endeavor

3. The detective struggled to solve the _____ that surrounded the mysterious disappearance.

   (A) endeavor   (B) enigma
   (C) equivocal   (D) evict

4. After being accused of an unfair statement, the speaker's response was vague and _____, leaving the audience confused.

   (A) equilibrium   (B) enunciate
   (C) evict   (D) equivocal

5. Yoga is said to help maintain a state of mental and physical _____, promoting overall well-being.

   (A) entourage   (B) enigma
   (C) equilibrium   (D) equivocal

💭 *Answers*

1. (C)   2. (A)   3. (B)   4. (D)   5. (C)

MIDDLE

1 2 3 4 5 6 7 8 9 10

UPPER

1 2 3 4 5 6 7 8 9 10

181 excruciating   186 extol

182 exculpate   187 extort

183 exhilarate   188 fabricate

184 exorbitant   189 fallow

185 explicate   190 fanciful

School Motto

"Whatsoever things are true"

- Lake Forest Academy

SSATKOREA.com

excruciating
[ik-**skroo**-shee-ey-ting]

adj. extremely painful
몹시 고통스러운, 극심한

*The pain was so **excruciating** that talking was difficult for the man.*

syn. torturous, painful, severe

exculpate
[**ek**-sk*uh*l-peyt]

v. to clear from a charge of guilt
무죄를 입증하다

*He was **exculpated** by the testimony of several witnesses.*

syn. excuse, justify, acquit

exhilarate
[ig-**zil**-uh-reyt]

v. to make someone feel very happy or elated
아주 기쁘게 만들다

*Car racing had **exhilarated** him.*

syn. excite, thrill, energize

exorbitant
[ig-**zawr**-bi-t*uh*nt]

adj. unreasonably high
과도한, 지나친

*The price of bottled water has become **exorbitant**.*

syn. excessive, overpriced, unreasonable

explicate
[**ek**-spli-keyt]

v. to make plain or clear
설명하다, 해석하다

*The scientist did his best to **explicate** the complex theory of the universe.*

syn. clarify, expand, untangle

extol
[ik-**stohl**]

v. to praise highly
극찬하다, 크게 칭찬하다

*He was **extolled** as a hero.*

syn. commend, praise, laud

extort
[ik-**stawrt**]

v. to obtain something by force or threats

갈취하다, 힘이나 나쁜 방법으로 뺏다

*The gang **extorted** money from several local businesses.*

syn. blackmail, cheat, wring

fabricate
[**fab**-ri-keyt]

v. to invent something typically with deceitful intent

조작하다, 위조하다

*The evidence was totally **fabricated**.*

syn. falsify, deceive, mislead

fallow
[**fal**-oh]

adj. left unsown for a period or unused

농지를 사용하지 않고 있는, 휴경지의

*Farmers let their lands lie **fallow**.*

syn. unused, resting, uncultivated

fanciful
[**fan**-si-f*uh*l]

adj. playfully unusual or overly imaginative

기발한, 독창적인

*The **fanciful** painting showed animals wearing hats.*

syn. whimsical, imaginative, unrealistic

ISEE Sentence Completion 4-4

Directions : Fill in the blanks to complete the sentences.

1. The reporter was accused of trying to _____ a story to attract more readers.

   (A) extort   (B) extol
   (C) fabricate   (D) exhilarate

2. In her speech, she sought to _____ the virtues of kindness and compassion to inspire others.

   (A) extol   (B) exhilarate
   (C) fallow   (D) fanciful

3. The lawyer worked hard to _____ the suspect by providing evidence of their innocence.

   (A) exhilarate   (B) explicate
   (C) extort   (D) exculpate

4. The professor took time to _____ the complex theory, breaking it down for the students.

   (A) exculpate   (B) explicate
   (C) fabricate   (D) extol

5. Many shoppers complained about the _____ prices of luxury goods at the new store.

   (A) extort   (B) fanciful
   (C) fallow   (D) exorbitant

Answers

1. (C) 2. (A) 3. (D) 4. (B) 5. (D)

191 tatigue	196 finesse
192 feasible	197 fluctuate
193 feign	198 galvanize
194 fiasco	199 garrulous
195 fickle	200 glut

School Motto

"Virtus Semper Viridis"
(Virtue Always Green)
- Lawrenceville School

SSATKOREA.com

fatigue
[fuh-**teeg**]

n. weariness from bodily or mental exertion

피로, 피로감

A bar of chocolate relieved her fatigue.

syn. exhaustion, tiredness, weariness

feasible
[**fee**-zuh-b*uh*l]

adj. capable of being done, effected, or accomplished

실현가능한

Do you think this project is feasible?

syn. possible, suitable, reasonable

feign
[feyn]

v. to represent fictitiously

가장하다, ~인 척하다

Some animals feign death when in danger.

syn. pretend, affect, fake

fiasco
[fee-**as**-koh]

n. a complete and ignominious failure

대 실패, 큰 실패

The enemy's plot ended in a fiasco.

syn. failure, disaster, debacle

fickle
[**fik**-*uh*l]

adj. likely to change

변덕스러운

The weather in this island is notoriously fickle.

syn. capricious, mercurial, whimsical

finesse
[fi-**ness**]

n. intricate and refined delicacy or skill

예리한 솜씨, 수완, 기교

He shows finesse in dealing with people.

syn. gimmick, maneuver, acumen

fluctuate

[**fluhk**-choo-eyt]

v. to change frequently between different levels or conditions unpredictably

변동하다, 오르내리다, 불규칙하게 변하다

The temperature tends to fluctuate a lot during spring, making it hard to choose what to wear.

syn. vary, oscillate, change

galvanize

[**gal**-v*uh*-nahyz]

v. to shock or excite someone into action

충격을 주거나 자극하여 행동하게 하다

The speech galvanized the students to start their new project.

syn. energize, motivate, inspire

garrulous

[**gar**-uh-l*uh*s]

adj. excessively talkative in a rambling manner

수다스러운, 말이 많은

The crowd grew garrulous before the speaker arrived.

syn. talkative, verbose, voluble

glut

[gluht]

n. an excessively abundant supply of something

과잉, 넘쳐나는 것

The potato glut is a real issue, and many farmers are dismayed.

syn. surplus, surfeit, excess, oversupply

ISEE Sentence Completion 4-5

Directions : Fill in the blanks to complete the sentences.

1. Their _____ neighbor often delayed conversations with long-winded and unnecessary stories.

   (A) garrulous   (B) fatigue
   (C) feign   (D) fiasco

2. The stock prices continued to _____ wildly, making investors anxious.

   (A) glut   (B) feign
   (C) fluctuate   (D) fatigue

3. After working for ten hours straight, he began to feel extreme _____ and needed rest.

   (A) fiasco   (B) fatigue
   (C) finesse   (D) feasible

4. The committee discussed whether the proposal was a _____ plan given the current budget constraints.

   (A) feasible   (B) fickle
   (C) galvanize   (D) fluctuate

5. She tried to _____ illness to avoid attending the meeting, but her boss saw through the act.

   (A) finesse   (B) fatigue
   (C) feign   (D) glut

Analogy 14. Action & Emotion

인간의 표정, 행동이 어떤 마음이나 감정을 표현하는지 매칭하는 문제 유형입니다.

A는 B를 표현하는 행동

grin : delight
싱긋 웃다 : 기쁨

frown : disgust
찡그리다 : 혐오

nod : assent
끄덕이다 : 동의

laughter : mirth
소리내어 웃다 : 즐거움

yawn : boredom
하품하다 : 지겨움

grumble : discontentment
투덜대다 : 불만

aplomb : confidence
침착함 : 자신감

cringe : fear
웅크리다 : 두려움

perspire : heat
땀 흘리다 : 더위

shiver : cold
떨다 : 추위

embrace : affection
껴안다 : 애정, 애착

sob : sorrow
흐느끼다, 울다 : 슬픔

salute : respect
경례하다 : 존경

jeer : contempt
비웃다 : 경멸

obeisance : submission
절하다, 머리 숙이다 : 복종

retort : defiance
말대꾸하다 : 반항

1. Grin is to delight as
   (A) aplomb is to excitement
   (B) jeer is to condolence
   (C) grumble is to inquiry
   (D) frown is to disgust
   (E) nod is to disapproval

2. Cringe is to fear as
   (A) salute is to respect
   (B) kneel is to defiance
   (C) shiver is to hot
   (D) perspire is to cold
   (E) shrug is to assent

Check-up 4-1

Directions   Each of the following questions consists of one word followed by five words or phrases.
You are to select the one word or phrase whose meaning is closest to the word in capital letters.

1. DIVERT
(A) badger
(B) segregate
(C) entertain
(D) starve
(E) appease

2. DIVULGE
(A) abandon
(B) burnish
(C) plunder
(D) debunk
(E) occupy

3. DOGMATIC
(A) luscious
(B) fruitful
(C) habitual
(D) cunning
(E) dictatorial

4. DUBIOUS
(A) adept
(B) capricious
(C) fearless
(D) doubtful
(E) tractable

5. EAVESDROP
(A) grumble
(B) baffle
(C) constrain
(D) snoop
(E) hail

6. ECCENTRIC
(A) benign
(B) unconventional
(C) misleading
(D) passionate
(E) avid

7. ECUMENICAL
(A) loaded
(B) triumphant
(C) universal
(D) laden
(E) perpetual

8. EDIFICE
(A) huge construction
(B) unusual idea
(C) social
(D) ancient form
(E) talkative person

9. EFFUSIVE
(A) overenthusiastic
(B) practical
(C) refined
(D) tacit
(E) amiable

10. EGREGIOUS
(A) harmful
(B) erratic
(C) productive
(D) outrageous
(E) guarded

243

Check-up 4-2

Each of the following questions consists of one word followed by five words or phrases. You are to select the one word or phrase whose meaning is closest to the word in capital letters.

1. ELATED
(A) overjoyed
(B) derogatory
(C) genial
(D) pertinent
(E) twisted

2. ELOQUENT
(A) covetous
(B) articulate
(C) magnificent
(D) hackneyed
(E) untamed

3. ELUCIDATE
(A) hesitate
(B) irritate
(C) explain
(D) hasten
(E) isolate

4. ELUSIVE
(A) heterogeneous
(B) evasive
(C) dormant
(D) tranquil
(E) hedonistic

5. EMANCIPATE
(A) shun
(B) liberate
(C) endow
(D) jabber
(E) litigate

6. EMBELLISH
(A) invade
(B) loathe
(C) commove
(D) arouse
(E) decorate

7. EMBEZZLE
(A) feign
(B) abhor
(C) hamper
(D) encroach
(E) misappropriate

8. EMINENT
(A) nimble
(B) inundated
(C) renowned
(D) intoxicating
(E) sobering

9. EMPATHY
(A) dilemma
(B) adversary
(C) neophyte
(D) understanding
(E) paradigm

10. EMPHATIC
(A) frivolous
(B) forceful
(C) hazardous
(D) agonizing
(E) furtive

Check-up 4-3

Directions   Each of the following questions consists of one word followed by five words or phrases.
You are to select the one word or phrase whose meaning is closest to the word in capital letters.

1. ENDEAVOR
(A) provoke
(B) attempt
(C) consider
(D) afflict
(E) illuminate

2. ENIGMA
(A) agility
(B) sanction
(C) exemplar
(D) mystery
(E) epoch

3. ENRAGE
(A) engage
(B) meander
(C) exhaust
(D) infuriate
(E) dwell

4. ENTOURAGE
(A) cascade
(B) loyalty
(C) attendants
(D) figment
(E) salute

5. ENUNCIATE
(A) babble
(B) articulate
(C) deceive
(D) enlarge
(E) beseech

6. EQUILIBRIUM
(A) fickleness
(B) epiphany
(C) fiasco
(D) balance
(E) epitome

7. EQUITABLE
(A) unreasonable
(B) fair
(C) fiscal
(D) biased
(E) dauntless

8. EQUIVOCAL
(A) flamboyant
(B) ambivalent
(C) vacant
(D) finicky
(E) ambiguous

9. EVICT
(A) blandish
(B) brandish
(C) relish
(D) polish
(E) banish

10. EXALT
(A) appease
(B) burgeon
(C) scowl
(D) fulfill
(E) glorify

Check-up 4-4

Directions   Each of the following questions consists of one word followed by five words or phrases. You are to select the one word or phrase whose meaning is closest to the word in capital letters.

1. EXCRUCIATING
- (A) extreme
- (B) torturous
- (C) glib
- (D) hypnotic
- (E) impromptu

2. EXCULPATE
- (A) broach
- (B) glance
- (C) dissent
- (D) separate
- (E) excuse

3. EXHILARATE
- (A) fumble
- (B) glower
- (C) excite
- (D) harass
- (E) imitate

4. EXORBITANT
- (A) deferential
- (B) excessive
- (C) laudatory
- (D) heinous
- (E) juvenile

5. EXPLICATE
- (A) oust
- (B) clarify
- (C) applaud
- (D) convey
- (E) excel

6. EXTOL
- (A) endure
- (B) commend
- (C) linger
- (D) speculate
- (E) perjury

7. EXTORT
- (A) mar
- (B) extract
- (C) lubricate
- (D) concede
- (E) blackmail

8. FABRICATE
- (A) intercede
- (B) permeate
- (C) invoke
- (D) falsify
- (E) placate

9. FALLOW
- (A) concise
- (B) unused
- (C) diverse
- (D) finite
- (E) limber

10. FANCIFUL
- (A) convoluted
- (B) ineffable
- (C) whimsical
- (D) lucrative
- (E) immutable

246

Check-up 4-5

Directions   Each of the following questions consists of one word followed by five words or phrases. You are to select the one word or phrase whose meaning is closest to the word in capital letters.

1. FATIGUE
- (A) exhaustion
- (B) hovel
- (C) genesis
- (D) moniker
- (E) impediment

2. FEASIBLE
- (A) irrelevant
- (B) baleful
- (C) malicious
- (D) truthful
- (E) possible

3. FEIGN
- (A) holler
- (B) mitigate
- (C) pretend
- (D) cancel
- (E) amass

4. FIASCO
- (A) failure
- (B) artifice
- (C) plateau
- (D) reverence
- (E) hue

5. FICKLE
- (A) temporary
- (B) ephemeral
- (C) obsolete
- (D) capricious
- (E) self-possessed

6. FINESSE
- (A) opulence
- (B) maxim
- (C) gimmick
- (D) alias
- (E) pioneer

7. FLUCTUATE
- (A) crave
- (B) abhor
- (C) employ
- (D) reproach
- (E) vary

8. GALVANIZE
- (A) taper
- (B) energize
- (C) prolong
- (D) ooze
- (E) enervate

9. GARRULOUS
- (A) talkative
- (B) outlandish
- (C) ignorant
- (D) sophisticated
- (E) ponderous

10. GLUT
- (A) gallantry
- (B) egress
- (C) surplus
- (D) repository
- (E) fortress

Answer: 1.A 2.E 3.C 4.A 5.D 6.C 7.E 8.B 9.A 10.C

201 gregarious   206 haggard

202 grimace   207 hallucination

203 grief   208 haphazard

204 gullible   209 hapless

205 hackneyed   210 haughty

School Motto

"Festina Lente"

(Make haste slowly)

- Madeira School

SSATKOREA.com

gregarious
[gri-**gair**-ee-uhs]

adj. fond of the company of others

사교적인, 다른 사람과 잘 어울리는

He is such a gregarious and outgoing person.

syn. sociable, amiable, affable

grimace
[**grim**-uhs]

n. a ugly or contortion, frown scowl

찡그린 표정

James' face formed a grimace when the dentist drilled into his tooth.

syn. contortion, frown scowl

grief
[greef]

n. intense sadness

슬픔, 비탄

He was overcome with grief and needed time to heal.

syn. sorrow, mourning, heartache

gullible
[**guhl**-uh-b*uh*l]

adj. easily fooled or deceived

남을 잘 믿는, 잘 속아 넘어가는

Sylvia's parents were worried that people might take advantage of their gullible daughter.

syn. credulous, ingenuous, innocent

hackneyed
[**hak**-need]

adj. repeated too often

진부한, 너무 많이 반복된

She doesn't like the hackneyed plots of television sit-coms.

syn. banal, commonplace, trite, clichéd

haggard
[**hag**-erd]

adj. having a gaunt, wasted, or exhausted appearance

수척한, 삐쩍 마른

The homeless man had a worn-out, haggard appearance.

syn. gaunt, emaciated, worn-looking

hallucination

[huh-loo-suh-**ney**-shuhn]

n. illusory perception

환각, 환영

A person experiencing a hallucination perceives things that aren't really there.

syn. delusion, mirage, illusion

haphazard

[hap-**haz**-erd]

adj. characterized by lack of order or planning

무계획적인, 되는 대로의

Files have been stored in such a haphazard manner that they are impossible to find.

syn. random, unorganized, chaotic

hapless

[**hap**-lis]

adj. unlucky or unfortunate

불운한, 불쌍한

Many children are hapless victims of the war.

syn. unlucky, luckless, unfortunate

haughty

[**haw**-tee]

adj. disdainfully proud

거만한, 오만한

She gave him a haughty look and walked away.

syn. arrogant, conceited, pompous

ISEE Sentence Completion 5-1

Directions : Fill in the blanks to complete the sentences.

1. Her _____ attitude towards her colleagues made her unpopular at work.

   (A) haphazard   (B) haughty
   (C) gregarious   (D) hackneyed

2. The scammer tricked the _____ customer into buying fake luxury goods.

   (A) gullible   (B) gregarious
   (C) haughty   (D) hapless

3. Her cheerful and _____ personality made her the life of every party.

   (A) haggard   (B) gullible
   (C) haughty   (D) gregarious

4. The office had a _____ organization, with papers and files scattered everywhere.

   (A) haphazard   (B) hackneyed
   (C) hapless   (D) haughty

5. The politician's speech was filled with _____ phrases, failing to make any real impact.

   (A) hallucination (B) haphazard
   (C) haggard   (D) hackneyed

MIDDLE 1 2 3 4 5 6 7 8 9 10

UPPER 1 2 3 4 5 6 7 8 9 10

211 hilarious	216 immerse
212 homogenous	217 imminent
213 idiosyncratic	218 impart
214 ignite	219 implicate
215 immaculate	220 implicit

School Motto

"Do It With Thy Might"

- Masters School

SSATKOREA.com

hilarious
[hi-**lair**-ee-*uh*s]

adj. extremely funny

아주 우스운, 정말 웃긴

*The movie was so **hilarious** that the entire audience couldn't stop laughing.*

syn. funny, comical, amusing

homogenous
[huh-**moj**-uh-nuhs]

adj. all of the same or similar kind or nature

같은 종류의, 동질의

*Stir the chemicals in the beaker until they become a **homogenous** mixture.*

syn. identical, uniform, akin

idiosyncratic
[id-ee-oh-sin-**krat**-ik]

adj. strange or peculiar

특이한, 특유한, 색다른

*Wearing two different socks was his **idiosyncratic** habit.*

syn. quirky, peculiar, eccentric

ignite
[ig-**nahyt**]

v. to set on fire

점화하다, 불을 붙이다

*A lightning strike **ignited** the forest fire.*

syn. kindle, set fire, light

immaculate
[ih-**mak**-yuh-lit]

adj. free from spot or stain

티 하나 없이 깔끔한, 완벽한

*Nancy's room must be **immaculate** before she can start studying.*

syn. impeccable, perfect, pure

immerse
[ih-**murs**]

v. to plunge into or place under a liquid

액체에 담그다

***Immerse** your sore ankle in a bowl of cold water.*

syn. submerge, sink, dip

imminent
[**im**-uh-nuhnt]

adj. about to happen

곧 닥칠, 임박한

*Judging by those dark clouds, rain is **imminent**.*

syn. impending, approaching, forthcoming

impart
[im-**pahrt**]

v. to make known

알리다, 전하다

*He **imparts** the secret to me.*

syn. tell, relate, reveal

implicate
[**im**-pli-keyt]

v. to show to be also involved

(범죄 등에) 연루되었음을 보여주다, 관련시키다

*Fingerprints on the weapon **implicated** Harold in the crime.*

syn. involve, relate to, connect with

implicit
[im-**plis**-it]

adj. implied, rather than expressly stated

암시된, 내포된

*Although they never discussed it, they had an **implicit** understanding.*

syn. implied, unspoken, inherent

ISEE Sentence Completion 5-2

Directions : Fill in the blanks to complete the sentences.

1. The inspirational speech managed to _____ a passion for learning in the students.

   (A) ignite   (B) implicate
   (C) immerse   (D) homogenous

2. The comedy was so _____ that the entire audience couldn't stop laughing throughout the movie.

   (A) implicit   (B) hilarious
   (C) immaculate   (D) immerse

3. His _____ habit of tapping his pen constantly annoyed his coworkers.

   (A) immaculate   (B) implicit
   (C) idiosyncratic   (D) hilarious

4. The weather report warned of _____ danger from the approaching hurricane.

   (A) imminent   (B) idiosyncratic
   (C) hilarious   (D) homogenous

5. A good teacher aims to _____ not just facts but also a love for knowledge to their students.

   (A) ignite   (B) immerse
   (C) impart   (D) implicate

Answers

1. (A) 2. (B) 3. (C) 4. (A) 5. (C)

221 impoverished 226 incumbent

222 incarcerate 227 indefatigable

223 incessant 228 indict

224 incite 229 indifferent

225 incompatible 230 indigent

School Motto

"Integritas, Virilitas, Fidelitas"

(Integrity, Virility, Fidelity)

- Mercersburg Academy

SSATKOREA.com

impoverished
[im-**pov**-er-isht]

adj. reduced to poverty

빈곤한, 결핍된

Many families became impoverished during the Great Depression.

syn. destitute, indigent, poor

incarcerate
[in-**kahr**-suh-reyt]

v. to lock up or confine, in or as in a jail

가두다, 투옥하다

After Mr. Smith was found guilty, he became incarcerated.

syn. imprison, confine, jail

incessant
[in-**ses**-uhnt]

adj. continuing without interruption

끊임없는, 계속되는

The incessant chatter among the students gave the teacher a headache.

syn. uninterrupted, ceaseless, unending

incite
[in-**sahyt**]

v. to stir, encourage, or urge on

자극하다, 선동하다

The cheers from the crowd incited the team to perform better.

syn. instigate, provoke, agitate

incompatible
[in-kuhm-**pat**-uh-b*uh*l]

adj. unable to exist together in harmony

공존할 수 없는, 호환성이 없는

Gail and Charlie broke up because they were incompatible.

syn. conflicting, mismatched, irreconcilable

incumbent
[in-**kuhm**-buhnt]

adj. holding an indicated position or role currently

현직의, 재직중인

The incumbent senator hopes to maintain her position.

syn. official, current, in office

indefatigable

[in-di-**fat**-i-guh-b*uh*l]

adj. incapable of being tired out

지치지 않는, 포기할 줄 모르는

*The **indefatigable** guide walked all day long.*

syn. tireless, persistent, unrelenting

indict

[in-**dahyt**]

v. to accuse formally of a crime

기소하다, 법원에 심판을 요구하다

*The grand jury **indicted** him for murder.*

syn. accuse, arraign, charge

indifferent

[in-**dif**-er-uhnt]

adj. showing no interest

무관심한

*People have become **indifferent** to the suffering of others.*

syn. apathetic, disinterested, aloof

indigent

[in-di-juhnt]

adj. lacking food or clothing because of poverty

가난한, 빈곤한

*Because she was **indigent**, the court appointed a lawyer to defend her.*

syn. impoverished, needy, poor

ISEE Sentence Completion 5-3

Directions : Fill in the blanks to complete the sentences.

1. The charity's mission was to provide clean water to the _____ village that lacked basic necessities.

   (A) indefatigable   (B) indifferent
   (C) indict   (D) impoverished

2. Their arguments stemmed from holding fundamentally _____ ideas about how the project should proceed.

   (A) incompatible   (B) incessant
   (C) incumbent   (D) indigent

3. It is _____ upon parents to ensure their children receive proper education.

   (A) indifferent   (B) incumbent
   (C) indefatigable   (D) indict

4. The _____ worker continued tirelessly despite the long hours and challenging conditions.

   (A) incompatible   (B) impoverished
   (C) incessant   (D) indefatigable

5. The grand jury chose to _____ the businessman for fraud after gathering substantial evidence.

   (A) incite   (B) indict
   (C) incarcerate   (D) indigent

231 indulgent   236 innocuous

232 infallible   237 insightful

233 inferno   238 integral

234 ingenious   239 interim

235 ingenuous   240 intermittent

School Motto

"Fides, Veritas, Labor"

(Faith, Truth, Effort)

- Middlesex School

SSATKOREA.com

indulgent
[in-**duhl**-j*uh*nt]

adj. showing excessive kindness or tolerance

지나치게 허용하는, 응석을 받아주는

Indulgent parents sometimes spoil their children unintentionally.

syn. permissive, lenient, tolerant

infallible
[in-**fal**-uh-b*uh*l]

adj. absolutely trustworthy or sure

틀림없는, 절대 확실한

No one is completely infallible.

syn. unerring, flawless, perfect

inferno
[in-**fur**-noh]

n. a place of great fire or destruction

거대한 화재, 지옥 같은 곳

The kitchen turned into an inferno when the stove caught fire.

syn. conflagration, blaze, firestorm

ingenious
[in-**jeen**-yuhs]

adj. very clever or creative

기발한, 독창적인

Jerry came up with an ingenious plan to raise funds for charity.

syn. inventive, creative, clever

ingenuous
[in-**jen**-yoo-uhs]

adj. naturally simple and artless

순진한, 솔직한, 꾸밈없는

The ingenuous man was tricked by the quack selling fake medicine.

syn. artless, innocent, naive

innocuous
[ih-**nok**-yoo-uhs]

adj. not harmful or injurious

무해한, 악의 없는

These mushrooms look innocuous but are in fact deadly.

syn. harmless, innocent, inoffensive

insightful
[**in**-sahyt-f*uh*l]

adj. characterized by or displaying insight, perceptive

통찰력 있는

The points in your essay were very insightful.

syn. discerning, perceptive, astute

integral
[**in**-ti-gr*uh*l]

adj. essential to the whole

필수적인, 필수불가결한

A strong thesis and clear topic sentences are integral to a successful essay.

syn. essential, vital, indispensable

interim
[**in**-ter-uhm]

adj. temporary or provisional

임시의, 잠정적인

We used an interim solution to fix the problem while waiting for expert help.

syn. provisional, temporary, tentative

intermittent
[in-ter-**mit**-nt]

adj. alternately ceasing and beginning again

간헐적인, 간간이 일어나는

We will have intermittent surprise quizzes in this class.

syn. sporadic, episodic, periodic

ISEE Sentence Completion 5-4

Directions : Fill in the blanks to complete the sentences.

1. The _____ parent often gave in to their child's every demand, rarely setting boundaries.

   (A) integral   (B) ingenious
   (C) indulgent   (D) ingenuous

2. His argument was based on _____ logic, leaving no room for error or doubt.

   (A) intermittent   (B) innocuous
   (C) interim   (D) infallible

3. The firefighters worked tirelessly to contain the raging _____ that consumed the building.

   (A) integral   (B) insightful
   (C) inferno   (D) indulgent

4. The _____ invention revolutionized the way people communicated across long distances.

   (A) ingenious   (B) ingenuous
   (C) innocuous   (D) infallible

5. The _____ rain disrupted outdoor events, as it came and went without warning.

   (A) insightful   (B) innocuous
   (C) intermittent   (D) indulgent

Answers
1. (C) 2. (D) 3. (C) 4. (A) 5. (C)

241 intervene	246 isolated
242 intrepid	247 jeer
243 intricate	248 jovial
244 intuition	249 judicious
245 invigorate	250 jurisdiction

School Motto

"Non Sibi Sed Cunctis"

(Not for oneself, but for all)

- Millbrook School

SSATKOREA.com

intervene
[in-ter-**veen**]

v. to come between disputing people or groups

끼어들다, 개입하다

He intervened in a heated argument between two of his friends.

syn. mediate, arbitrate, interlope

intrepid
[in-**tre**-pid]

adj. resolutely fearless

용감한, 두려움을 모르는

My intrepid grandfather was always brave and bold.

syn. valiant, dauntless, courageous

intricate
[**in**-tri-kit]

adj. hard to understand, work, or make

복잡한, 난해한

The plot of that novel was too intricate to keep track of.

syn. complicated, complex, difficult

intuition
[in-too-**ish**-uhn]

n. direct perception of truth

직관, 직각

Tara made decisions based on her intuition rather than on known facts.

syn. instinct, hunch, insight

invigorate
[in-**vig**-uh-reyt]

v. to give strength or energy to something or someone

기운나게 하다, 활기차게 하다

Drinking cold water invigorated him.

syn. stimulate, energize, enliven

isolated
[**ahy**-suh-ley-tid]

adj. separated from other persons or things

외떨어진, 외딴, 고립된

He was isolated from all the other prisoners.

syn. remote, solitary, lonely

jeer

[jeer]

v. to speak or shout derisively

조소하다, 조롱하다

The crowd jeered him when he missed several shots in a row.

syn. sneer, ridicule, scoff

jovial

[**joh**-vee-*uhl*]

adj. endowed with or characterized by a joyous humor

쾌활한, 명랑한, 즐거운

Santa Claus is depicted as a large, jovial man with a white beard.

syn. cheerful, happy, jolly

judicious

[joo-**dish**-uhs]

adj. showing good judgment

현명한

We should make judicious use of the resources available to us.

syn. prudent, sensible, discreet

jurisdiction

[joor-is-**dik**-shuhn]

n. the extent of right or power to administer justice

관할권, 사법권

A police officer from Canada does not have jurisdiction to arrest someone in America.

syn. authority, control, power

ISEE Sentence Completion 5-5

Directions : Fill in the blanks to complete the sentences.

1. The motivational speech managed to _____ the team, boosting their morale before the big game.

   (A) intervene (B) jeer
   (C) invigorate (D) jurisdiction

2. Some fans began to _____ at the player after a series of mistakes during the game.

   (A) jeer (B) invigorate
   (C) intervene (D) intuition

3. The police stated that the crime occurred outside their _____, limiting their ability to act.

   (A) intuition (B) intervene
   (C) jurisdiction (D) invigorate

4. The holiday party was filled with laughter and a _____ atmosphere that brought everyone together.

   (A) jeer (B) isolated
   (C) intricate (D) jovial

5. The manager emphasized the _____ use of resources to ensure the project stayed within budget.

   (A) judicious (B) jovial
   (C) intricate (D) intrepid

Analogy 15. List & Collection

하나하나가 모여 만들어진 전체를 연결시키는 문제입니다. 문제가 많이 나오지는 않아도 빠지지 않고 출세되는 유형이지요.

menu : food
메뉴 : 음식

catalog : goods
카탈로그 : 물품

cookbook : recipe
요리책 : 조리법

atlas : map
지도책 : 지도

receipt : item
영수증 : 구매 품목

lexicon : word
어휘집, 사전 : 단어

suite : tune
모음곡 : 곡, 음악

anthology : work
문집, 작품 모음집 : 작품

manifest : cargo
화물 목록 : 화물

ledger : transaction
장부 : 거래

inventory : merchandise
재고목록 : 상품

index : topic
색인 : 주제

roster : name
명단 : 이름

tally : sum
(총계나 총액을 누적해나가는) 기록 : 총합

bibliography : book
참고 문헌 : 책

program : performance
프로그램 : 공연

POP QUIZ

1. Suite is to tune as
(A) anthology is to work
(B) inventory is to debt
(C) roster is to transaction
(D) tally is to tale
(E) cookbook is to deed

2. Index is to topic as
(A) menu is to diner
(B) receipt is to customer
(C) catalog is to shopper
(D) atlas is to chart
(E) lexicon is to word

Check-up 5-1

Directions — Each of the following questions consists of one word followed by five words or phrases. You are to select the one word or phrase whose meaning is closest to the word in capital letters.

1. GREGARIOUS
(A) sociable
(B) abject
(C) callous
(D) enervated
(E) hapless

2. GRIMACE
(A) empathy
(B) contortion
(C) retaliation
(D) surfeit
(E) travesty

3. GRIEF
(A) belief
(B) tune
(C) sorrow
(D) feature
(E) elegy

4. GULLIBLE
(A) pithy
(B) noxious
(C) credulous
(D) magnanimous
(E) lithe

5. HACKNEYED
(A) complicit
(B) algid
(C) envious
(D) banal
(E) gluttonous

6. HAGGARD
(A) irascible
(B) harrowing
(C) familial
(D) divisive
(E) gaunt

7. HALLUCINATION
(A) indignation
(B) delusion
(C) modicum
(D) penchant
(E) repose

8. HAPHAZARD
(A) reprehensible
(B) static
(C) random
(D) uniform
(E) vivacious

9. HAPLESS
(A) laminated
(B) helpless
(C) dismayed
(D) sumptuous
(E) unlucky

10. HAUGHTY
(A) arrogant
(B) histrionic
(C) fatuous
(D) benign
(E) acute

259

Check-up 5-2

1. HILARIOUS

(A) highly creative
(B) totally unnecessary
(C) extremely funny
(D) absolutely stunning
(E) fairly decent

2. HOMOGENOUS

(A) meager
(B) obdurate
(C) novel
(D) identical
(E) placid

3. IDIOSYNCRATIC

(A) precarious
(B) quirky
(C) remiss
(D) scathing
(E) complicit

4. IGNITE

(A) kindle
(B) concede
(C) abbreviate
(D) mediate
(E) ratiocinate

5. IMMACULATE

(A) seminal
(B) impeccable
(C) tortuous
(D) ubiquitous
(E) voluminous

6. IMMERSE

(A) rectify
(B) wane
(C) abhor
(D) submerge
(E) berate

7. IMMINENT

(A) truculent
(B) winsome
(C) impending
(D) accommodating
(E) boisterous

8. IMPART

(A) aggregate
(B) conduct
(C) tell
(D) forsake
(E) manifest

9. IMPLICATE

(A) obfuscate
(B) demolish
(C) revise
(D) satisfy
(E) involve

10. IMPLICIT

(A) calm
(B) scathing
(C) overwhelming
(D) redoubtable
(E) implied

Check-up 5-3

Directions   Each of the following questions consists of one word followed by five words or phrases.
You are to select the one word or phrase whose meaning is closest to the word in capital letters.

1. IMPOVERISHED
(A) destitute
(B) formidable
(C) pervasive
(D) malevolent
(E) judicious

2. INCARCERATE
(A) urge
(B) praise
(C) imprison
(D) diminish
(E) combine

3. INCESSANT
(A) cogent
(B) apparent
(C) pellucid
(D) uninterrupted
(E) flexible

4. INCITE
(A) appease
(B) gratify
(C) satiate
(D) whet
(E) instigate

5. INCOMPATIBLE
(A) poised
(B) conflicting
(C) radiant
(D) significant
(E) original

6. INCUMBENT
(A) truculent
(B) unvarying
(C) official
(D) vicarious
(E) charming

7. INDEFATIGABLE
(A) tireless
(B) reprehensible
(C) indistinct
(D) hostile
(E) frenetic

8. INDICT
(A) enlighten
(B) shorten
(C) accuse
(D) enhance
(E) bid

9. INDIFFERENT
(A) numerous
(B) apathetic
(C) reserved
(D) spectral
(E) baleful

10. INDIGENT
(A) brazen
(B) unpredictable
(C) cogent
(D) agreeable
(E) impoverished

261

Check-up 5-4

Each of the following questions consists of one word followed by five words or phrases. You are to select the one word or phrase whose meaning is closest to the word in capital letters.

1. INDULGENT
(A) demanding
(B) permissive
(C) inquisitive
(D) petulant
(E) insightful

2. INFALLIBLE
(A) complicit
(B) impulsive
(C) superficial
(D) unerring
(E) daunting

3. INFERNO
(A) conflagration
(B) menagerie
(C) resource
(D) trauma
(E) synopsis

4. INGENIOUS
(A) diligent
(B) exhausted
(C) urgent
(D) fatuous
(E) inventive

5. INGENUOUS
(A) distinct
(B) mistaken
(C) artless
(D) elated
(E) fertile

6. INNOCUOUS
(A) untamed
(B) harmless
(C) fickle
(D) astounded
(E) hopeless

7. INSIGHTFUL
(A) extraordinary
(B) discerning
(C) hapless
(D) dramatic
(E) idolatrous

8. INTEGRAL
(A) immutable
(B) penetrated
(C) angered
(D) essential
(E) jubilant

9. INTERIM
(A) provisional
(B) judicious
(C) intricate
(D) admiring
(E) improper

10. INTERMITTENT
(A) lethargic
(B) vulgar
(C) sporadic
(D) lawless
(E) generous

Check-up 5-5

Directions   Each of the following questions consists of one word followed by five words or phrases. You are to select the one word or phrase whose meaning is closest to the word in capital letters.

1. INTERVENE
(A) accentuate
(B) mediate
(C) gratify
(D) mollify
(E) exclude

2. INTREPID
(A) noble
(B) valiant
(C) patent
(D) fruitful
(E) indecent

3. INTRICATE
(A) eager
(B) abundant
(C) soiled
(D) fixed
(E) complicated

4. INTUITION
(A) instinct
(B) partiality
(C) irritability
(D) repose
(E) conflict

5. INVIGORATE
(A) abscond
(B) reserved
(C) pacify
(D) stimulate
(E) flourish

6. ISOLATED
(A) celestial
(B) arranged
(C) remote
(D) viable
(E) intimidating

7. JEER
(A) sneer
(B) approach
(C) defame
(D) fortify
(E) manifest

8. JOVIAL
(A) sarcastic
(B) cheerful
(C) habitual
(D) sentimental
(E) morose

9. JUDICIOUS
(A) negligent
(B) rustic
(C) prudent
(D) enormous
(E) compassionate

10. JURISDICTION
(A) capability
(B) outcast
(C) sympathy
(D) tragedy
(E) authority

263

251	juxtapose	256	lampoon
252	kindle	257	languid
253	kinetic	258	latent
254	lackluster	259	laudable
255	lament	260	lavish

School Motto

"Dare to be True"

- Milton Academy

SSATKOREA.com

juxtapose
[**juhk**-stuh-pohz]

v. to place close together or side by side

옆으로 나란히 늘어놓다

Juxtaposed against a red backdrop, your blue painting really stands out.

syn. appose, bring near, pair

kindle
[**kin**-dl]

v. to start a fire

불을 피우다, 불 붙이다

Knowing how to kindle a fire is an important survival skill.

syn. ignite, inflame, set fire

kinetic
[ki-**net**-ik]

adj. caused by motion

운동의, 운동에 의해 생기는

A roller coaster has a lot of kinetic energy when it rolls down the big dip.

syn. moving, active, energetic

lackluster
[**lak**-luhs-ter]

adj. lacking brilliance or vitality

광택이 없는, 흐리멍덩한

His lackluster life was without brilliance, shine, or vitality.

syn. dull, lifeless, flat

lament
[luh-**ment**]

v. To feel or express sorrow or regret for

슬퍼하다, 애도하다

Josh lamented not studying harder when he received a C on his test.

syn. grieve, mourn, sorrow

lampoon
[lam-**poon**]

n. a sharp, often virulent satire

풍자시, 풍자문

Stacey and Helen performed a lampoon making fun of the school principal.

syn. satire, parody, mockery

languid
[**lang**-gwid]

adj. lacking in vigor or vitality

나른한, 움직임에 힘이 없는

Helen felt languid from the heat and humidity.

syn. shiftless, listless, torpid

latent
[**leyt**-nt]

adj. present but not visible

잠재하는, 숨어 있는

Without training, his musical talent remained latent.

syn. hidden, dormant, inert

laudable
[**law**-duh-b*uhl*]

adj. deserving praise

칭찬할 만한

His noble ideas and polite behavior are laudable.

syn. commendable, estimable, praiseworthy

lavish
[**lav**-ish]

adj. extremely generous

풍성한, 호화로운, 후한

The mayor threw a lavish party for his daughter on her 16th birthday.

syn. luxurious, extravagant, opulent

ISEE Sentence Completion 6-1

Directions : **Fill in the blanks to complete the sentences.**

1. The actor's _____ performance disappointed the audience, who had expected much more from him.

   (A) lampoon   (B) kinetic
   (C) languid   (D) lackluster

2. The demonstration explained how _____ energy is transformed into potential energy in motion.

   (A) kinetic   (B) lackluster
   (C) laudable   (D) latent

3. Her _____ efforts to raise funds for the charity were recognized and applauded by everyone.

   (A) munificent   (B) laudable
   (C) lackluster   (D) lampoon

4. He led a _____ lifestyle, spending money extravagantly on luxury and leisure.

   (A) lavish   (B) latent
   (C) languid   (D) laudable

5. The young singer's _____ talent was finally discovered when she performed at the local event.

   (A) kinetic   (B) laudable
   (C) lavish   (D) latent

Answers
1. (D)   2. (A)   3. (B)   4. (A)   5. (D)

MIDDLE 1 2 3 4 5 6 7 8 9 10

UPPER 1 2 3 4 5 6 7 8 9 10

261	legacy	266	liberal
262	legible	267	lineage
263	legitimate	268	literate
264	lethargic	269	lucrative
255	liaison	270	ludicrous

School Motto

"Discere et Vivere"

(To Learn and to Live)

- Northfield Mount Hermon School

━━━━ SSATKOREA.com

legitimate
[li-**jit**-uh-mit]

adj. according to law

합법의, 정당한

*I hope you had a **legitimate** reason for missing yesterday's science class.*

syn.   lawful, legible, licit

lethargic
[luh-**thahr**-jik]

adj. affected with lethargy

무기력한, 축 처진

*Because he had the flu,
he felt **lethargic**.*

syn.   sluggish, listless, lazy

legacy
[**leg**-uh-see]

n. anything handed down from the past

(선조 등이 남긴) 유산

*He received a large **legacy** from
his uncle.*

syn.   heritage, inheritance, endowment

liaison
[lee-ey-**zawn**]

n. a link between people or groups

연락, 연락 담당자, 연락책

*The negotiator provided a **liaison**
with the guerrillas.*

syn.   contact, channel, connection

legible
[**lej**-uh-b*uh*l]

adj. easy to read

글자를 알아 볼 수 있게 쓰여진, 또렷한

*His handwriting is clearly **legible**.*

syn.   readable, clear, understandable

liberal
[**lib**-er-*uh*l]

adj. giving and generous in temperament or behavior

관대한, 후한

*I like it sweet, so pour a **liberal**
amount of sugar into my lemonade.*

syn.   generous, progressive, open-minded

lineage
[**lin**-ee-ij]

n. lineal descent from an ancestor

혈통

*Dave's **lineage** includes Charles Dickens.*

syn. pedigree, ancestry, family tree

literate
[**lit**-er-it]

adj. able to read and write

읽고 쓸 수 있는

*I hope that someday all people on Earth can become **literate**.*

syn. educated, erudite, learned

lucrative
[**loo**-kruh-tiv]

adj. producing a lot of money or profit

수익성이 좋은, 돈이 잘 벌리는

*The company decided to invest in a **lucrative** business opportunity.*

syn. profitable, rewarding, money-making

ludicrous
[**loo**-di-kruh]

adj. causing laughter because of absurdity

우스꽝스러운, 터무니없는

*The whole idea is absolutely **ludicrous**!*

syn. ridiculous, absurd, laughable

ISEE Sentence Completion 6-2

Directions : Fill in the blanks to complete the sentences.

1. The teacher praised the student for their neat and _____ handwriting on the essay.

   (A) lethargic   (B) ludicrous
   (C) legible   (D) liberal

2. The philanthropist left a _____ that will benefit future generations for years to come.

   (A) legacy   (B) liaison
   (C) lineage   (D) lucrative

3. The court ruled in favor of the plaintiff, stating that they had a _____ claim to the property.

   (A) liaison   (B) lineage
   (C) lucrative   (D) legitimate

4. After the long hike, she exhibited _____ behavior, barely able to move from exhaustion.

   (A) lethargic   (B) liberal
   (C) ludicrous   (D) literate

5. The _____ officer facilitated communication between the two departments to ensure smooth operations.

   (A) legacy   (B) liaison
   (C) lineage   (D) lucrative

1. (C) 2. (A) 3. (D) 4. (A) 5. (B)
Answers

271	lull	276	mar
272	magnificent	277	meander
273	malady	278	meddle
274	mandatory	279	mediocre
275	manifest	280	meditate

School Motto

"Lumen, Fides, Labor, Facta"

(Light, Faith, Work, and Deeds)

- Eaglebrook School

SSATKOREA.com

lull
[lu*h*l]

n. a pause during which things are calm

소강상태, 잠잠한 시기, 고요해진 상태

*Then came the **lull** before the storm.*

syn. pause, calm, hiatus

magnificent
[mag-**nif**-uh-suhnt]

adj. making a splendid appearance

매우 훌륭하고 멋진

*The view from the top of the Empire State Building is **magnificent**.*

syn. extraordinary, glorious, grand

malady
[**mal**-uh-dee]

n. any disorder or disease

병, 병폐

*Manuel's aunt has a **malady** that causes her pain in her knees.*

syn. ailment, disease, affliction

mandatory
[**man**-duh-tawr-ee]

adj. authoritatively ordered

의무적인, 법에 정해진

*Attendance at the meeting is **mandatory**.*

syn. compulsory, obligatory, required

manifest
[**man**-uh-fest]

adj. readily perceived by the eye or the understanding

명백한, 분명한

*It is **manifest** that Jack is in love with Diane.*

syn. evident, obvious, apparent

mar
[mahr]

v. to make imperfect

흠집을 내다, 손상시키다

*The pen mark **mars** his crisp, white shirt.*

syn. spoil, damage, ruin

meander

[mee-**an**-der]

v. to wander aimlessly

거닐다, 구불구불하다

*He **meandered** through the playground and then the mall instead of coming directly home from school.*

syn. ramble, saunter, wander

meddle

[med-l]

v. to involve oneself in a matter without invitation

간섭하다

*Susan always **meddles** in other people's business.*

syn. interfere, intrude, tamper

mediocre

[mee-dee-**oh**-ker]

adj. neither good nor bad

보통 밖에 안 되는, 썩 좋지는 않은

*He knew his essay only deserved a **mediocre** grade.*

syn. average, commonplace, ordinary

meditate

[med-i-teyt]

v. to engage in transcendental meditation

명상하다

*He **meditated** over what he should major in at college.*

syn. contemplate, ponder, reflect

ISEE Sentence Completion 6-3

Directions : Fill in the blanks to complete the sentences.

1. The sailors prepared for the approaching hurricane during the brief _____ before the storm.

   (A) lull   (B) mar
   (C) manifest   (D) meditate

2. Attendance at the meeting is _____, and all employees are expected to participate.

   (A) magnificent   (B) mediocre
   (C) mandatory   (D) meditate

3. The vandals managed to _____ the surface of the statue, leaving permanent damage.

   (A) mar   (B) lull
   (C) manifest   (D) meditate

4. The doctor diagnosed him with a serious _____ that required immediate attention.

   (A) meddle   (B) lull
   (C) malady   (D) manifest

5. Critics described the actor's latest film as a _____ performance, lacking both energy and depth.

   (A) magnificent   (B) mediocre
   (C) mandatory   (D) malady

Answers

1. (A)   2. (C)   3. (A)   4. (C)   5. (B)

281	memento	286	mesmerize
282	mentor	287	meticulous
283	mercenary	288	mimic
284	mercurial	289	minute
285	meritorious	290	misconstrue

School Motto

"Non Sibi"

(Not for Self)

- Phillips Academy/ Phillips Exeter Academy

SSATKOREA.com

memento
[muh-**men**-toh]

n. an object item that serves to remind past

기념물, 기념품

Elisa bought a colorful shell as a memento of her trip to Hawaii.

syn. souvenir, keepsake, token

mentor
[**men**-tawr]

n. a wise and trusted counselor or teacher

정신적 스승, 조언자

Todd's mentor taught him how to be a good person.

syn. advisor, role model

mercenary
[**mur**-suh-ner-ee]

adj. working merely for money

돈 버는 데만 관심이 있는, 돈이 목적인

The mercenary soldiers were only loyal to the person who paid them.

syn. venal, avaricious, greedy

mercurial
[mer-**kyoor**-ee-*uhl*]

adj. changeable and erratic

변덕스러운

Debra's mercurial mood swings always kept Ray on his toes.

syn. capricious, fickle, whimsical

meritorious
[mer-i-**tawr**-ee-uhs]

adj. deserving praise, reward, esteem

칭찬할 만한

He was praised for his meritorious contributions to the city.

syn. praiseworthy, admirable, heroic

mesmerize
[**mez**-muh-rahyz]

v. to compel by fascination

매혹시키다, 마음을 사로잡다

The cat was mesmerized by the feather on a string.

syn. fascinate, captivate, enchant

meticulous
[muh-**tik**-yuh-luhs]

adj. taking extreme care about minute details

꼼꼼한, 세심한

*I want my surgeon to be **meticulous**.*

syn. fastidious, precise, thorough

mimic
[**mim**-ik]

v. to copy or imitate someone's actions, speech, or behavior

(웃기려고) 흉내내다, 모방하다

*The parrot can **mimic** human speech perfectly.*

syn. imitate, mock, replicate

minute
[**min**-it]

adj. extremely small

극히 작은, 매우 상세한

*Compared to an elephant, a mouse is a **minute** creature.*

syn. tiny, microscopic, infinitesimal

misconstrue
[mis-kuhn-**stroo**]

v. to misunderstand the meaning of

오해하다, 잘못 이해하다

*She **misconstrued** her brother's intentions.*

syn. misinterpret, distort, misunderstand

ISEE Sentence Completion 6-4

Directions : Fill in the blanks to complete the sentences.

1. The committee recognized her _____ efforts in organizing the event, awarding her a medal of honor.

   (A) meritorious   (B) mercenary
   (C) mimic   (D) misconstrue

2. The actor's _____ personality often made him unpredictable but fascinating to watch.

   (A) mesmerize   (B) meticulous
   (C) mercurial   (D) memento

3. The young professional sought guidance from her _____, who offered valuable career advice.

   (A) memento   (B) mentor
   (C) meticulous   (D) misconstrue

4. She kept the locket as a _____ of her late grandmother, treasuring it dearly.

   (A) mercurial   (B) mentor
   (C) memento   (D) mimic

5. The magician was able to _____ the audience with his stunning tricks and illusions.

   (A) meticulous   (B) mentor
   (C) misconstrue   (D) mesmerize

Answers

1. (A)   2. (C)   3. (B)   4. (C)   5. (D)

291	miserly	296	muddle
292	monotonous	297	mundane
293	moor	298	munificent
294	morose	299	mutual
295	mourn	300	myriad

School Motto

"Finis andorigine pendet"

(The end is the beginning)

- Phillips Academy/ Phillips Exeter Academy

SSATKOREA.com

miserly
[**mahy**-zer-lee]

adj. extremely reluctant to spend money or share resources

구두쇠 같은, 인색한

The miserly old man refused to donate even a single dollar to the charity.

syn. stingy, tightfisted, penny-pinching

monotonous
[muh-**not**-n-uhs]

adj. tediously unvarying

단조로운, 변함없는

Students complain about the teacher's uninteresting and monotonous lectures.

syn. tedious, boring, dull

moor
[moor]

v. to secure a ship or boat in a particular place

(배를) 정박시키다, 잡아매다

You'd better moor the canoe to shore so it doesn't float away.

syn. anchor, berth, dock

morose
[muh-**rohs**]

adj. gloomily as a person or mood

시무룩한, 뚱한

You seem morose today; is something wrong?

syn. gloomy, melancholy, somber

mourn
[mawrn]

v. to feel or express sorrow or grief

애도하다, 슬퍼하다

He mourned the loss of a beloved pet.

syn. grieve, sorrow, lament

muddle
[**muh**-dl]

v. to mix up in a confused or bungling manner

혼란스럽게 만들다, 갈피를 못 잡게 하다

She felt muddled when she first woke from a deep sleep.

syn. jumble, confuse, disorganize

mundane
[muhn-**deyn**]

adj. common or ordinary

평범한, 일상적인, 재미없는

> When I feel like my life is becoming too mundane, I like to take a small trip.

syn.   ordinary, common, prosaic

munificent
[myoo-**nif**-uh-suhnt]

adj. very generous

매우 인자한, 아낌없이 주는

> My **munificent** friend is very lavish when it comes to giving gifts.

syn.   generous, lavish, bountiful

mutual
[**myoo**-choo-*uhl*]

adj. experienced by each of two or more with respect

상호간의, 서로의

> The two competing nations have a **mutual** distrust.

syn.   reciprocal, communal, bilateral

myriad
[**mir**-ee-uhd]

adj. of an indefinitely great number

무수한, 무수히 많은

> We could see the **myriad** stars of a summer night.

syn.   innumerable, countless, untold

ISEE Sentence Completion 6-5

Directions : **Fill in the blanks to complete the sentences.**

1. She found herself distracted by the _____ chores of everyday life, longing for adventure.

   (A) mundane   (B) miserly
   (C) morose   (D) myriad

2. His _____ attitude often prevented him from sharing even when he had more than enough.

   (A) morose   (B) myriad
   (C) miserly   (D) munificent

3. The employees complained about their _____ routine, wishing for more variety in their work.

   (A) mentor   (B) miserly
   (C) mutual   (D) monotonous

4. They reached a _____ agreement, ensuring both parties were satisfied with the outcome.

   (A) mutual   (B) monotonous
   (C) muddle   (D) myriad

5. The sailor skillfully managed to _____ the boat to the dock before the storm hit.

   (A) miserly   (B) moor
   (C) myriad   (D) mourn

1. (A) 2. (C) 3. (D) 4. (A) 5. (B)

Answers

Analogy 16. Place

장소와 장소에 보관되거나 장소에서 하는 일이 연결되는 유형도 자주 출제됩니다. 문제를 풀 때 'A에 B가 있다'라고 생각하지 말고 [A는 B를 보관하기 위해 만든 공간] 또는 [A는 B를 하기 위해 만든 공간]으로 장소의 '목적'에 집중해서 풀어보세요. 더 답이 확실하게 보일 것입니다.

A는 B를 보관하기 위해 만든 장소

library : book 도서관 : 책	morgue : corpse 시체보관소 : 시체
archive : record 기록 보관소 : 기록	silo : grain 곡물 저장고 : 곡물
pantry : food 식료품 저장실 : 음식	armory : weapons 무기고 : 무기

A를 하기 위해 만든 장소 B

tennis : court 테니스 : 테니스 코트	golf : course 골프 : 골프 코스
soccer : pitch 축구 : 축구 경기장 (필드)	baseball : diamond 야구 : 야구장
bowling : lane 볼링 : 레인	skate : rink 스케이트 : 아이스 링크장
chess : board 체스 : 체스보드	basketball : court 농구 : 농구 코트
football : gridiron 미식축구 : 그리드아이언 (경기장)	fencing : piste 펜싱 : 피스트 (펜싱 경기장)

POP QUIZ

1. Court is to tennis as
(A) rink is to billiard
(B) pool is to table
(C) club is to golf
(D) puck is to hockey
(E) diamond is to baseball

2. Pantry is to food as
(A) museum is to curator
(B) silo is to grain
(C) exhibit is to painter
(D) recital is to pianist
(E) galley is to kitchen

Check-up 6-1

Directions   Each of the following questions consists of one word followed by five words or phrases. You are to select the one word or phrase whose meaning is closest to the word in capital letters.

1. JUXTAPOSE
(A) appose
(B) rant
(C) spurn
(D) pander
(E) oscillate

2. KINDLE
(A) mitigate
(B) harbinger
(C) ignite
(D) foster
(E) corrupt

3. KINETIC
(A) hackneyed
(B) moving
(C) frugal
(D) eloquent
(E) docile

4. LACKLUSTER
(A) congenial
(B) expendable
(C) ineffable
(D) kinetic
(E) dull

5. LAMENT
(A) incite
(B) sever
(C) patent
(D) grieve
(E) abolish

6. LAMPOON
(A) shrewdness
(B) censure
(C) distend
(D) satire
(E) expedite

7. LANGUID
(A) obtuse
(B) shiftless
(C) cryptic
(D) fastidious
(E) gratuitous

8. LATENT
(A) dubious
(B) hidden
(C) generic
(D) humane
(E) indignant

9. LAUDABLE
(A) judicious
(B) ambiguous
(C) commendable
(D) relevant
(F) trivial

10. LAVISH
(A) luxurious
(B) caustic
(C) sage
(D) insignificant
(E) obdurate

275

Check-up 6-2

Each of the following questions consists of one word followed by five words or phrases. You are to select the one word or phrase whose meaning is closest to the word in capital letters.

1. LEGACY
(A) odyssey
(B) amity
(C) heritage
(D) praise
(E) ephemeral

2. LEGIBLE
(A) genetic
(B) hypocritical
(C) indolent
(D) listless
(E) readable

3. LEGITIMATE
(A) laconic
(B) mobile
(C) haphazard
(D) lawful
(E) narcissistic

4. LETHARGIC
(A) nonchalant
(B) observable
(C) affording
(D) precise
(E) sluggish

5. LIAISON
(A) motive
(B) contact
(C) sharpness
(D) equality
(E) probity

6. LIBERAL
(A) queasy
(B) reciprocal
(C) generous
(D) firm
(E) sardonic

7. LINEAGE
(A) pedigree
(B) stimulus
(C) tangent
(D) venality
(E) brevity

8. LITERATE
(A) refined
(B) educated
(C) venerable
(D) convivial
(E) affable

9. LUCRATIVE
(A) provocative
(B) forlorn
(C) seditious
(D) indulgent
(E) profitable

10. LUDICROUS
(A) opaque
(B) ironic
(C) hideous
(D) ridiculous
(E) greedy

Check-up 6-3

Directions   Each of the following questions consists of one word followed by five words or phrases.
              You are to select the one word or phrase whose meaning is closest to the word in capital letters.

1. LULL
(A) pause
(B) fidelity
(C) liveliness
(D) accolade
(E) blunder

2. MAGNIFICENT
(A) stable
(B) churlish
(C) extraordinary
(D) bizarre
(E) decorous

3. MALADY
(A) drawback
(B) ailment
(C) edict
(D) foible
(E) genre

4. MANDATORY
(A) complimentary
(B) refractory
(C) decrepit
(D) compulsory
(E) brazen

5. MANIFEST
(A) vigorous
(B) habitual
(C) evident
(D) tolerant
(E) ineffective

6. MAR
(A) spoil
(B) dispose
(C) seize
(D) dwindle
(E) control

7. MEANDER
(A) destroy
(B) jeer
(C) incline
(D) ramble
(E) perceive

8. MEDDLE
(A) replete
(B) placate
(C) abdicate
(D) belittle
(E) interfere

9. MEDIOCRE
(A) humane
(B) overt
(C) vulgar
(D) copious
(E) average

10. MEDITATE
(A) contemplate
(B) galvanize
(C) reinforce
(D) compensate
(E) revitalize

277

Check-up 6-4

1. MEMENTO
(A) nostalgia
(B) counterbalance
(C) souvenir
(D) oblivion
(E) parity

2. MENTOR
(A) dictum
(B) speech
(C) advisor
(D) quality
(E) hybrid

3. MERCENARY
(A) innocuous
(B) unrestrained
(C) blatant
(D) venal
(E) apocryphal

4. MERCURIAL
(A) capricious
(B) bucolic
(C) occupied
(D) didactic
(E) erudite

5. MERITORIOUS
(A) expendable
(B) famished
(C) germane
(D) insolent
(E) praiseworthy

6. MESMERIZE
(A) fascinate
(B) alleviate
(C) provoke
(D) deviate
(E) rebuke

7. METICULOUS
(A) efficient
(B) distant
(C) gullible
(D) fastidious
(E) irrefutable

8. MIMIC
(A) deceive
(B) imitate
(C) resign
(D) abdicate
(E) baffle

9. MINUTE
(A) harmonious
(B) evanescent
(C) tiny
(D) fallow
(E) conspicuous

10. MISCONSTRUE
(A) misinterpret
(B) rugged
(C) disprove
(D) kindle
(E) levitate

Check-up 6-5

Directions   Each of the following questions consists of one word followed by five words or phrases.
You are to select the one word or phrase whose meaning is closest to the word in capital letters.

1. MISERLY
(A) bashful
(B) miserable
(C) judicious
(D) stingy
(E) philanthropic

2. MONOTONOUS
(A) unnerving
(B) revitalizing
(C) poised
(D) bewildered
(E) tedious

3. MOOR
(A) declare
(B) evoke
(C) ruffle
(D) hinder
(E) anchor

4. MOROSE
(A) furtive
(B) appropriate
(C) gloomy
(D) spontaneous
(E) unyielding

5. MOURN
(A) retract
(B) grieve
(C) disavow
(D) scour
(E) pollute

6. MUDDLE
(A) unveil
(B) jumble
(C) oust
(D) crave
(E) expel

7. MUNDANE
(A) willful
(B) omnipresent
(C) superior
(D) magnificent
(E) ordinary

8. MUNIFICENT
(A) boisterous
(B) hectic
(C) generous
(D) miserable
(E) dormant

9. MUTUAL
(A) superb
(B) exasperating
(C) deft
(D) reciprocal
(E) ample

10. MYRIAD
(A) nagging
(B) beloved
(C) innumerable
(D) baleful
(E) deported

279

301	naive	306	neutralize
302	narcissistic	307	nonchalant
303	nebulous	308	noncommittal
304	negate	309	nostalgia
305	nemesis	310	nuance

School Motto

"Certa Viriliter"

(Strive Valiantly)

- Pomfret School

SSATKOREA.com

naive
[nah-**eev**]

adj. lacking sophistication or street smarts

세상 물정을 너무 모르는, 잘 속는

*It's **naive** of you to believe he'll do what he says.*

syn. credulous, childlike, ignorant

narcissistic
[nahr-suh-**sis**-tik]

adj. hazy, vague, indistinct, or confused

자기애적인, 자기중심적인, 자아도취적인

*The character in the story was so **narcissistic** that she didn't care about anyone else's feelings.*

syn. self-centered, egotistical, arrogant

nebulous
[neb-**yuh**-l*uh*s]

adj. unclear, vague, or ill-defined

흐릿한, 모호한

*His explanation was so **nebulous** that no one understood his point.*

syn. vague, obscure, ambiguous

negate
[ni-**geyt**]

v. to deny the existence, evidence, or truth of

효력이 없게 만들다, 무효화하다

*Forgetting to save your game **negates** all your progress.*

syn. nullify, invalidate, cancel

nemesis
[**nem**-uh-sis]

n. a long-standing rival or enemy

이기기 어려운 상대, 응징

*The superhero finally defeated his greatest **nemesis**, bringing peace to the city.*

syn. foe, adversary, opponent

neutralize
[**noo**-truh-lahyz]

v. to make something ineffective

무효화시키다, 상쇄시키다

*Acids **neutralize** alkalis and vice versa.*

syn. counteract, nullify, offset

nonchalant

[non-shuh-**lahnt**]

adj. coolly unconcerned, indifferent, or unexcited

무심한, 태연한 척하는

Tyler always seems nonchalant about his assignments.

syn. indifferent, apathetic, casual

noncommittal

[non-kuh-**mit**-l]

adj. not committing oneself to a particular view

주장을 밝히지 않는, 태도가 애매한

The White House spokesman was noncommittal on this question.

syn. indefinite, vague, equivocal

nostalgia

[no-**stal**-juh]

n. pleasant remembrances

향수 (고향이나 지난 과거를 그리워하는 마음)

Photos of my favorite childhood bring on nostalgia.

syn. reminiscence, longing, wistfulness

nuance

[**noo**-ahns]

n. a subtle differnce

미묘한 차이, 뉘앙스

This painting is famous in part for its nuances of shading.

syn. subtlety, shade, distinction

ISEE Sentence Completion 7-1

Directions : Fill in the blanks to complete the sentences.

1. His _____ tendencies often made him prioritize his own needs above everyone else's.

   (A) narcissistic   (B) nebulous
   (C) negate   (D) neutralize

2. The young intern made a _____ assumption about how easy the project would be, not realizing its complexity.

   (A) nuance   (B) nostalgia
   (C) nemesis   (D) naive

3. The superhero faced off against his arch _____, determined to stop their latest plan for destruction.

   (A) nuance   (B) nemesis
   (C) nebulous   (D) nonchalant

4. The government worked to _____ the threat before it could cause any significant harm.

   (A) neutralize   (B) nuance
   (C) narcissistic   (D) negate

5. The professor explained the _____ concept in a way that was easier for the students to grasp.

   (A) nonchalant   (B) naive
   (C) nuance   (D) nebulous

Answers
1. (A) 2. (D) 3. (B) 4. (A) 5. (D)

311 null

312 oblique

313 obliterate

314 oblivious

315 obsessive

316 obstinate

317 obstruct

318 occupy

319 officious

320 ominous

School Motto

"Veritas"

(Truth)

- Portsmouth Abbey School

SSATKOREA.com

null
[n*uh*l]

adj. without value, effect, consequence, or significance

아무 가치, 영향, 중요성 등이 없는

*The contract was proved to be **null** and void.*

syn. zero value, ineffectual, valueless

oblique
[uh-**bleek**]

adj. indirectly stated or expressed

비스듬한, 완곡한 표현을 하는

*Not directly stating their names, the principal made an **oblique** reference.*

syn. indirect, roundabout, slanting

obliterate
[uh-**blit**-uh-reyt]

v. to remove or destroy all

없애나

*Our school soccer team **obliterated** the other team by a score of 7-0.*

syn. eliminate, decimate, eradicate

oblivious
[uh-**bliv**-ee-uhs]

adj. lacking remembrance, memory, or mindful attention

의식하지 못하는

*Absorbed in her work, she was totally **oblivious** of her surroundings.*

syn. unmindful, unconscious, unaware

obsessive
[uhb-**ses**-iv]

adj. being, pertaining to, or resembling an obsession

(어떤 생각에 심하게) 사로잡혀 있는, 강박적인

*Dave is so **obsessive** about baseball.*

syn. compulsive, fixated, preoccupied

obstinate
[**ob**-stuh-nit]

adj. firmly or stubbornly adhering to one's purpose

고집 센, 완강한

*I was confused by her **obstinate** refusal to comply with my request.*

syn. dogmatic, stubborn, unwilling

obstruct
[uhb-**struhkt**]

v. to block or close up with an obstacle

막다, 차단하다

*The accident is **obstructing** traffic on Main Street.*

syn. block, hinder, impede

occupy
[**ok**-yuh-pahy]

v. to take or fill up

(공간을) 차지하다, 거주하다

*The paintings of Andy Warhol **occupied** a prominent place on her walls.*

syn. inhabit, reside, use

officious
[uh-**fish**-uhs]

adj. objectionably aggressive in offering one's unrequested and unwanted services

거들먹거리는, 위세를 부리는

*His clients are mostly rude and **officious**.*

syn. overbearing, meddlesome, intrusive

ominous
[**om**-uh-nuhs]

adj. portending evil or harm

불길한, 나쁜 징조의

*Those **ominous** clouds means we might get a storm soon.*

syn. foreboding, threatening, inauspicious

ISEE Sentence Completion 7-2

Directions : Fill in the blanks to complete the sentences.

1. The powerful explosion managed to _____ all evidence of the crime.

   (A) occupy   (B) obstruct
   (C) officious   (D) obliterate

2. She was so immersed in her thoughts that she seemed completely _____ to the chaos around her.

   (A) ominous   (B) oblivious
   (C) officious   (D) obstinate

3. His _____ behavior of repeatedly checking the locks worried his family.

   (A) null   (B) oblique
   (C) obsessive   (D) ominous

4. The contract was declared _____ after it was found to violate federal laws.

   (A) null   (B) ominous
   (C) officious   (D) obsessive

5. His _____ interference in their discussion irritated everyone, as he kept giving unwanted advice.

   (A) obstinate   (B) oblivious
   (C) officious   (D) oblique

Answers
1. (D) 2. (B) 3. (C) 4. (A) 5. (C)

321 onerous	326 ostentatious
322 opinionated	327 outlandish
323 optimum	328 outrageous
324 opulent	329 overbearing
325 oratory	330 overlook

School Motto

"Ea discamus in terris quorum scientia perseveret in coelis"
(Let us learn those things on Earth the knowledge of which continues in Heaven)
- St.Paul's School

SSATKOREA.com

onerous
[**on**-er-uhs]

adj. burdening and difficult

아주 힘든, 부담되는

*Ms. Han gave us an **onerous** amount of homework this weekend.*

syn. burdensome, taxing, difficult

opinionated
[uh-**pin**-yuh-ney-tid]

adj. conceitedly dogmatic

자기 의견을 고집하는, 독선적인

*William is very **opinionated** when it comes to politics.*

syn. bigoted, dogmatic, stubborn

optimum
[**op**-tuh-muhm]

adj. the best quality and quantity

최고의, 최적의

*The **optimum** result on my report card would be straight A's.*

syn. best, ideal, peak

opulent
[**op**-yuh-luhnt]

adj. abundant or plentiful

부유한, 풍부한, 풍족한

*The president usually stays in **opulent** hotels when she travels.*

syn. wealthy, luxurious, extravagant

oratory
[**awr**-uh-tawr-ee]

n. skill or eloquence in public speaking

웅변술

*During her speech on third-world poverty, Lisa moved her classmates with her **oratory**.*

syn. rhetoric, speaking skill, articulation

ostentatious
[os-ten-**tey**-shuhs]

adj. showy or flashy

과시하는, 허세부리는, 화려한

*The house was decorated in an **ostentatious** style, with gold furniture and enormous chandeliers.*

syn. showy, flashy, pretentious

outlandish
[out-**lan**-dish]

adj. freakishly or grotesquely strange or odd

이상한, 기이한

*Donna's **outlandish** outfit drew stares from the other students.*

syn. bizarre, weird, eccentric

outrageous
[out-**rey**-juhs]

adj. greatly exceeding bounds of reason

너무나 충격적인, 터무니 없는

*The culprit's **outrageous** remarks caused public outrage.*

syn. shocking, extreme, ridiculous

overbearing
[oh-ver-**bair**-ing]

adj. haughty or rudely arrogant

고압적인, 남을 지배하려 드는

*The coach can sometimes be **overbearing** toward his athletes.*

syn. haughty, dictatorial, domineering

overlook
[oh-ver-**look**]

v. to fail to notice, perceive, or consider

못 보고 넘어가다, 간과하다

*Making to-do list prevent you from **overlooking** any details.*

syn. disregard, neglect, omit

ISEE Sentence Completion 7-3

Directions : Fill in the blanks to complete the sentences.

1. His _____ argument left no room for discussion, as he refused to consider anyone else's perspective.

   (A) ostentatious   (B) opinionated
   (C) onerous   (D) outlandish

2. The billionaire's _____ mansion was adorned with gold fixtures and priceless artwork.

   (A) opulent   (B) overbearing
   (C) optimum   (D) outlandish

3. The celebrity's _____ display of wealth included wearing diamond-encrusted shoes.

   (A) outrageous   (B) opinionated
   (C) onerous   (D) ostentatious

4. Her _____ outfit turned heads at the gala, as it was unlike anything anyone had seen before.

   (A) optimum   (B) outlandish
   (C) overbearing   (D) opulent

5. The manager's _____ attitude made it difficult for employees to voice their opinions.

   (A) opinionated   (B) outlandish
   (C) overbearing   (D) oratory

1. (B) 2. (A) 3. (D) 4. (B) 5. (C)
Answers

331	overrule	336	parch
332	pacific	337	parody
333	palatable	338	parry
334	paltry	339	patron
335	paramount	340	patronizing

School Motto

"Pistis Kai Episteme"

(Faith and Learning)

- St. Andrew's School

SSATKOREA.com

overrule
[oh-ver-**rool**]

v. to decide against or reject a decision, ruling, or opinion
(결정, 판결 등을) 기각하다, 뒤엎다

*The judge **overruled** the objection.*

syn. override, reverse, annul

pacific
[puh-**sif**-ik]

adj. calm and peaceful
평화로운, 온화한

*Bruce always feels **pacific** after a long bike ride.*

syn. peaceful, calm, tranquil

palatable
[**pal**-uh-tuh-b*uhl*]

adj. tasty or savory
맛있는, 맛 좋은

*Ian thinks chicken curry is a very **palatable** dish.*

syn. appetizing, delectable, luscious

paltry
[**pawl**-tree]

adj. ridiculously or insultingly small
보잘 것 없는, 쥐꼬리만한

*Sarah earned a **paltry** 66% on her biology quiz.*

syn. insignificant, meager, scanty

paramount
[**par**-uh-mount]

adj. chief in importance or impact
최고의, 다른 무엇보다 중요한

*It is **paramount** that students have a variety of extracurricular activities if they want to enter an Ivy League school.*

syn. supreme, primary, essential

parch
[pahrch]

v. to wither or dry out from exposure to heat
바짝 말리다, 물기 하나 없이 건조시키다

*American Indians **parched** corn to preserve it for the winter.*

syn. dehydrate, dry out, scorch

parody
[par-uh-dee]

n. a humorous or satirical imitation

패러디, 풍자 모방

*Matthew's **parody** of Hamlet's soliloquy is sarcastic but brilliant.*

syn. imitation, satire, spoof

parry
[par-ee]

v. to impede the movement of

(공격하는 무기를) 쳐내다, 막다

*The shot was **parried** by the goalie.*

syn. ward off, deflect, counter

patron
[pey-truhn]

n. a person who supports with money

후원자, 단골 고객

*The great **patrons** of the arts donate money to artists every year.*

syn. benefactor, backer, sponsor

patronizing
[pey-truh-nahy-zing]

adj. displaying an offensively condescending manner

잘난체하는, 생색내는, 베푸는 척하는

*Students don't like it when teachers speak to them in a **patronizing** tone.*

syn. condescending, arrogant, pretentious

ISEE Sentence Completion 7-4

Directions : Fill in the blanks to complete the sentences.

1. The chef prepared a _____ meal that even the pickiest eater enjoyed.

   (A) patron   (B) parody
   (C) parch   (D) palatable

2. The bonus offered by the company was a _____ amount compared to the employees' expectations.

   (A) paltry   (B) overrule
   (C) patronizing (D) pacific

3. She managed to _____ the journalist's difficult question with a clever response.

   (A) paltry   (B) parry
   (C) paramount   (D) overrule

4. Ensuring the safety of the children was a matter of _____ importance for the school administration.

   (A) parry   (B) parody
   (C) paltry   (D) paramount

5. The bookstore's most loyal _____ was a retired professor who visited daily to browse for rare books.

   (A) patron   (B) pacific
   (C) parody   (D) paltry

Answers

1. (D) 2. (A) 3. (B) 4. (D) 5. (A)

341	pensive	346	pernicious
342	penury	347	perspicacious
343	perch	348	pertain
344	perjury	349	peruse
345	permeate	350	pervade

School Motto

"Sapientia Utriusque Vitae Lumen"
(Wisdom, the light of every life)

- St. George's School

SSATKOREA.com

pensive
[**pen**-siv]

adj. deep in thought, often in a way that is reflective, wistful, or slightly sad

깊은 생각에 잠긴, 수심 어린

She sat by the window, looking pensive as she reflected on her past decisions.

syn. thoughtful, reflective, contemplative

penury
[**pen**-yuh-ree]

n. extreme poverty

극빈, 빈곤

After losing his job, he fell into penury and struggled to provide for his family.

syn. poverty, destitution, indigence

perch
[purch]

v. to sit or rest on something, especially in a high or precarious place

(높거나 불안정한 곳에) 앉다, 자리 잡다

The cat perched on the windowsill, watching the birds outside.

syn. sit, rest, balance

perjury
[**pur**-juh-ree]

n. the willful giving of false testimony under oath

위증, 위증죄

She was charged with perjury when it was discovered she had lied in court.

syn. dishonesty, falsehood, forswearing

permeate
[**pur**-mee-eyt]

v. to be diffused through

스며들다, 침투하다

A sense of anxiety permeated the classroom as the students arrived for their final exam.

syn. pervade, saturate, infiltrate

pernicious
[per-**nish**-uhs]

adj. deadly or fatal

치명적인

AIDS is a pernicious disease affecting millions of Africans.

syn. deadly, fatal, lethal

perspicacious
[pur-spi-**key**-shuhs]

adj. having keen mental perception and understanding

총명한, 명민한

*He was **perspicacious** to realize that things were soon going to change.*

syn. discerning, keen, perceptive

pertain
[per-**teyn**]

v. to have reference or relation

(특정한 상황이나 때에) 존재하다, 속하다

*Ensure your response **pertains** to the actual question asked.*

syn. belong, relate, refer

peruse
[puh-**rooz**]

v. to read through with thoroughness or care

정독하다, 꼼꼼히 읽다

*Rina's mother **perused** magazines while Rina spoke to the doctor.*

syn. examine, scrutinize, study

pervade
[per-**veyd**]

v. to become spread throughout all parts of

널리 퍼지다, 배어 스며들다

*A sense of excitement **pervaded** the arena as sudden-death overtime began.*

syn. diffuse, impregnate, infiltrate

ISEE Sentence Completion 7-5

Directions : **Fill in the blanks to complete the sentences.**

1. Please take your time to _____ the report thoroughly before making any decisions.

   (A) pertain   (B) permeate
   (C) peruse   (D) perjury

2. The family was forced to live in _____ after losing all their savings in the economic crash.

   (A) penury   (B) pernicious
   (C) permeate   (D) perspicacious

3. Lying under oath is a serious crime, and anyone who commits _____ can face severe penalties.

   (A) penury   (B) perjury
   (C) pertain   (D) permeate

4. His _____ influence on the team caused tension and a lack of trust among its members.

   (A) perch   (B) pervade
   (C) pensive   (D) pernicious

5. The author captured the character's _____ mood as he reflected on his life's decisions.

   (A) perch   (B) penury
   (C) pensive   (D) perjury

🍎 **Answers**

1. (C)   2. (A)   3. (B)   4. (D)   5. (C)

Analogy 17. Verse & Prose

글의 유형은 크게 Prose 산문과 Verse 운문으로 이루어 집니다. 글의 유형과 그 내용을 묻는 문제도 Analogy를 풀기 위해 꼭 알아야 하는 내용입니다.

Prose 산문	
fiction 소설, 허구, 지어낸 이야기	nonfiction 전기, 역사, 사건 기록
biography 전기, 위인전	essay 수필
memoir 회고록	narrative 이야기
editorial 사설 (신문이나 잡지에서 글쓴이의 주장이나 의견을 써내는 논설)	propaganda 프로파간다 (사상이나 교의 따위의 선전)

Verse 운문	
epic 서사시	lyric 서정시
lampoon 풍자시	limerick 5행의 짧고 재미있는 내용의 시
sonnet 소네트, 소곡, 14행시	haiku 일본 단시 형태를 띤 일상적이고 짧은 시
dirge 비가, 슬픔의 시	ode (특정한 사람, 사물 등에 부치는) 시, 송시
ballad 발라드, 감상적인 유행가	chant 구호, 성가, 주문처럼 반복되는 노래

POP QUIZ

1. Lampoon is to satire as
- (A) epic is to hero
- (B) haiku is to religion
- (C) ballad is to logic
- (D) limerick is to grief
- (E) sonnet is to moral

2. Memoir is to memory as
- (A) journal is to review
- (B) editorial is to opinion
- (C) autobiography is to criticism
- (D) propaganda is to satire
- (E) campaign is to mount

3. Haiku is to epic as
- (A) ode is to sonnet
- (B) obituary is to death
- (C) lyric is to emotion
- (D) ditty is to opera
- (E) memoir is to biography

4. Editorial is to opinion as
- (A) propaganda is to misinformation
- (B) billboard is to post
- (C) narrative is to expository
- (D) book is to ledger
- (E) volume is t encyclopedia

Check-up 7-1

Directions — Each of the following questions consists of one word followed by five words or phrases. You are to select the one word or phrase whose meaning is closest to the word in capital letters.

1. NAIVE
(A) laconic
(B) credulous
(C) pithy
(D) inactive
(E) reticent

2. NARCISSISTIC
(A) mutual
(B) evident
(C) self-centered
(D) capricious
(E) subsequent

3. NEBULOUS
(A) explicit
(B) taciturn
(C) vague
(D) bombastic
(E) ambiguous

4. NEGATE
(A) confirm
(B) approve
(C) nullify
(D) reinforce
(E) pine

5. NEMESIS
(A) negotiator
(B) demon
(C) camaraderie
(D) companion
(E) foe

6. NEUTRALIZE
(A) counteract
(B) hoax
(C) avert
(D) peel
(E) vibrate

7. NONCHALANT
(A) complacent
(B) disdainful
(C) egotistical
(D) indifferent
(E) ostentatious

8. NONCOMMITTAL
(A) undecided
(B) contemptuous
(C) haughty
(D) presumptuous
(E) supercilious

9. NOSTALGIA
(A) bankruptcy
(B) apologia
(C) reminiscence
(D) empathy
(F) compassion

10. NUANCE
(A) evidence
(B) iniquity
(C) maxim
(D) pariah
(E) subtlety

291

Check-up 7-2

1. NULL
(A) zero value
(B) turning point
(C) open
(D) highest
(E) frequent visit

6. OBSTINATE
(A) choreographed
(B) belligerent
(C) dogmatic
(D) abject
(E) hasty

2. OBLIQUE
(A) indirect
(B) tedious
(C) unique
(D) vivacious
(E) winsome

7. OBSTRUCT
(A) ramble
(B) dictate
(C) feign
(D) block
(E) advance

3. OBLITERATE
(A) swagger
(B) eliminate
(C) prattle
(D) rant
(E) digress

8. OCCUPY
(A) inhabit
(B) hail
(C) fabricate
(D) narrate
(E) peregrinate

4. OBLIVIOUS
(A) stagnant
(B) unmindful
(C) reprehensible
(D) portentous
(E) lithe

9. OFFICIOUS
(A) dilapidated
(B) fecund
(C) overbearing
(D) profuse
(E) rife

5. OBSESSIVE
(A) immaculate
(B) forlorn
(C) exorbitant
(D) conciliatory
(E) compulsive

10. OMINOUS
(A) favorable
(B) foreboding
(C) timorous
(D) revered
(E) unilateral

Check-up 7-3

Directions   Each of the following questions consists of one word followed by five words or phrases.
You are to select the one word or phrase whose meaning is closest to the word in capital letters.

1. ONEROUS
(A) burdensome
(B) figurative
(C) truculent
(D) compassionate
(E) bloated

2. OPINIONATED
(A) amiable
(B) contemptible
(C) gracious
(D) gregarious
(E) bigoted

3. OPTIMUM
(A) deceit
(B) ingenuity
(C) originality
(D) best
(E) fidelity

4. OPULENT
(A) innocuous
(B) wealthy
(C) venerated
(D) pervasive
(E) redoubtable

5. ORATORY
(A) criterion
(B) dominion
(C) repose
(D) guile
(E) rhetoric

6. OSTENTATIOUS
(A) tart
(B) clad
(C) showy
(D) indelible
(E) murky

7. OUTLANDISH
(A) copious
(B) diminutive
(C) scandalous
(D) bizarre
(E) heinous

8. OUTRAGEOUS
(A) susceptible
(B) facile
(C) shocking
(D) dreary
(E) marvelous

9. OVERBEARING
(A) impecunious
(B) haughty
(C) jubilant
(D) tedious
(E) earnest

10. OVERLOOK
(A) oblige
(B) raze
(C) stuff
(D) disregard
(E) astound

293

Check-up 7-4

1. OVERRULE
(A) suture
(B) vend
(C) override
(D) concede
(E) acclaim

6. PARCH
(A) petrify
(B) dehydrate
(C) scavenge
(D) acknowledge
(E) perch

2. PACIFIC
(A) grateful
(B) incisive
(C) harrowing
(D) flabbergasted
(E) peaceful

7. PARODY
(A) credulity
(B) libel
(C) imitation
(D) folklore
(E) indignation

3. PALATABLE
(A) growled
(B) comatose
(C) appetizing
(D) viable
(E) reproachful

8. PARRY
(A) put off
(B) turn off
(C) ward off
(D) take off
(E) get off

4. PALTRY
(A) vital
(B) baleful
(C) audacious
(D) plentiful
(E) insignificant

9. PATRON
(A) benefactor
(B) pathfinder
(C) vanguard
(D) entrepreneur
(E) magnate

5. PARAMOUNT
(A) cosmopolitan
(B) transparent
(C) divisive
(D) supreme
(E) extravagant

10. PATRONIZING
(A) sophisticated
(B) diverse
(C) brusque
(D) condescending
(E) abject

Check-up 7-5

Directions   Each of the following questions consists of one word followed by five words or phrases. You are to select the one word or phrase whose meaning is closest to the word in capital letters.

1. PENSIVE
(A) pricey
(B) wooden
(C) thoughtful
(D) stilted
(E) radiant

2. PENURY
(A) greed
(B) poverty
(C) excess
(D) truism
(E) sanction

3. PERCH
(A) create
(B) imitate
(C) imbibe
(D) sit
(E) bear

4. PERJURY
(A) hierarchy
(B) salutation
(C) fib
(D) tendency
(E) dishonesty

5. PERMEATE
(A) search
(B) urge
(C) compel
(D) pervade
(E) extort

6. PERNICIOUS
(A) inveterate
(B) deadly
(C) furious
(D) chronic
(E) lethargic

7. PERSPICACIOUS
(A) malicious
(B) discerning
(C) insane
(D) benign
(E) frigid

8. PERTAIN
(A) groan
(B) defame
(C) construct
(D) belong
(E) contrive

9. PERUSE
(A) scan
(B) extol
(C) impede
(D) mislead
(E) examine

10. PERVADE
(A) clarify
(B) stroll
(C) promote
(D) infuse
(E) diffuse

295

351 petition   356 poignant

352 petty   357 polish

353 philanthropy 358 pompous

354 plagiarize   359 ponder

355 plummet   360 porous

School Motto

"Age Quod Agis"

(Drive because you are driven)

- St. Mark's School

SSATKOREA.com

petition
[puh-**tish**-*uh*n]

n. a formally drawn request

탄원서, 진정서

We're collecting signatures for a petition.

syn. appeal, plea, request

petty
[**pet**-ee]

adj. not important and not worth giving attention to

사소한, 하찮은, 중요하지 않은

Students complain about too many petty rules and restrictions.

syn. trivial, trifling, insignificant

philanthropy
[fi-**lan**-thruh-pee]

n. the activity of helping the poor, especially by giving them money

자선활동, 박애주의

She has been acclaimed by people for his works of public philanthropy.

syn. charity, generosity, humanitarianism

plagiarize
[**pley**-juh-rahyz]

v. to take and use ideas or passages from another's work

표절하다

He was accused of plagiarizing his roommate's writing.

syn. steal, copy, pirate

plummet
[**pluhm**-it]

v. drop sharpy

곤두박질치다

Share prices plummeted to an all-time low.

syn. plunge, collapse, dive

poignant
[**poi**-nuhnt]

adj. causing a very sharp feeling of sadness

슬픔으로 가슴 아픈, 가슴 저린

The photograph awakens poignant memories of refugees.

syn. heartrending, painful, touching

polish
[pol-ish]

v. to make smooth and glossy

광택내다, 윤을 내다

It was her job to polish the silverware.

syn. burnish, shine, brighten

pompous
[pom-puhs]

adj. overly self-important

거만한, 잘난 척 하는

He was a little pompous when he talks about film directing.

syn. arrogant, overbearing, imperious

ponder
[pon-der]

v. to think carefully about something, especially for a noticeable length of time

깊이 생각하다, 숙고하다

He sat back to ponder his next chess move.

syn. contemplate, meditate, speculate

porous
[pawr-uhs]

adj. full of pores

구멍이 많이 나 있는, 다공성의

The word "osteoporosis" means porous bone.

syn. absorbent, absorptive, penetrable

ISEE Sentence Completion 8-1

Directions : Fill in the blanks to complete the sentences.

1. She devoted her life to _____, organizing charitable events and donating to causes worldwide.

   (A) polish   (B) petition
   (C) ponder   (D) philanthropy

2. The teacher warned students never to _____ someone else's work, as it is a serious offense.

   (A) plagiarize   (B) plummet
   (C) porous   (D) petition

3. The novel tells a _____ story of love and sacrifice that left readers deeply moved.

   (A) porous   (B) pompous
   (C) poignant   (D) philanthropy

4. His _____ attitude made him unpopular among his peers, as he often acted superior to others.

   (A) petition   (B) porous
   (C) philanthropy   (D) pompous

5. He took time to _____ the decision, carefully considering all possible outcomes before acting.

   (A) ponder   (B) plummet
   (C) plagiarize   (D) petition

1. (D) 2. (A) 3. (C) 4. (D) 5. (A)

🍒 *Answers*

361	posterity	366	pragmatic
362	posthumous	367	precocious
363	posture	368	premonition
364	potable	369	preposterous
365	potent	370	pretentious

School Motto

"Poteris Modo Velis"

(You Can If You Will)

- Fay School

SSATKOREA.com

posterity
[po-**ster**-i-tee]

n. the people who will exist in the future

후손, 후대

Natural habitats must be left to posterity.

syn. progeny, descendants, offspring

posthumous
[**pos**-chuh-muhs]

adj. arising after one's death

사후의

His posthumous work has just been published.

syn. after death, postmortem, belated

posture
[**pos**-cher]

n. the relative disposition of the parts of something

자세

The model is practicing her walking posture.

syn. stance, aspect, pose

potable
[**poh**-tuh-buhl]

adj. fit or suitable for drinking

마셔도 되는, 음용이 가능한

This tap water is potable.

syn. drinkable, safe to drink

potent
[**poht**-nt]

adj. powerful or mighty

강한, 강력한

The nation has a potent weapons system.

syn. powerful, mighty, forceful

pragmatic
[**prag**-mat-ik]

adj. dealing with problems or situations in a practical, realistic way

실용적인, 현실적인

When the bus broke down, the principal's pragmatic decision kept things on time.

syn. practical, realistic, sensible

precocious

[pri-**koh**-sh*uh*s]

adj. unusually advanced
or mature in development

조숙한, 아이 같지 않은

*The child is too precocious
for her age.*

syn. advanced, mature, intelligent

premonition

[pree-**muh**-nish-*uh*n]

n. a feeling that something, especially
something unpleasant, is going to
happen

예감, 특히 안 좋은 일이 일어날 것 같은 예감

*He had a premonition of what the
future might bring.*

syn. forewarning, omen, foreboding

preposterous

[pri-**pos**-ter-*uh*s]

adj. very silly or stupid

말도 안되는, 터무니 없는, 어리석은

*Her claims are absolutely
preposterous!*

syn. absurd, ridiculous, ludicrous

pretentious

[pri-**ten**-sh*uh*s]

adj. characterized by assumption
of dignity or importance

허세부리는, 가식적인

*He has a pretentious style of writing,
using very difficult words.*

syn. snobbish, conceited, exaggerated

ISEE Sentence Completion 8-2

Directions : Fill in the blanks to
complete the sentences.

1. The campers brought a portable
filter to ensure access to _____
water in the wilderness.

   (A) potent   (B) preposterous
   (C) potable   (D) pretentious

2. The author received a _____
award for her contributions to
literature, years after her death.

   (A) posthumous   (B) premonition
   (C) pretentious   (D) precocious

3. She had a sudden sense of
_____, feeling something bad
was about to happen.

   (A) preposterous   (B) premonition
   (C) pragmatic   (D) potable

4. This new pain reliever is a
_____ medicine, offering relief
almost instantly.

   (A) posterity   (B) pragmatic
   (C) potent   (D) potable

5. The _____ child amazed
everyone by solving advanced
math problems at the age of five.

   (A) potent   (B) posthumous
   (C) pretentious   (D) precocious

1. (C) 2. (A) 3. (B) 4. (C) 5. (D)
Answers

371	prevalent	376	prudent
372	pristine	377	prune
373	procrastinate	378	pseudonym
374	prolific	379	pugnacious
375	promenade	380	pun

School Motto

"Suaviter in Modo Fortiter in Re"

(resolute in execution, gentle in manner)
- Stevenson School

SSATKOREA.com

prevalent
[**prev**-uh-l*uh*nt]

adj. widespread or in general use

일반적인

*This condition is more **prevalent** in men than in women.*

syn. common, widespread, accepted

pristine
[**pris**-teen]

adj. uncorrupted or unsullied

완전 새것 같은, 아주 깨끗한

*The car is in **pristine** condition.*

syn. intact, clean, immaculate

procrastinate
[proh-**kras**-tuh-neyt]

v. to delay

미루다

*You **procrastinated**.*
You should have done it little by little.

syn. delay, suspend, dawdle

prolific
[pruh-**lif**-ik]

adj. highly fruitful

생산성이 많은, 다량을 생산하는, 다작의

*She is a **prolific** writer of novels.*

syn. productive, fruitful, fertile

promenade
[prom-*uh*-**neyd**]

n. a stroll or walk as for pleasure or a path for walkingn. the original model

산책, 산책로

*The girls strolled along on the **promenade** eating ice creams.*

syn. stroll, leisurely walk, boardwalk

prudent
[**prood**-nt]

adj. wise or judicious in practical affairs

신중한

*I don't think he is **prudent** in his behavior.*

syn. discreet, wise, cautious

prune

[proon]

v. to cut or lop off

잘라내다, 가지를 치다

*When should we **prune** our rose bushes?*

syn. trim, crop, shave

pseudonym

[sood-n-im]

n. a fictitious name to conceal his or her identity

필명, 가명

*Robert Galbraith is a **pseudonym** for J.K. Rowling*

syn. alias, pen name, nickname

pugnacious

[puhg-**ney**-sh*uh*s]

adj. inclined to quarrel or fight readily

싸우기 좋아하는, 공격적인

*English sparrows are **pugnacious** birds.*

syn. belligerent, combative, aggressive

pun

[puhn]

n. the humorous use of a word or phrase

말장난

*A good **pun** brings the smaller excellencies of conversation.*

syn. wordplay, play on words, double entendre

ISEE Sentence Completion 8-3

Directions : Fill in the blanks to complete the sentences.

1. The comedian's routine was filled with clever jokes and the occasional _____ that delighted the audience.

   (A) pun   (B) prune
   (C) pseudonym   (D) procrastinate

2. Tourists enjoyed a leisurely walk along the _____, taking in the scenic views.

   (A) prevalent   (B) prune
   (C) promenade   (D) pseudonym

3. Students who _____ on tasks often find themselves overwhelmed as deadlines approach.

   (A) prevalent   (B) prune
   (C) promenade   (D) procrastinate

4. She was a _____ writer, producing several bestsellers in a short span of time.

   (A) pun   (B) prolific
   (C) pseudonym   (D) pugnacious

5. The artifact was found in a _____ condition, untouched by the passage of time.

   (A) prune   (B) prudent
   (C) pristine   (D) pugnacious

Answers

1. (A) 2. (C) 3. (D) 4. (B) 5. (C)

381 pungent	386 quell
382 puzzle	387 quench
383 quaint	388 quixotic
384 qualm	389 rampant
385 quarantine	390 ratify

School Motto

"Esse Quam Videri"

(To be, rather than to seem)

- Suffield Academy

SSATKOREA.com

pungent
[**puhn**-ju*h*nt]

adj. sharply affecting the organs of taste or smell

(맛이나 냄새가) 심하게 자극적인

*Garlic has a **pungent** taste and odor.*

syn. sharp, acrid, tart

puzzle
[**puhz**-*uh*l]

v. be a mystery or bewildering to

어리둥절하게 만들다

*What **puzzles** me is why he left the country without telling anyone.*

syn. baffle, confuse, frustrate

quaint
[kweynt]

adj. having an old-fashioned attractiveness or charm

진기한, 매력 있게 예스러운

*He has a **quaint** way of speaking.*

syn. bizarre, strange, odd

qualm
[kwahm]

n. an uneasy feeling of conscience as to conduct

양심의 가책, 거리낌

*He had been working very hard so he had no **qualms** about taking a few days off*

syn. misgiving, anxiety, suspicion

quarantine
[**kwawr**-*uh*n-teen]

n. a strict isolation

격리

*This is a biohazard **quarantine** area.*

syn. isolation, detention, separation

quell
[kwel]

v. to stop something, especially by using force

진압하다, 평정하다, 가라앉히다

*The troops **quelled** the rebellion quickly.*

syn. suppress, defeat, extinguish

quench

[kwench]

v. to satisfy a need or wish

(갈증을) 풀다, 해소하다

His thirst for knowledge will never be quenched.

syn. satisfy, sate, satiate

quixotic

[kwik-**sot**-ik]

adj. extravagantly chivalrous or romantic

비현실적인, 이상주의적인

*The heroes are **quixotic** and romantic.*

syn. idealistic, foolish, unrealistic

rampant

[**ram**-p*uh*nt]

adj. spreading uncontrollably, especially something negative

(나쁜 것이) 걷잡을 수 없는, 만연한

*Cheating on tests became **rampant** in the school, so the teachers decided to take stricter measures.*

syn. widespread, uncontrolled, unrestrained

ratify

[**rat**-uh-fahy]

v. to confirm by expressing consent

승인하다, 허가하다

*All the members have voted to **ratify** the treaty.*

syn. approve, confirm, endorse

Directions : Fill in the blanks to complete the sentences.

1. They enjoyed their stay in a _____ village with cobblestone streets and charming cottages.

   (A) quixotic   (B) quaint
   (C) pungent   (D) quarantine

2. Despite initial support, she began to have _____ about the decision as the consequences became clear.

   (A) quell   (B) quench
   (C) qualms   (D) quaint

3. The committee dismissed the plan as a _____ project, deeming it too impractical to implement.

   (A) quixotic   (B) pungent
   (C) ratify   (D) quell

4. In the wake of the scandal, rumors were _____ throughout the company, undermining trust among the employees.

   (A) quench   (B) rampant
   (C) ratify   (D) ravenous

5. The military was deployed to _____ the rebellion before it spread to neighboring cities.

   (A) puzzle   (B) quench
   (C) pungent   (D) quell

1. (B)   2. (C)   3. (A)   4. (B)   5. (D)

Answers

391	rational	396	rectify
392	ravenous	397	recuperate
393	recalcitrant	398	refute
394	reciprocal	399	reiterate
395	recluse	400	relegate

School Motto

"Vincit Semper Veritas"

(Truth Always Conquers)

- Tabor Academy

SSATKOREA.com

rational
[**rash**-uh-nl]

adj. having its source in or being guided by the intellect

합리적인

*Don't jump to conclusions.
Be rational.*

syn. sensible, reasonable, judicious

ravenous
[**rav**-uh-n*uh*s]

adj. extremely hungry

몹시 굶주린, 게걸스러운, 탐욕스러운

*The lions have not eaten for
four days and are ravenous.*

syn. gluttonous, greedy, voracious

recalcitrant
[ri-**kal**-si-tr*uh*nt]

adj. resisting authority or control

반항하는, 다루기 힘든

*At last, the recalcitrant leader engaged
in talks towards reconciliation.*

syn. obstinate, disobedient, uncontrollable

reciprocal
[ri-**sip**-ruh-k*uh*l]

adj. given or felt by each toward the other

상호적인, 서로간의

*She was hoping for some reciprocal
respect.*

syn. mutual, alternate, exchanged

recluse
[**rek**-loos]

n. a person living in seclusion or apart
from society

은둔자

*He has led the life of a recluse since
his wife died.*

syn. hermit, solitaire, introvert

rectify
[**rek**-t*uh*-fahy]

v. to correct something or make
something right

바로잡다, 정정하다, 고치다

*We must rectify any mistakes before
the book is printed.*

syn. fix, correct, amend

recuperate
[ri-**koo**-*puh*-reyt]

v. to recover from sickness or exhaustionv.

회복하다, 건강을 되찾다

He spent several months recuperating after the operation.

syn. convalesce, recover, get well

refute
[ri-**fyoot**]

v. to prove to be false

반박하다

It was the kind of rumor that it is impossible to refute.

syn. rebut, contradict, oppose

reiterate
[ree-**it**-*uh*-reyt]

v. to say or do again or repeatedly

반복하다, 되풀이하다

The president reiterated refusal to compromise with terrorists.

syn. repeat, echo, restate

relegate
[**rel**-i-geyt]

v. to send or consign to an interior position

좌천하다, 계급을 떨어뜨리다, 강등시키다

He was relegated to the role of assistant.

syn. demote, downgrade, dismiss

ISEE Sentence Completion 8-5

Directions : Fill in the blanks to complete the sentences.

1. The programmer worked tirelessly to _____ the error in the system before the deadline.

   (A) relegate   (B) rectify
   (C) recuperate   (D) rational

2. The manager made a _____ decision based on logic and data rather than emotions.

   (A) rational   (B) recluse
   (C) reciprocal   (D) ravenous

3. The teacher struggled to deal with the student's _____ attitude, as they constantly resisted authority.

   (A) reciprocal   (B) recuperate
   (C) relegate   (D) recalcitrant

4. The two companies formed a _____ relationship, agreeing to share resources for mutual benefit.

   (A) rational   (B) ravenous
   (C) reciprocal   (D) reiterate

5. After skipping breakfast, he sat down to lunch with a _____ appetite.

   (A) refute   (B) rational
   (C) reiterate   (D) ravenous

Analogy 18. Literary Devices

01. The world is your oyster.

Metaphor 은유법
A figure of speech that identifies something as being the same as some unrelated thing for rhetorical effect, thus highlighting the similarities between the two

02. The king was as brave as a lion.

Simile 직유법
A figure of speech involving the comparison of one thing with another thing of a different kind, used to make a description more emphatic or vivid. "As" and "like" are used

03. The pen is mightier than the sword.

Metonymy 환유법
A figure of speech in which a thing or concept is called not by its own name but rather by the name of something associated in meaning with that thing

04. The stars dance in the sky.

Personification 의인법
A rhetorical device in which a thing or animal is given human characteristics

05. The traffic cop got his license suspended for unpaid parking tickets.

Irony 반어법
The expression of one's meaning by using language that normally signifies the opposite, typically for humorous or emphatic effect

06. To ensure peace, the two countries must continue to build weapons.

Paradox 역설법
A statement that apparently contradicts itself and yet might be true

07. Bam! Splash!! Slam!!!

Onomatopoeia 의성어
A word that phonetically imitates, resembles or suggests the source of the sound that it describes

08. Peter Piper Picked a Peck of Pickled Peppers.

Alliteration 두운법
A stylistic literary device identified by the repeated sound of the first consonant in a series of multiple words at the beginning of words

09. Humpty Dumpty sat on a wall Humpty Dumpty had a great fall.

Rhyme 각운법
Correspondence of sound between words or the endings of words, especially when these are used at the ends of lines of poetry

10. Life is short, but art is long.

Contrast 대조법
Device used to describe difference(s) between two or more entities

Check-up 8-1

Directions — Each of the following questions consists of one word followed by five words or phrases. You are to select the one word or phrase whose meaning is closest to the word in capital letters.

1. PETITION
- (A) appeal
- (B) elixir
- (C) glut
- (D) connoisseur
- (E) repose

2. PETTY
- (A) forlorn
- (B) innate
- (C) sensible
- (D) trivial
- (E) temperate

3. PHILANTHROPY
- (A) despotism
- (B) charity
- (C) euphemism
- (D) aristocracy
- (E) epiphany

4. PLAGIARIZE
- (A) chatter
- (B) abstain
- (C) steal
- (D) nod
- (E) indulge

5. PLUMMET
- (A) abdicate
- (B) disparage
- (C) hinder
- (D) immerse
- (E) plunge

6. POIGNANT
- (A) pithy
- (B) reserved
- (C) irate
- (D) heartrending
- (E) saved

7. POLISH
- (A) burnish
- (B) tether
- (C) wander
- (D) revere
- (E) appease

8. POMPOUS
- (A) humble
- (B) beneficial
- (C) overdue
- (D) unassuming
- (E) arrogant

9. PONDER
- (A) bellow
- (B) contemplate
- (C) rehearse
- (D) clasp
- (E) escalate

10. POROUS
- (A) minute
- (B) ponderous
- (C) dumbfounded
- (D) impromptu
- (E) absorbent

Check-up 8-2

Each of the following questions consists of one word followed by five words or phrases.
You are to select the one word or phrase whose meaning is closest to the word in capital letters.

1. POSTERITY
(A) progeny
(B) boor
(C) cooper
(D) bumpkin
(E) erudite

2. POSTHUMOUS
(A) assailant
(B) tepid
(C) after death
(D) shallow
(E) poach

3. POSTURE
(A) rivulet
(B) leniency
(C) augment
(D) stance
(E) solace

4. POTABLE
(A) lukewarm
(B) strewn
(C) vigilant
(D) laconic
(E) drinkable

5. POTENT
(A) powerful
(B) pliable
(C) illegible
(D) pungent
(E) amusing

6. PRAGMATIC
(A) fanciful
(B) absurd
(C) muddled
(D) practical
(E) quixotic

7. PRECOCIOUS
(A) superficial
(B) forethought
(C) advanced
(D) repulsive
(E) contradictory

8. PREMONITION
(A) forewarning
(B) pitfall
(C) pinnacle
(D) hilarious
(E) luminescence

9. PREPOSTEROUS
(A) exotic
(B) absurd
(C) pernicious
(D) narcissistic
(E) floundering

10. PRETENTIOUS
(A) headstrong
(B) snobbish
(C) muddled
(D) enthusiastic
(E) pecuniary

Check-up 8-3

Directions Each of the following questions consists of one word followed by five words or phrases.
You are to select the one word or phrase whose meaning is closest to the word in capital letters.

1. PREVALENT
(A) common
(B) phlegmatic
(C) treasonous
(D) culinary
(E) shared

2. PRISTINE
(A) ecumenical
(B) distasteful
(C) stubborn
(D) abominable
(E) intact

3. PROCRASTINATE
(A) remit
(B) sprinkle
(C) sully
(D) delay
(E) tarnish

4. PROLIFIC
(A) reluctant
(B) confident
(C) courageous
(D) productive
(E) concerned

5. PROMENADE
(A) stroll
(B) turncoat
(C) claim
(D) finale
(E) apostate

6. PRUDENT
(A) ornate
(B) eminent
(C) discreet
(D) despicable
(E) lithe

7. PRUNE
(A) rustle
(B) bellow
(C) grieve
(D) trim
(E) misconstrue

8. PSEUDONYM
(A) memorandum
(B) insomnia
(C) dissertation
(D) strongbox
(E) alias

9. PUGNACIOUS
(A) belligerent
(B) complimentary
(C) amiable
(D) ingenuous
(E) fair minded

10. PUN
(A) sonnet
(B) wordplay
(C) syntax
(D) amnesia
(E) brawl

Check-up 8-4

1. PUNGENT
- (A) exemplary
- (B) gentle
- (C) sharp
- (D) mild
- (E) predictable

2. PUZZLE
- (A) retract
- (B) abbreviate
- (C) baffle
- (D) withdraw
- (E) misjudge

3. QUAINT
- (A) bizarre
- (B) avaricious
- (C) mortified
- (D) delighted
- (E) humiliated

4. QUALM
- (A) alms
- (B) subpoena
- (C) obeisance
- (D) misgiving
- (E) royalty

5. QUARANTINE
- (A) swarm
- (B) din
- (C) mob
- (D) understatement
- (E) isolation

6. QUELL
- (A) broach
- (B) suppress
- (C) elicit
- (D) blackmail
- (E) loom

7. QUENCH
- (A) direct
- (B) motivate
- (C) satisfy
- (D) vitalize
- (E) weld

8. QUIXOTIC
- (A) earnest
- (B) recurrent
- (C) nimble
- (D) idealistic
- (E) diligent

9. RAMPANT
- (A) antithetical
- (B) comparable
- (C) malnourished
- (D) widespread
- (E) identical

10. RATIFY
- (A) scatter
- (B) rectify
- (C) extinguish
- (D) coordinate
- (E) approve

Check-up 8-5

Directions   Each of the following questions consists of one word followed by five words or phrases.
You are to select the one word or phrase whose meaning is closest to the word in capital letters.

1. RATIONAL
- (A) overblown
- (B) vivid
- (C) sensible
- (D) withdrawn
- (E) obscure

2. RAVENOUS
- (A) reserved
- (B) vibrant
- (C) arcane
- (D) gluttonous
- (E) prudish

3. RECALCITRANT
- (A) obstinate
- (B) habitable
- (C) tranquil
- (D) docile
- (E) gullible

4. RECIPROCAL
- (A) palatable
- (B) olfactory
- (C) mutual
- (D) illustrious
- (E) boorish

5. RECLUSE
- (A) anarchist
- (B) iconoclast
- (C) stipend
- (D) burglar
- (E) hermit

6. RECTIFY
- (A) snoop
- (B) commence
- (C) aggravate
- (D) reassure
- (E) fix

7. RECUPERATE
- (A) convalesce
- (B) reminisce
- (C) remit
- (D) repudiate
- (E) chastise

8. REFUTE
- (A) skitter
- (B) glance
- (C) rebut
- (D) exonerate
- (E) exempt

9. REITERATE
- (A) reproduce
- (B) confiscate
- (C) purloin
- (D) repeat
- (E) chide

10. RELEGATE
- (A) impound
- (B) demote
- (C) jabber
- (D) scrutinize
- (E) renounce

Answer 1.C 2.D 3.A 4.C 5.E 6.E 7.A 8.C 9.D 10.B

401 relentless	406 replica
402 relinquish	407 reproach
403 reminisce	408 repulsive
404 remorse	409 requisite
405 reparation	410 rescind

School Motto

"Non ut sibi ministretur sed ut ministret"

(Not to be served but to serve)

- Taft School

SSATKOREA.com

relentless
[ri-**lent**-lis]

adj. unyieldingly severe, strict, or harsh

끈질긴, 수그러들지 않는

This relentless pressure began to wear down their resistance.

syn. persistent, harsh, cruel

relinquish
[ri-**ling**-kwish]

v. to renounce or surrender

(마지못해 소유권 등을) 포기하다, 내주다

No one wants to relinquish power once they have it.

syn. renounce, surrender, yield

reminisce
[rem-uh-**nis**]

v. to recall past experiences or events

추억에 잠기다, 회상하다

She likes to reminisce about her childhood.

syn. retrospect, recollect, recall

remorse
[ri-**mawrs**]

n. a feeling of deep regret

후회, 회한

She felt remorse when she saw the outcome of her action.

syn. regret, guilt, sorrow

reparation
[rep-uh-**rey**-sh*uh*n]

n. the making of amends for wrong or injury done

배상, 보상

Offenders must make reparation for their crimes.

syn. compensation, restitution, amends

replica
[**rep**-li-kuh]

n. an exact copy

복사, 복제품

She made a 1:5 scale replica of a real ship.

syn. facsimile, copy, duplicate

reproach
[ri-**prohch**]

v. to find fault with

비난하다, 야단치다

Do not reproach yourself, it was not your fault.

syn. reprove, reprimand, reprehend

repulsive
[ri-**puhl**-siv]

adj. causing intense dislike or disgust

역겨운, 혐오스러운

The smell coming from the garbage was absolutely repulsive.

syn. disgusting, revolting, offensive

requisite
[**rek**-wuh-zit]

n. a required or necessary thing for a particular purpose

필수품, 꼭 필요한 것

Self-confidence is the first requisite to great undertakings.

syn. requirement, necessity, precondition

rescind
[ri-**sind**]

v. to invalidate an act or measure

(법률, 계약 등을) 폐지하다, 철회하다

You cannot rescind the contract simply because our payment is delayed by one day.

syn. annul, revoke, repeal

ISEE Sentence Completion 9-1

Directions : **Fill in the blanks to complete the sentences.**

1. The government demanded that the company pay _____ for the environmental damage it caused.

   (A) relentless   (B) requisite
   (C) reparation   (D) reproach

2. They gathered around the fireplace to _____ about the past, sharing memories of their youth.

   (A) replica   (B) relentless
   (C) requisite   (D) reminisce

3. The museum displayed an exact _____ of the ancient artifact to protect the original from damage.

   (A) replica   (B) repulsive
   (C) requisite   (D) reminisce

4. He felt deep _____ for his actions, realizing the hurt he caused to his loved ones.

   (A) repulsive   (B) remorse
   (C) reparation   (D) rescind

5. Despite multiple failures, her _____ pursuit of success inspired those around her.

   (A) replica   (B) remorse
   (C) requisite   (D) relentless

1. (C) 2. (D) 3. (A) 4. (B) 5. (D)

Answers

411 resilient   416 retort

412 restitution   417 retract

413 restrain   418 retribution

414 resuscitate   419 retrospect

415 retaliate   420 revere

School Motto

"Non sibi sed aliis"

(Not for self, but for others)

- The Governor's Academy

SSATKOREA.com

resilient
[ri-**zil**-y*uh*nt]

adj. returning to the original form

회복력이 있는, 탄성이 있는

He was so resilient that he could recover quickly from unfortunate circumstances.

syn.   elastic, bouncy, flexible

restitution
[res-ti-**too**-sh*uh*n]

n. the act of restoring something to the rightful owner

배상, 보상

He had to make restitution for the broken window, paying for its replacement.

syn.   compensation, reimbursement, repayment

restrain
[ri-streyn]

v. to keep under control

저지하다, 제지하다

When she found herself face to face with a dessert case, she had to restrain herself.

syn.   hold back, constrain, restrict

resuscitate
[ri-**suhs**-i-teyt]

v. to revive, especially from apparent death

소생시키다, 다시 살리다

Ambulance workers are skilled at resuscitating heart and lungs.

syn.   revive, rejuvenate, revitalize

retaliate
[ri-**tal**-ee-eyt]

v. to return like for like, especially evil for evil

보복하다, 앙갚음하다

When Ellen tripped Tanya in the schoolyard, Tanya retaliated by pulling Ellen's hair.

syn.   revenge, repay, avenge

retort
[ri-**tawrt**]

v. to reply in a sharp or retaliatory way

쏘아붙이다, 대꾸하다

'Mind your own business,' Jamie retorted angrily.

syn.   repartee, retaliate, respond

retract

[ri-**trakt**]

v. to draw back or in

(속으로) 들어가다, 움츠리다, 취소하다

*A tiger **retracts** its claw.*

syn. withdraw, revoke, renounce

retribution

[re-truh-**byoo**-sh*uh*n]

n. punishment for offenses

보복, 징벌

*She speaks the truth to the public without fear of **retribution**.*

syn. vengeance, reprisal, revenge

retrospect

[**re**-truh-spekt]

n. looking back and contemplating the past

회상, 회고, 추억

*In **retrospect**, she found herself wishing that she had done some things differently.*

syn. recollection, reminiscence, hindsight

revere

[ri-**veer**]

v. to regard with respect tinged with awe

숭배하다, 경외하다, 존경하다

*Lance **reveres** his favorite author, Ernest Hemingway.*

syn. venerate, worship, exalt

ISEE Sentence Completion 9-2

Directions : **Fill in the blanks to complete the sentences.**

1. Despite the hardships she endured, her _____ nature allowed her to overcome every challenge.

   (A) resilient   (B) restitution
   (C) restrain   (D) retrospect

2. The politician was forced to _____ the false statement after public outrage.

   (A) resilient   (B) retaliate
   (C) retract   (D) resuscitate

3. The soldiers planned to _____ against the enemy's sudden and unexpected attack.

   (A) retract   (B) restrain
   (C) restitution   (D) retaliate

4. Her sharp _____ silenced her critic, who had been making unfair accusations.

   (A) retort   (B) retribution
   (C) resuscitate   (D) retrospect

5. The court ordered the _____ of the stolen property to its rightful owner.

   (A) retribution   (B) revere
   (C) restrain   (D) restitution

421	revert	426	ruthless
422	revile	427	sabotage
423	robust	428	sage
424	rotund	429	sanctimonious
425	rugged	430	sanguine

School Motto

"Whatsoever things are true."

- The Hill School

SSATKOREA.com

revert
[ri-**vurt**]

v. to return to a former habit or condition

(본래 상태나 습관으로) 되돌아가다

*House cats will **revert** to a wild, feral state if they are left outside.*

syn. backslide, lapse, regress

revile
[ri-**vahyl**]

v. to scold abusively

심하게 꾸짖다, 심하게 욕하다

*No one likes spam calls, and they are widely **reviled**.*

syn. vilify, berate, castigate

robust
[roh-**buhst**]

adj. strong and healthy

원기 왕성한, 건강한

*His **robust** strength made him survive the disaster.*

syn. healthy, strong, vigorous

rotund
[roh-**tuhnd**]

adj. plump or round

둥근, 퉁퉁하게 살찐

*My chubby Aunt Margie is **rotund** like a teapot.*

syn. plump, round, portly

rugged
[**ruhg**-id]

adj. Strong and tough

강인한, 튼튼한

*He had a **rugged** look, with a strong jawline and a sun-tanned face.*

syn. tough, masculine, weathered

ruthless
[**rooth**-lis]

adj. without pity or compassion

잔인한, 무자비한

*She is **ruthless** in her dealings with competitors.*

syn. cruel, merciless, truculent

sabotage

[**sab**-uh-tahzh]

n. a deliberate act of destruction

고의적인 방해, 고의적인 파괴

*If you don't believe in yourself, you cause **sabotage** to yourself.*

syn. destruction, damage, vandalism

sage

[seyj]

n. a profoundly wise person

현명한 사람, 지혜로운 사람

*Warren Buffett, an American business magnate, is often called the **Sage** of Omaha.*

syn. wise person, mentor, guru

sanctimonious

[sangk-tuh-**moh**-nee-*uh*s]

adj. making a hypocritical show of religious devotion

독실한 체하는

*The **sanctimonious** religious leader preached about morality.*

syn. hypocritical, preachy, self-righteous

sanguine

[**sang**-gwin]

adj. cheerfully optimistic, hopeful, or confident

낙관적인, 자신감이 넘치는

*He tends to take a **sanguine** view of the problems involved.*

syn. optimistic, hopeful, positive

ISEE Sentence Completion 9-3

Directions : Fill in the blanks to complete the sentences.

1. His _____ behavior in business often led to success, but at the cost of losing trust from his peers.

   (A) ruthless   (B) sanguine
   (C) sanctimonious   (D) robust

2. The new software was praised for being a _____ system that could handle heavy workloads.

   (A) sage   (B) robust
   (C) ruthless   (D) rugged

3. After weeks of discipline, he began to _____ to his old habits of procrastination and lateness.

   (A) revert   (B) revile
   (C) rugged   (D) sabotage

4. The cartoon featured a jolly character with a distinctly _____ figure, adding to their comedic appeal.

   (A) revert   (B) sanctimonious
   (C) rotund   (D) sanguine

5. The spy was caught attempting to _____ the enemy's plan by leaking false information.

   (A) sage   (B) revert
   (C) rugged   (D) sabotage

431	sarcastic	436	sedentary
432	satiate	437	seditious
433	scrutinize	438	segregate
434	secede	439	sequester
435	sedate	440	shirk

School Motto

"Virtus Scientia"

(Virtue through knowledge)

- The Hockaday School

SSATKOREA.com

sarcastic
[sahr-**kas**-tik]

adj. expressing irony or mockery

비꼬는, 풍자적인, 빈정대는

*His **sarcastic** tone made it hard to tell if he was serious.*

syn.   ironic, mocking, snarky

satiate
[**sey**-shee-yet]

v. to satisfy fully

(욕구를 충분히) 채우다

*The more the heart is **satiated** with joy, the more it becomes insatiable.*

syn.   satisfy, gratify, indulge

scrutinize
[**skroot**-n-ahyz]

v. to examine in detail with careful attontion

세심히 살피다, 면밀히 조사하다

*Be sure to **scrutinize** your essays for spelling and grammar errors.*

syn.   examine, inspect, observe

secede
[si-**seed**]

v. to withdraw from an alliance, federation, or association

(동맹, 연합, 협회 등에서) 탈퇴하다, 분리 독립하다

*Britain decided to **secede** from the European Union.*

syn.   withdraw, separate, break away

sedate
[si-**deyt**]

adj. calm, quiet, or composed

차분한, 조용한

*We set off again at a more **sedate** pace.*

syn.   calm, collected, placid

sedentary
[**sed**-n-ter-ee]

adj. characterized by or requiring a sitting posture

주로 앉아서 하는, 좌식의

*Humans adopted a **sedentary** rather than a mobile lifestyle after learning how to farm.*

syn.   fixed, immobile, inactive

seditious

[si-**dish**-*uhs*]

adj. encouraging rebellion or resistance against authority

선동적인, 반란을 부추기는

*The leader was arrested for making **seditious** speeches against the government.*

syn. rebellious, subversive, incendiary

segregate

[**seg**-ri-geyt]

v. to separate or set apart

분리하다, 차별하다

*The teacher decided to **segregate** the students into groups based on their skill levels.*

syn. separate, isolate, divide

sequester

[si-**kwes**-ter]

v. to remove or withdraw into solitude or retirement

격리시키다, 떨어뜨려 놓다

*The jury is expected to be **sequestered** for at least two months.*

syn. isolate, seclude, quarantine

shirk

[shurk]

v. to get out of responsibility

(의무를) 피하다, 안 하려하다

*If you **shirk** your responsibilities duties now, the situation will just be that much harder.*

syn. avoid, evade, elude

ISEE Sentence Completion 9-4

Directions : Fill in the blanks to complete the sentences.

1. The editor took extra time to _____ the details of the manuscript before it was sent to print.

   (A) shirk　　　　(B) secede
   (C) satiate　　　(D) scrutinize

2. A _____ lifestyle can lead to various health problems, including obesity and heart disease.

   (A) satiate　　　(B) sedentary
   (C) sedate　　　(D) scrutinize

3. The region decided to _____ from the union due to political and economic disagreements.

   (A) secede　　　(B) segregate
   (C) sequester　　(D) sedate

4. The government arrested individuals involved in _____ activity aimed at overthrowing the administration.

   (A) sarcastic　　(B) sequester
   (C) seditious　　(D) segregate

5. The controversial policy served to further _____ communities, rather than fostering unity.

   (A) sedate　　　(B) shirk
   (C) satiate　　　(D) segregate

 Answers

1. (D)　2. (B)　3. (A)　4. (C)　5. (D)

441 simultaneous 446 sneer

442 skirmish 447 snub

443 slander 448 sojourn

444 smear 449 speculate

445 smolder 450 stipulation

School Motto

"Moniti Meliora Sequamur"

(Guided by each other, let us seek better paths)

- The Hotchkiss School

SSATKOREA.com

simultaneous
[sahy-m*uh*l-**tey**-nee-*uhs*]

adj. existing , occurring, or operating at the same time

동시의, 동시에 일어나는

The explosion was almost simultaneous with the announcement.

syn. concurrent, contemporaneous, concomitant

skirmish
[**skur**-mish]

n. a fight between small bodies of troops

소규모 접전, 충돌

Today, every skirmish in every part of the planet is broadcast straight into your living room live.

syn. clash, scuffle, fight

slander
[**slan**-der]

n. the act of making a false or negative statement

악의적인 소문을 퍼뜨림, 비방

She does not care about rumors full of slander.

syn. defamation, libel, smear

smear
[smeer]

v. to tarnish a reputation

(명예나 명성을) 더럽히다, 실추시키다

His arm was smeared with dirt.

syn. sully, tarnish, taint

smolder
[**smohl**-der]

v. to burn slowly without flames

(불꽃 없이 서서히) 타다

The logs smoldered in the fireplace.

syn. burn, smoke, glow

sneer
[sneer]

v. to express through a scornful smile

비웃다, 조롱하다

Although some may sneer, working as a secretary is for many the fastest route to career success.

syn. mock, condemn, jeer

snub

[snuhb]

v. to rebuff, ignore, or spurn disdainfully

모욕하다, 무시하다

I tried to be friendly, but she snubbed me completely.

syn. ignore, disregard, boycott

sojourn

[**soh**-jurn]

n. a temporary stay

체류, 일시적인 머무름

Next weekend, we're going to take a sojourn into Nicaragua.

syn. stay, visit, stopover

speculate

[**spek**-yuh-leyt]

v. to think about deeply and theorize

추측하다, 짐작하다

I wouldn't like to speculate on the reasons for her resignation.

syn. guess, surmise, theorize

stipulation

[stip-yuh-**ley**-shuhn]

n. a condition, demand, or promise in an agreement or contract

(계약이나 법률상의) 조항, 조건

You must be careful of any stipulation before accepting it.

syn. condition, clause, specification

ISEE Sentence Completion 9-5

Directions : Fill in the blanks to complete the sentences.

1. The two explosions were _____ and caused widespread panic in the city.

   (A) stipulation   (B) sojourn
   (C) smear   (D) simultaneous

2. The diplomat decided to _____ the invitation, sending a clear message of disapproval to the host.

   (A) snub   (B) skirmish
   (C) smolder   (D) simultaneous

3. The contract included a strict _____ that all work must be completed by the end of the month.

   (A) smear   (B) sojourn
   (C) stipulation   (D) smolder

4. His rivals tried to _____ his reputation by spreading baseless rumors about his past.

   (A) smear   (B) simultaneous
   (C) skirmish   (D) stipulation

5. During his short _____ in the countryside, he found the peace he had been longing for.

   (A) sneer   (B) sojourn
   (C) speculate   (D) stipulation

1. (D) 2. (A) 3. (C) 4. (A) 5. (B)

💣 **Answers**

Analogy 19. Symbols

[상징 : 의미] 관계는 상징으로 사용되는 단어가 특정 의미를 나타내거나 연결되는 관계를 의미합니다. 이러한 관계는 상징과 의미 사이의 문화적, 역사적, 또는 보편적으로 이해되는 연관성에 기반합니다. 특히, 기독교 문화나 그리스-로마 신화와 같은 배경 지식이 있다면 이러한 관계를 더 쉽게 이해할 수 있습니다.

A는 B의 내용이나 감정을 담은 작품

dove : peace
비둘기 : 평화

owl : wisdom
올빼미 : 지혜

ant : diligence
개미 : 근면함

fox : cunning
여우 : 교활함

crown : authority
왕관 : 권력

flag : nation
국기 : 국가

chain : bondage
사슬 : 속박

feather : freedom
깃털 : 자유

scales : justice
저울 : 정의

cross : faith
십자가 : 신앙

skull : danger
해골 : 위험

olive branch : truce
올리브 가지 : 휴전

bridge : connection
다리 : 연결

path : journey
길 : 여정

POP QUIZ

1. Olive branch is to truce as
- (A) chain is to bondage
- (B) war is to wage
- (C) love is to hate
- (D) hope is to pessimism
- (E) light is to darkness

2. Fox is to cunning as
- (A) rose is to greed
- (B) bird is to aviary
- (C) dog is to pedigree
- (D) ant is to colony
- (E) owl is to wisdom

Check-up 9-1

1. RELENTLESS

(A) innate
(B) persistent
(C) incredible
(D) genuine
(E) inflammable

2. RELINQUISH

(A) moor
(B) hoax
(C) renounce
(D) envelop
(E) insist

3. REMINISCE

(A) gaze
(B) stare
(C) dissent
(D) retrospect
(E) glimpse

4. REMORSE

(A) regret
(B) habitat
(C) malfunction
(D) route
(E) fatigue

5. REPARATION

(A) expedition
(B) boycott
(C) caliber
(D) aplomb
(E) compensation

6. REPLICA

(A) vitality
(B) facsimile
(C) onslaught
(D) budget
(E) recital

7. REPROACH

(A) captivate
(B) renounce
(C) corrode
(D) deceive
(E) reprove

8. REPULSIVE

(A) amiable
(B) buoyant
(C) elastic
(D) disgusting
(E) merciful

9. REQUISITE

(A) crusade
(B) pantomime
(C) reputation
(D) requirement
(E) misgiving

10. RESCIND

(A) loom
(B) err
(C) contend
(D) annul
(E) detract

323

Check-up 9-2

1. RESILIENT
(A) elastic
(B) heedful
(C) solitary
(D) meager
(E) rational

2. RESTITUTION
(A) integrity
(B) fidelity
(C) oracle
(D) compensation
(E) liability

3. RESTRAIN
(A) get off
(B) hold back
(C) pull up
(D) carry on
(E) take apart

4. RESUSCITATE
(A) soar
(B) recede
(C) debunk
(D) revive
(E) agitate

5. RETALIATE
(A) mediate
(B) commence
(C) devastate
(D) revenge
(E) compromise

6. RETORT
(A) recourse
(B) replenish
(C) resort
(D) repartee
(E) renovate

7. RETRACT
(A) perceive
(B) compel
(C) implicate
(D) withdraw
(E) involve

8. RETRIBUTION
(A) prowess
(B) vengeance
(C) garland
(D) maneuver
(E) proximity

9. RETROSPECT
(A) era
(B) debut
(C) recollection
(D) locomotion
(E) component

10. REVERE
(A) repulse
(B) ebb
(C) annihilate
(D) wax
(E) venerate

Check-up 9-3

Directions   Each of the following questions consists of one word followed by five words or phrases. You are to select the one word or phrase whose meaning is closest to the word in capital letters.

1. REVERT
(A) petrify
(B) hover
(C) backslide
(D) flourish
(E) enlighten

2. REVILE
(A) vilify
(B) dominate
(C) eliminate
(D) dispatch
(E) enroll

3. ROBUST
(A) formidable
(B) haughty
(C) dilapidated
(D) fluctuate
(E) healthy

4. ROTUND
(A) grueling
(B) plump
(C) illiterate
(D) benevolent
(E) drastic

5. RUGGED
(A) tender
(B) skeptical
(C) pedestrian
(D) digressive
(E) tough

6. RUTHLESS
(A) invincible
(B) lucrative
(C) cruel
(D) polyglot
(E) sacred

7. SABOTAGE
(A) jest
(B) destruction
(C) ecstasy
(D) revelry
(E) theme

8. SAGE
(A) a wise person
(B) a sense of pride
(C) an antique jewelry
(D) a massive attack
(E) a streaming cold

9. SANCTIMONIOUS
(A) restful
(B) curious
(C) hypocritical
(D) tedious
(E) religious

10. SANGUINE
(A) colossal
(B) toxic
(C) pathetic
(D) ultimate
(E) optimistic

325

Check-up 9-4

Each of the following questions consists of one word followed by five words or phrases. You are to select the one word or phrase whose meaning is closest to the word in capital letters.

1. SARCASTIC
(A) tactful
(B) demure
(C) ironic
(D) still
(E) wistful

2. SATIATE
(A) locate
(B) ponder
(C) fascinate
(D) satisfy
(E) unveil

3. SCRUTINIZE
(A) depart
(B) lurk
(C) perish
(D) examine
(E) consent

4. SECEDE
(A) ensure
(B) don
(C) scoff
(D) manipulate
(E) withdraw

5. SEDATE
(A) tropical
(B) intrepid
(C) credulous
(D) gullible
(E) calm

6. SEDENTARY
(A) impetuous
(B) fixed
(C) epidemic
(D) ravenous
(E) dismal

7. SEDITIOUS
(A) rebellious
(B) poignant
(C) invincible
(D) unfeasible
(E) emphatic

8. SEGREGATE
(A) separate
(B) reprehend
(C) biodegrade
(D) splice
(E) diffuse

9. SEQUESTER
(A) intervene
(B) fathom
(C) isolate
(D) dissuade
(E) gratify

10. SHIRK
(A) inherit
(B) avoid
(C) intimidate
(D) oppress
(E) procure

326

Check-up 9-5

Directions   Each of the following questions consists of one word followed by five words or phrases.
You are to select the one word or phrase whose meaning is closest to the word in capital letters.

1. SIMULTANEOUS
(A) intermittent
(B) concurrent
(C) veteran
(D) dreadful
(E) privileged

2. SKIRMISH
(A) sovereign
(B) jest
(C) clash
(D) revelry
(E) comfort

3. SLANDER
(A) defamation
(B) collusion
(C) drought
(D) poverty
(E) indifference

4. SMEAR
(A) sully
(B) table
(C) suspend
(D) ruminate
(E) exude

5. SMOLDER
(A) burn
(B) waft
(C) alter
(D) dispute
(E) extinguish

6. SNEER
(A) impede
(B) mock
(C) sink
(D) thrive
(E) flourish

7. SNUB
(A) subjugate
(B) ignore
(C) elevate
(D) deflate
(E) conscientious

8. SOJOURN
(A) abhor
(B) confer
(C) stay
(D) distinguish
(E) cull

9. SPECULATE
(A) endure
(B) muffle
(C) guess
(D) plead
(E) suffocate

10. STIPULATION
(A) query
(B) rabble
(C) salvage
(D) condition
(E) stipend

Answer 1.B 2.C 3.A 4.A 5.A 6.B 7.B 8.C 9.C 10.D

451	sublime	456	summit
452	submissive	457	sumptuous
453	substantiate	458	supercilious
454	succumb	459	superfluous
455	sully	460	supple

School Motto

"Ne Cede Malis"

(Yield not to evil)

- The Loomis Chaffee School

SSATKOREA.com

sublime
[suh-**blahym**]

adj. impressing the mind with a sense of grandeur or power

숭고한, 절묘한

There is but one step from the sublime to the ridiculous.

syn. magnificent, exquisite, transcendent

submissive
[suhb-**mis**-iv]

adj. unresistingly or humbly obedient

순종적인, 고분고분한

When animals live in packs, one animal is usually the dominant leader, while the others fall into more submissive roles.

syn. compliant, meek, obedient

substantiate
[suhb-**stan**-shee-eyt]

v. to establish by proof or competent evidence

입증하다

If you accuse someone of committing a crime, you should have proof to substantiate the claim.

syn. authenticate, confirm, corroborate

succumb
[suh-**kuhm**]

v. to yield to or surrender

굴복하다, 무릎을 꿇다

She tried to study all night, but eventually succumbed to sleep around 3 a.m.

syn. surrender, yield, accede

sully
[**suhl**-ee]

v. to try to ruin one's reputation

(명예나 이미지를) 훼손하다, 더럽히다

Joan's good reputation was sullied by the false rumors.

syn. tarnish, stain, defile

summit
[**suhm**-it]

n. the highest point

꼭대기, 절정, 최고점

It took us hours to climb to the summit of the mountain, but the view was worth it.

syn. apex, pinnacle, peak

sumptuous
[**suhmp**-choo-uhs]

adj. rich and superior in quality

호화로운, 화려한

The chefs prepared a sumptuous meal for the wedding.

syn. lavish, luxurious, deluxe

supercilious
[soo-per-**sil**-ee-uhs]

adj. having arrogant superiority

거만한, 남을 얕보는

Her supercilious sister acts snobby by raising her eyebrow.

syn. haughty, arrogant, rude

superfluous
[soo-**pur**-floo-uhs]

adj. being more than is sufficient or required

(더 이상) 필요치 않은, 불필요한

Since each student will be carrying his or her own supplies, try not to bring anything superfluous.

syn. unnecessary, needless, excessive

supple
[**suhp**-uhl]

adj. limber and flexible

유연한, 탄력 있는

The belt was made of a soft, supple leather.

syn. limber, pliant, malleable

ISEE Sentence Completion 10-1

Directions : Fill in the blanks to complete the sentences.

1. The landscape was breathtaking, filled with _____ beauty that left the hikers in awe.

   (A) summit   (B) submissive
   (C) sublime   (D) sumptuous

2. Her _____ behavior made her an easy target for manipulation in the workplace.

   (A) submissive   (B) supercilious
   (C) supple   (D) sully

3. After days of climbing, the team finally managed to reach the _____, celebrating their achievement.

   (A) sublime   (B) sumptuous
   (C) summit   (D) submissive

4. The host prepared a _____ feast for the guests, with dishes from around the world.

   (A) sumptuous   (B) sublime
   (C) supple   (D) superfluous

5. His _____ attitude alienated his peers, as they found his arrogance unbearable.

   (A) sully   (B) submissive
   (C) summit   (D) supercilious

 Answers

1. (C) 2. (A) 3. (C) 4. (A) 5. (D)

461 surmise	466 taint
462 susceptible	467 tarnish
463 tacit	468 taut
464 taciturn	469 tenacious
465 tactful	470 tenure

School Motto

"Honor. Virtue. Humility."

- The Pennington School

SSATKOREA.com

surmise
[ser-**mahyz**]

n. a matter of conjecture

추측, 추정

*Her **surmise** turned out to be right.*

syn. conjecture, guess, assumption

susceptible
[suh-**sep**-tuh-b*uh*l]

adj. easily affected by

민감한, 예민한

*The operation had left her **susceptible** to infection.*

syn. impressionable, sensitive, vulnerable

tacit
[**tas**-it]

adj. not openly said but implied

암묵적인, 무언의

*Your silence implies **tacit** consent to these proposals.*

syn. implied, implicit, understood

taciturn
[**tas**-i-turn]

adj. inclined to silence

과묵한, 말수가 적은

*The ship's captain was a **taciturn** man who spoke only to give orders.*

syn. reserved, laconic, quiet

tactful
[**takt**-f*uh*l]

adj. having or manifesting tact

수완이 좋은, 요령 있는, 눈치가 좋은

*She is extremely **tactful** in dealing with the finance.*

syn. diplomatic, thoughtful, careful

taint
[teynt]

v. to sully or tarnish

(평판 등을) 더럽히다, 오염시키다

*The warm weather will **taint** the food.*

syn. stain, sully, tarnish

tarnish
[**tahr**-nish]

v. to dull the luster of something

(광택을 잃고) 흐려지다, 변색되다

*The affair could **tarnish** the reputation of the prime minister.*

syn. smear, spoil, corrupt

taut
[tawt]

adj. tightly stretched

팽팽한

*The skin of the drum is **taut**.*

syn. tight, drawn, tense

tenacious
[tuh-**ney**-sh*uh*s]

adj. stubborn or persistent

집요한, 완강한

*He is regarded as a **tenacious** and persistent interviewer.*

syn. unyielding, persistent, stubborn

tenure
[**ten**-yer]

n. time in position of responsibility

재임 기간

*During his **tenure** as dean, he had a real influence on the students.*

syn. regime, reign, term

ISEE Sentence Completion 10-2

Directions : Fill in the blanks to complete the sentences.

1. Her _____ efforts to complete the project ahead of schedule earned her the admiration of her colleagues.

   (A) surmise   (B) tarnish
   (C) tenacious   (D) taciturn

2. People with weakened immune systems are more _____ to common illnesses during flu season.

   (A) tactful   (B) taut
   (C) tenure   (D) susceptible

3. His silent nod was taken as _____ approval for the plan.

   (A) tacit   (B) surmise
   (C) tarnish   (D) tenacious

4. Her _____ response helped to ease tensions and pave the way for constructive discussion.

   (A) surmise   (B) tactful
   (C) susceptible   (D) tenacious

5. The detective was able to _____ a motive based on the clues left at the crime scene.

   (A) surmise   (B) tarnish
   (C) taint   (D) taciturn

471	tepid	476	trite
472	torrid	477	trivial
473	trait	478	tumult
474	tranquil	479	unanimous
475	transcend	480	unattainable

School Motto

"Principes non Homines"

(Leaders, not Ordinary Men)

- The Webb School of California

SSATKOREA.com

tepid
[**tep**-id]

adj. characterized by a lack of force or enthusiasm

미지근한, 열의 없는, 성의 없는

He got a tepid response to his suggestion.

syn. lukewarm, halfhearted, unenthusiastic

torrid
[**tawr**-id]

adj. extremely hot

몹시 덥고 건조한

She was sitting on the rocks in the torrid sun.

syn. sweltering, parched, blazing

trait
[treyt]

n. distinguishing characteristic of one's personal nature

특색, 특성

Persistence is the common trait of anyone who has had a significant impact on the world.

syn. disposition, attribute, characteristic

tranquil
[**trang**-kwil]

adj. free from commotion or tumult

평온한, 고요한

She stared at the tranquil surface of the water.

syn. placid, calm, pacific

transcend
[tran-**send**]

v. to rise above or go beyond

초월하다, 능가하다

The best novels are those which transcend national or cultural barriers.

syn. surpass, exceed, outdo

trite
[trahyt]

adj. lacking in freshness because of excessive repetition

진부한, 독창적이지 못한

Her remarks sounded trite and ill-informed.

syn. hackneyed, stale, stereotyped

trivial

[**triv**-ee-*uhl*]

adj. of very small importance

사소한, 하찮은

*She showed her inexperience by asking lots of **trivial** questions.*

syn. insignificant, trifling, paltry

tumult

[**too**-m*uh*lt]

n. a state of great commotion, confusion or disturbance

소란, 혼란

*They waited for the **tumult** to die down.*

syn. commotion, disturbance, agitation

unanimous

[yoo-**nan**-uh-m*uhs*]

adj. in complete agreement

만장일치의, 모든 찬성표를 받은

*The jury reached a **unanimous** verdict of 'not guilty'.*

syn. united, agreed, harmonious

unattainable

[un-uh-**tey**-nuh-b*uhl*]

adj. hard to be achieved

달성하기 어려운, 불가능한

*This is not an **unattainable** ideal, but a goal which you must pursue.*

syn. impossible, inaccessible, unreachable

ISEE Sentence Completion 10-3

Directions : Fill in the blanks to complete the sentences.

1. He grew frustrated with the constant discussions over _____ matters that seemed unimportant in the grand scheme of things.

   (A) torrid   (B) trivial
   (C) transcend   (D) tepid

2. His _____ response to the invitation showed little enthusiasm or interest.

   (A) tepid   (B) torrid
   (C) unanimous   (D) tranquil

3. The peaceful countryside offered a _____ environment that allowed for deep relaxation and reflection.

   (A) tepid   (B) tumult
   (C) tranquil   (D) trite

4. The phrase had become so overused that it felt like a _____ expression, losing all its impact.

   (A) trite   (B) tepid
   (C) transcend   (D) torrid

5. The artist's work seemed to _____ all previous expectations, breaking new ground in the art world.

   (A) torrid   (B) tepid
   (C) trivial   (D) transcend

Answers
1. (B) 2. (A) 3. (C) 4. (A) 5. (D)

481 undermine	486 veritable
482 unflinching	487 vex
483 vandalism	488 vie
484 venerate	489 vigilant
485 verbose	490 vindictive

School Motto

"Dat Deus Incrementum"

(God Gives the Increase)

- Westminster School

SSATKOREA.com

undermine
[uhn-der-**mahyn**]

v. to injure or destroy

(자신감이나 권위 등을) 약화시키다

*He constantly tried to **undermine** her self-confidence.*

syn.   weaken, blunt, injure

unflinching
[uhn-**flin**-ching]

adj. not shrinking from danger

위축되지 않는, 수그러들지 않는

*They are strong, brave and **unflinching** to fight again this disaster.*

syn.   resolute, courageous, steadfast

vandalism
[**van**-dl-iz-*uh*m]

n. intentional destruction or damage of property

공공기물 파손, 기물 파괴

*Acts of **vandalism**, like breaking windows, are punishable by law.*

syn.   destruction, damage, sabotage

venerate
[**ven**-uh-reyt]

v. to regard or treat with reverence

숭배하다, 경외하다, 존경하다

*The monk was **venerated** as a saint.*

syn.   revere, honor, admire

verbose
[ver-**bohs**]

adj. using or containing too many words

수다스러운, 말이 많은

*His writing is often unclear and **verbose**.*

syn.   loquacious, wordy, talkative

veritable
[**ver**-i-t*uh*-b*uh*l]

adj. true or real:

진정한, 실제의, 참된

*The attic was a **veritable** treasure of old photographs and letters.*

syn.   true, genuine, authentic

vex

[vex]

v. to annoy, frustrate, or worry someone, often repeatedly

괴롭히다, 짜증나게 하다

The constant noise from the construction site vexed Sarah, making it hard to focus on her homework.

syn. annoy, irritate, badger

vie

[vahy]

v. to strive in competition or rivalry with another

경쟁하다, 다투다

The state champions will vie for the national title.

syn. compete, contend, strive

vigilant

[**vij**-uh-l*uh*nt]

adj. keenly watchful to detect danger

경계하는, 조심하는

He warned the public to be vigilant and report anything suspicious.

syn. watchful, wary, chary

vindictive

[vin-**dik**-tiv]

adj. disposed or inclined to revenge

앙심을 품은, 보복하려 하는

A vindictive man will look for occasions for resentment.

syn. revengeful, spiteful, resentful

ISEE Sentence Completion 10-4

Directions : Fill in the blanks to complete the sentences.

1. The soldier demonstrated _____ courage in the face of danger, never wavering in his mission.

   (A) veritable   (B) vex
   (C) verbose   (D) unflinching

2. The discovery of the ancient artifacts was a _____ treasure, with immense historical value.

   (A) vigilant   (B) veritable
   (C) vindictive   (D) undermine

3. The constant criticism served to _____ his confidence, making him doubt his abilities.

   (A) vigilant   (B) venerate
   (C) undermine   (D) vindictive

4. The security guard remained _____ throughout the night, ensuring no one entered the building after hours.

   (A) vigilant   (B) verbose
   (C) vex   (D) undermine

5. The constant interruptions during the meeting began to _____ the speaker, making it difficult to continue.

   (A) verbose   (B) vigilant
   (C) vex   (D) vindictive

491	vociferous	496	wither
492	vulnerable	497	wrath
493	wail	498	writhe
494	waive	499	zany
495	wince	500	zealous

School Motto

"Cogitare Agere Esse"

(To think, to do, to be)

- Westover School

SSATKOREA.com

vociferous
[vo-**sif**-er-*uhs*]

adj. conspicuously and offensively loud

소리 높여 표현하는, 강하게 외치는

Max was vociferous in his support of the proposal.

syn.   clamorous, strident, boisterous

vulnerable
[**vuhl**-ner-uh-b*uhl*]

adj. capable of being physically or emotionally wounded

상처받기 쉬운, 연약한

Jack was very vulnerable after his divorce.

syn.   assailable, susceptible, defenseless

wail
[weyl]

v. to express sorrow audibly

울부짖다, 통곡하다, 흐느끼다

The child started wailing after she stumbled and fell.

syn.   cry, howl, grieve

waive
[weyv]

v. to give up

(권리 등을) 포기하다

Many banks waive online transaction fees.

syn.   relinquish, forgo, surrender

wince
[wins]

v. to shrink back involuntarily as from pain

움찔하고 놀라다, 움찔하다

Tom winced as the nurse gave him an injection.

syn.   cower, cringe, flinch

wither
[**with**-er]

v. to become dry and sapless

시들다, 말라죽다

The plants withered and died.

syn.   shrivel, wilt, droop

wrath
[rath]

n. strong vengeful anger or indignation

심한 분노, 노여움

When the critic wrote a harsh review of the play, he earned the wrath of the playwright's fans.

syn. fury, rage, indignation

writhe
[rahyth]

v. to twist into coils or folds

비비 꼬다, 온몸을 비틀다

She lay on the floor, writhing in pain.

syn. contort, wrest, squirm

zany
[**zey**-nee]

adj. ludicrously or whimsically comical

엉뚱한, 괴짜 같은

There's a fine line between zany and crazy.

syn. wacky, eccentric, quirky

zealous
[**zel**-*uhs*]

adj. marked by active interest and enthusiasm

열성적인, 열광적인

No one was more zealous than her in that work.

syn. ardent, passionate, fervent

Directions : Fill in the blanks to complete the sentences.

1. He was a _____ supporter of the team, attending every game and cheering with passion.

   (A) vulnerable   (B) zealous
   (C) wrath   (D) vociferous

2. The company decided to _____ the membership fee for loyal customers.

   (A) wail   (B) wrath
   (C) wither   (D) waive

3. She could not help but _____ in pain when the doctor administered the injection.

   (A) zany   (B) wince
   (C) wither   (D) vulnerable

4. The patient began to _____ in agony after the surgery, unable to find comfort.

   (A) writhe   (B) wail
   (C) zealous   (D) waive

5. The children performed _____ antics during the party, making everyone laugh with their silly tricks.

   (A) wince   (B) zealous
   (C) zany   (D) vociferous

Answers
1. (B)   2. (D)   3. (B)   4. (A)   5. (C)

Analogy 20. Math Terms

Math Section 고득점을 위해서는 Math 용어를 정확히 익히고 문제를 충분히 풀어야 합니다. 본문에는 Arithmetic/ Algebra/ Geometry 핵심 어휘와 Math Lexicon 수학용어사전까지 포함되어 있습니다. 수학 용어가 약하다면 본문을 꼼꼼히 익히고 연습문제를 풀어야 합니다.

absolute value 절대값	average 평균값
digit 숫자	distinct digit 서로 다른 숫자
even number 짝수	odd number 홀수
decimal 소수	fraction 분수
sequence 수열	consecutive number 연속하는 수
factor 인수	integer 정수
greatest common factor 최대공약수	least common multiple 최소공배수
in terms of x x로 나타내면	whole number 0을 포함한 양의 정수
prime number 소수 (1과 자기 자신만으로 나누어지는 수)	factorization 인수분해
numerator 분자	denominator 분모
lowest term 기약분수	mixed number 대분수
average 평균	reciprocal 역수
median 중간 값	mode 최빈값, 가장 자주 나오는 수
ratio 비, 비율	rate 속도, 비율
rounding off 반올림	x-axis | y-axis x 축 | y 축
slope 기울기	x-intercept | y-intercept x 절편 | y 절편
set 집합	subset 부분집합
union 합집합	null set 공집합
intersection 교집합	sum of sets 합집합
perimeter 둘레길이	circumference 원의 둘레길이
radius 반지름	diameter 지름
diagonal 대각선	vertex 꼭지점
Pythagorean theorem 피타고라스의 정리	scalene triangle 부등변 삼각형 (모든 변의 길이가 다른 삼각형)
isosceles triangle 이등변 삼각형 (두 변의 길이가 같은 삼각형)	parallelogram 평행사변형

Check-up 10-1

Directions   Each of the following questions consists of one word followed by five words or phrases.
You are to select the one word or phrase whose meaning is closest to the word in capital letters.

1. SUBLIME
(A) patient
(B) magnificent
(C) frigid
(D) dormant
(E) aghast

2. SUBMISSIVE
(A) compliant
(B) visible
(C) stupendous
(D) aloof
(E) eloquent

3. SUBSTANTIATE
(A) alleviate
(B) captivate
(C) employ
(D) inflict
(E) authenticate

4. SUCCUMB
(A) illuminate
(B) slither
(C) relieve
(D) surrender
(E) apologize

5. SULLY
(A) scold
(B) exist
(C) tarnish
(D) vacate
(E) accelerate

6. SUMMIT
(A) cacophony
(B) terrain
(C) apex
(D) hangar
(E) adversary

7. SUMPTUOUS
(A) lavish
(B) unfeeling
(C) arranged
(D) frugal
(E) elaborate

8. SUPERCILIOUS
(A) circumspect
(B) viable
(C) desperate
(D) puny
(E) haughty

9. SUPERFLUOUS
(A) ravenous
(B) unnecessary
(C) elusive
(D) lethargic
(E) minute

10. SUPPLE
(A) limber
(B) complicit
(C) ferocious
(D) grim
(E) efficient

339

Check-up 10-2

Each of the following questions consists of one word followed by five words or phrases. You are to select the one word or phrase whose meaning is closest to the word in capital letters

1. SURMISE
(A) kindle
(B) despise
(C) conjecture
(D) employ
(E) adopt

2. SUSCEPTIBLE
(A) lavish
(B) momentous
(C) nomadic
(D) impressionable
(E) inevitable

3. TACIT
(A) implied
(B) rare
(C) inhibited
(D) banned
(E) occupied

4. TACITURN
(A) transparent
(B) vacant
(C) threadbare
(D) reserved
(E) scarce

5. TACTFUL
(A) level
(B) accurate
(C) furious
(D) humble
(E) diplomatic

6. TAINT
(A) overwhelm
(B) stain
(C) perturb
(D) slaughter
(E) abduct

7. TARNISH
(A) rejoice
(B) burnish
(C) halt
(D) smear
(E) abate

8. TAUT
(A) mediocre
(B) tight
(C) perpetual
(D) extravagant
(E) brisk

9. TENACIOUS
(A) ignorant
(B) keen
(C) esteemed
(D) unyielding
(E) intelligent

10. TENURE
(A) chamber
(B) tempo
(C) meter
(D) entourage
(E) regime

Check-up 10-3

Directions   Each of the following questions consists of one word followed by five words or phrases.
You are to select the one word or phrase whose meaning is closest to the word in capital letters.

1. TEPID
(A) lukewarm
(B) conspicuous
(C) trepid
(D) exotic
(E) impromptu

2. TORRID
(A) immaculate
(B) laden
(C) sweltering
(D) rancorous
(E) pensive

3. TRAIT
(A) diction
(B) visage
(C) homage
(D) disposition
(E) stance

4. TRANQUIL
(A) paltry
(B) unctuous
(C) discreet
(D) placid
(F) inept

5. TRANSCEND
(A) muffle
(B) dissent
(C) incinerate
(D) surpass
(E) decimate

6. TRITE
(A) hackneyed
(B) marvelous
(C) tranquil
(D) enormous
(E) flimsy

7. TRIVIAL
(A) insignificant
(B) accurate
(C) mysterious
(D) grandiose
(E) untamed

8. TUMULT
(A) token
(B) umpire
(C) trek
(D) commotion
(E) turncoat

9. UNANIMOUS
(A) traumatic
(B) ubiquitous
(C) tenable
(D) unified
(E) cardinal

10. UNATTAINABLE
(A) irate
(B) obsolete
(C) mere
(D) impossible
(E) lethargic

341

Check-up 10-4

Directions   Each of the following questions consists of one word followed by five words or phrases.
You are to select the one word or phrase whose meaning is closest to the word in capital letters.

1. UNDERMINE
(A) weaken
(B) classify
(C) accelerate
(D) beseech
(E) restrain

2. UNFLINCHING
(A) resolute
(B) daunted
(C) jubilant
(D) deft
(E) indistinct

3. VANDALISM
(A) intention
(B) destruction
(C) prophesy
(D) capitalism
(E) dystopia

4. VENERATE
(A) hibernate
(B) revere
(C) intimidate
(D) compel
(E) assimilate

5. VERBOSE
(A) comprehensive
(B) loquacious
(C) secondary
(D) considerable
(E) exclusive

6. VERITABLE
(A) true
(B) decent
(C) stunning
(D) noticeable
(E) charming

7. VEX
(A) debunk
(B) annoy
(C) diminish
(D) concur
(E) rejuvenate

8. VIE
(A) concede
(B) enrage
(C) modify
(D) compete
(E) entice

9. VIGILANT
(A) watchful
(B) ambivalent
(C) ephemeral
(D) feasible
(E) superior

10. VINDICTIVE
(A) fatigued
(B) amiable
(C) spontaneous
(D) revengeful
(E) condescending

Check-up 10-5

Directions   Each of the following questions consists of one word followed by five words or phrases.
You are to select the one word or phrase whose meaning is closest to the word in capital letters.

1. VOCIFEROUS
(A) austere
(B) impulsive
(C) clamorous
(D) fatigued
(E) revengeful

2. VULNERABLE
(A) assailable
(B) humorous
(C) integrated
(D) flamboyant
(E) stagnant

3. WAIL
(A) slander
(B) excavate
(C) cry
(D) fortify
(E) depict

4. WAIVE
(A) daunt
(B) remunerate
(C) intimidate
(D) seize
(E) relinquish

5. WINCE
(A) fumble
(B) cower
(C) grope
(D) furnish
(E) sharpen

6. WITHER
(A) shrivel
(B) nourish
(C) renovate
(D) hinder
(E) inhale

7. WRATH
(A) retribution
(B) feint
(C) havoc
(D) fury
(E) distinction

8. WRITHE
(A) harry
(B) pester
(C) badger
(D) contort
(E) consecrate

9. ZANY
(A) wacky
(B) fastidious
(C) gargantuan
(D) complimentary
(F) ferocious

10. ZEALOUS
(A) hollow
(B) futile
(C) conceited
(D) ardent
(E) sympathetic

343

한세희의 SSAT
HIT VOCABULARY

초판 발행   2020년 6월 5일
개정 3쇄   2025년 4월 30일

지은이 한세희
감수자 이준, 구영원, 이지은, Phillip Lim
펴낸이 최영민
디자인 이연수
Contributors Yewon Lee, Jeongwon Han

펴낸곳 헤르몬하우스
출판등록 제406-2015-31호
주소 경기도 파주시 신촌로 16
전화 031-8071-0088
Fax 031-942-8688
이메일 hermonh@naver.com

ISBN 979-11-94085-44-7   (13740)

■ 헤르몬하우스는 피앤피북의 임프린트입니다.
■ 책값은 뒤표지에 있습니다. 잘못된 책은 구입하신 곳에서 교환해드립니다.